The
Wri  ok

college

Pool Redruth ...

From the same publishers:

The Creative Writing Handbook (2nd edition)
Edited by John Singleton and Mary Luckhurst

Creative Writing : A Practical Guide (2nd edition)
Julia Casterton

The Creative Writing Workbook

JOHN SINGLETON

palgrave

First published 2001 by
PALGRAVE
Houndmills, Basingstoke, Hampshire RG21 6XS and
175 Fifth Avenue, New York, N.Y. 10010
Companies and representatives throughout the world

PALGRAVE is the new global academic imprint of St. Martin's
Press LLC Scholarly and Reference Division and Palgrave
Publishers Ltd (formerly Macmillan Press Ltd).

ISBN 0-333-79216-5

This book is printed on paper suitable for recycling and made from
fully managed and sustained forest sources.

A catalogue record for this book is available
from the British Library.

10 9 8 7 6 5 4 3 2 1
10 09 08 07 06 05 04 03 02 01

Printed in Malaysia

Contents

Abbreviations

CC   *Close Company*, ed. Christine Park and Caroline Heaton (Virago, 1993).

EK   *Emergency Kit*, ed. Jo Shapcott and Matthew Sweeney (Faber and Faber, 1996).

FB   *The Firebox*, ed. Sean O'Brien (Picador, 1998).

FBP   *The Forward Book of Poetry 2000* (Forward Publishing, 1999).

MBSS   *Modern British Short Stories*, ed. Malcolm Bradbury (Penguin, 1988).

NP   *The New Poetry*, ed. Michael Hulse, David Kennedy and David Morley (Bloodaxe, 1993).

OBV   *The Oxford Book of Verse 1945–1980*, ed. D. J. Enright (OUP, 1995).

PBPBI   *The Penguin Book of Poetry from Britain and Ireland since 1945*, ed. Simon Armitage and Robert Crawford (Penguin, 1998).

20WP   *The Faber Book of 20th Century Women's Poetry*, ed. Fleur Adcock (Faber and Faber, 1987).

RB   *The Rattlebag*, ed. Seamus Heaney and Ted Hughes (Faber and Faber, 1982).

SB   *The School Bag*, ed. Seamus Heaney and Ted Hughes (Faber and Faber, 1997).

SS1   *The Secret Self, Vol. 1*, ed. Hermione Lee (Dent, 1993).

SS2   *The Secret Self, Vol. 2*, ed. Hermione Lee (Dent, 1993).

These abbreviations are widely used throughout the *Workbook* for ease of reference.

Using The Creative Writing Workbook

The Creative Writing Workbook contains nearly a thousand original and practical ideas for writing, and is designed for writers everywhere; from kitchen-table enthusiasts and armchair addicts dreaming of writing steaming romances to purposeful and ambitious students working their way through a school, college or university course.

Some of the material will overlap, some ideas are repeated; not for emphasis but because good meat has a wider appeal when cooked in a variety of ways and users can take what they want and leave the rest. Thus, where actual titles for writing are suggested they are no more than that, *suggestions*, readily open to substitution, and in their deliberate ambiguity they open up possibility.

Inevitably the content of *The Creative Writing Workbook* reflects the taste of the writer. The book is based on the idea of 'model' writing; on the belief that accomplished writing by successful writers offers 'templates' for new writers, and enthuses them into 'daring to be different'. Thus the hundreds of exemplary poems and short stories, scripts and novels cited or quoted here could and should be replaced by teachers or students with their own favoured texts.

The Creative Writing Workbook uses a critical vocabulary and refers to ideas *about* writing. This is because it assumes that art is a product both of the imagination and of reflective thinking. Many writers are quoted who have thought long and hard about their craft, and the book encourages new writers to do likewise by keeping a reflective journal and by trying out a number of exercises involving expository and analytic writing. No doubt serious and enthusiastic writers and teachers, users of this book, will inevitably 'measure and reason out' the art of writing through their journals and notes, or through group discussions in workshops and Internet chat rooms. New writers, however, flourish best in a group context where there is an open and anxiety-free exchange of ideas for and about writing, and though this book is about getting down to business it presumes teachers will oxygenate the process of writing with rich and effervescing talk.

Guiding Principles

The Creative Writing Workbook is based on five principles.

1 'An unexamined life is not worth living,' wrote Socrates, and a similar humanist purpose lies at the core of this book. In this sense it accords with the ambition Matthew Arnold saw in writing when he said that 'literature is a criticism of life'. By criticism he meant the intelligent scrutiny of life with intent to find value and worth in human behaviour. Lynne Sharon Schwartz, a contemporary American novelist, echoes Arnold and the argument behind *The Creative Writing Workbook* when she pleads with young writers to 'Do something with your spirit and your relationship with the world'.

2 Writing is about vision and re-vision. The Arnoldian scrutiny I am thinking of means not just looking at the world quizzically but examining one's own precepts and concepts in the same sceptical light. Writing is not about holding onto ideas but of letting them go and following their risky trail. In her essay 'When We Dead Awaken' the American feminist and poet Adrienne Rich, argues that women writers must wake up and begin seeing 'with fresh eyes'. And not just women. Men have sat in the sun so long they are the more blind. William Blake's 'mind-forged manacles' apply to all writers, all people.

　　In the same piece Rich wrote about the challenge of writing. Imagination is the way to see *into* things and the truths that elude our rational grasp. It is the revisionary, active force transforming reality. To be transformative, Rich says 'the imagination has to question, to challenge, to conceive of alternatives, perhaps to the life you are leading at the moment... to play around with the notion that day may be night, love might be hate.'

3 Though *The Creative Writing Workbook* opens by considering the writer the core ambition is to improve writing by informed practice, because practice makes perfect. There is, however, more to this proverbial advice than making fine phrases and polished prose. Writing is explorative. It reveals as it opens up. As Adrienne Rich says of poems: 'They are like dreams. In them you put what you don't know you know.' This applies to all forms of honest writing. So doing it is the only way to reach those parts others have hidden from you. The point is well made by the novelist Kate Braverman. 'You *make* yourself a writer,' she says.

4 Though the book acknowledges the primal power of the imagination it also emphasises the central role of craft in the writing process. Craft and technique are stressed because by sympathetic constraint they release the forces of the imagination just as shaft and rein release horsepower. The issue for new writers is not that they don't have any technique, but that at times they have too much. Technique takes over and writing becomes an empty display. This book tries to introduce the craft of writing as a servant of content and purpose; *how* serves *what* serves *why*. Unless this is so no art is made, and 'Writing has to be art before it can be real'.

5 Good readers make good writers. Here new writers are encouraged to read and to keep on reading until books have body-snatched them and the pulse of language put-puts in their veins, for reading supplies the life-blood of writing – words. It also lights the way and guides the craft. 'Until you can read,' argues Lynne Schwartz, 'you don't know what you want to do with your writing.'

SECTION 1
THE WRITING SELF

1 | Deep Roots

Ancestral Voices

- R. S. Thomas, in his poem *Here* (RB), imagines himself, twentieth-century man, sitting in the top branches of the tree of life looking back down the millennia and seeing 'The footprints that led up to me'. I like this image; lookout man searching his past, finding only ancestral traces, the ape antecedents of his evolutionary ascent. I like the irony of man climbing into the canopy not realising he's back again where monkeys live.

According to Wordsworth, man arrives on the earth 'trailing clouds of glory'. On one level this phrase can be read as a poetic description of the afterbirth, but it is primarily a Christian view of man's origins and contrasts strongly with the Darwinian tinge of Thomas's metaphor. Just as evolution is like looking at ourselves through the wrong end of the telescope, so history is a turning of the lens on ourselves and our individual life-span. In biological terms we each have our niche, and when it's a matter of knowing who we are and where we've come from we need to account for both the long-shot and the close-up of ourselves; catch ourselves in the niche of time as it were. Much writing is about looking at ourselves and placing ourselves.

To get used to the long-shot view of 'mankind' find some ancient artefact. Try a fossil, a picture of a hominid, something archaeological: a pebble, shard of rock, geological map/calendar even. Recall pictures of that disappearing trail of primeval footprints fossilised for a million years in

3

the African mud. **Write** on it. Tumble it around in your mind. Hear the echoes. Reverberations. Write whatever comes into your head. Write quickly. Let the writing take over, not the writer, and certainly not the reader. Forget the reader.

- Biologists say we retain crucial vestiges of distant ancestral experiences in our psyches. Fear of the dark is one such inheritance; fear of being swallowed up is another. Possibly both terrors derive from the time when our early relatives were cave-dwellers and were regularly devoured by sabre-tooths springing out of the depths. It is said dreams are the echoes of such times, colourful resonances of a dawning consciousness. Neuro-biologists argue that we retain vestiges in our bodies too. The brain, for instance, is in two parts. One is of recent development, and constitutes the upper layers containing the cerebral cortex which controls the higher human functions, language, reasoning, and so on. The underlying part is the 'reptilian' brain, primordial, instinctual and derived from a time when we lived as oceanic beings, scaly and cold-blooded. Under extreme conditions the upper layers of the brain shut down. Only the reptilian stays on alert controlling, controlling. Can you think of a dream you've had that sounds primordial, something emerging from way back? **Write** it down trying to bring some kind of order to the disruptions of the original dream narrative. If you can't think of such a dream, create one. Fall back on the mind. Go back and back and back and imagine. Go reptilian even.

- Some writers have explored man's early state of being. William Golding, in his novel *The Inheritors*, attempted to capture the primitive self. The same writer traced the descent of the civilised into barbarity and debased tribalism in *Lord of the Flies*. Russell Hoban dramatised startling primitivistic patterns in *Riddley Walker*, a novel set in a distant future. Both these latter two books and novels like *The Clockwork Orange* are based on catastrophic and apocalyptic events that drive man back to his dark roots.

    Ideas of the savage lurking below the urbane and civilised exterior underwrite much fiction. Remember Caliban? Remember the Yahoos? Alexander Pope, the eighteenth-century poet, said man 'bestrode an isthmus'. On one foot he stood like an angel; on the other like a beast. Beast and angel. Is the folk story *Beauty and the Beast* yet another variant? Are we made up of such simple dualities? Is Frankenstein's monster our father? Grendel our mother? Are we still at heart savages? Have you any reason to believe this is true? What's the evidence? **Write** a story or poem based on this theme. If you want a model read some of the stories from Angela Carter's collection *The Bloody Chamber*.

- 'Savage' is an interesting word. (Aren't they all?) It comes from the Latin *silva* meaning wood or forest, an uncultivated and wild place. People who lived in forests were thought to be mad. (Anyone who chose to live away from the companionship and comforts of the city had to be.) *Wood* also meant lunatic in Shakespeare's time. Perhaps it comes from *Wodan*, the wild Norse god. The word 'city' derives from *civis* in Latin, which provides us with our 'civilisation' and 'civilising' ways. So cities are places of order and reason, woods of wildness and danger and irrationality. *A Midsummer Night's Dream* has it all – woodland insanities, Athenian civilities, destructive jealousies, men turned into beasts, man-eating animals. Imagine a man or a woman has a sudden near-irresistible urge to eat someone. Stunned by this compulsion he/she prays for help. Help arrives – of a sort. **Write** on. Invent some other perverse drive for your shocked character.

- Have you ever witnessed totally irrational behaviour? Someone flipping? Recall the event(s). **Write** as faithful an account of it as memory will allow. Imagine you are telling this story to a psychologist. At the end of your account write down her explanation of the behaviour you have described. You ought to attempt both pieces of writing.

- Another variant on this theme is man regressing and emerging as a lower order of life, sliding down the evolutionary ladder. Kafka's 'Metamorphosis' supposes a man has turned into a giant beetle. In Homer's *Odyssey* Circe, the witch, turns Odysseus' men into swine. Nothing changes!

For instance, women today frequently swear men into swine. Imagine that an angry girlfriend's insult – 'you swine' – has had a literal effect. Is it a sudden or slow transformation? What happens? **Write** the story or any variant on this theme that comes to mind. Is it turning into a horror story or a moral fable or just a comforting fantasy?

Family Portraits

- As we backtrack from the beginning and approach present times our scrutiny becomes more intense and our lives come up in sharp detail. We can put bits under the microscope, trace lines, map ourselves, see the forces that gave rise to us. Thomas Hardy, who knew a thing or two about the uprooting forces of nature, wrote a poem on a similar theme. He called it 'Heredity' (RB). It was written before the elegant acrobatics of spiralling chromosomes had become the new hieroglyphs of life.

  > I am the family face;
  > Flesh perishes, I live on,
  > Projecting trait and trace
  > Through time to times anon,
  > And leaping from place to place
  > Over oblivion.

  There are ironies to relish here. The metaphor of leaping suggests playground games, but not playfulness. There is no suggestion of childlike innocence either, unless you accept self-absorption as innocence. The selfish gene only persists by first destroying its SELF. Hardy allows Heredity a voice in the poem. This pre-nominal 'I', cuckooing the poet, takes over his words and boasts of the principle that will efface the creator and his sad syllables for ever. Perversely, the principle is LIFE!

  Maybe you've never really bothered to look back at yourself, at what made you. Try it. First, identify family traits – physical, temperamental. Is there a 'family face', to use Hardy's phrase? Do biological traces run through the generations? Do people in your family claim you all share a common character? Is there a family pattern of behaviour/beliefs you are expected to comply with, adhere to? Does the origin of your surname give a clue to the family personality? **Write** a *Family Portrait* and say how you are part of it and not part of it. Are you inside or outside?

- In the writing of her first book *That's How It Was*, Maureen Duffy says she 'was trying to make psychological sense of myself and to do this I was rerunning those events and emotions that formed me'. The events and emotions she reruns are those of a hard working-class childhood, a deep relationship with her mother, an escape from poverty through education, and the alienation from her background and from 'family roots'. The world of school and home were in continuous conflict for her.

  Do you see any of these kinds of conflicts in your own life? Has there been any incident/period/encounter that brought this conflict into particularly sharp focus? **Write** about it. Now, this is a hard but a worthwhile thing to do. After you've finished, try and work out what this piece has done to the experience you've just described, and what it has done to you? Has the writing changed anything in you? What?

- Are there any key events/episodes in your life that you would focus on if you were trying to make 'psychological sense of yourself'? Examine one or more in detail and **write** about it.

- The novelist Margaret Forster has remarked that 'Family is something you have to struggle against'. Do you see any truth in this comment? Jot down some first thoughts. Is it the *idea* of family she sees as repressive/oppressive? Apart from the obvious idea of adolescent rebellion what else is she thinking about? What else are you thinking about? **Write** yourself out of ideas. Exhaust your ideas. Try shaping them into an opinion-style magazine article entitled *The Real Truth About Families*.

- In her *Journals* Sylvia Plath explores the influence of family on her. She sees the family as having an identity of its own. She writes: ' ... for you are all an inexplicable unity – this family group with its twisted tensions, unreasoning loves and solidarity and loyalty born and bred in blood. These people are the ones most basically responsible for what you are.' What does she mean by the phrase: 'born and bred in blood'? Just what are 'blood ties'? That's a good title for a poem especially with the question mark. **Write** a poem called *Blood Ties?*

- Who in your family would you say had the most influence on you? Brother? Sister? Mother? Father? Grandparent? **Write** about this, exploring any crucial events that illustrate the precise nature of that influence.

- 'Identity is not a given. It is something you carve out of resistance.' True or false? Or half-true and half-false? **Write** a piece entitled *Resistance* or *Resisting* or *Resisted* or *Carving*.

- You've surely observed families other than your own. You've observed the pressures, the contrarieties, the submissions and oppositions, the surface behaviour, and the subterranean emotions. Often the underlife, the reefs of family life are more evident to the outsider than the participants. **Write** a short story based on an incident/relationship within a family outside your own. Try and show the deeper currents.

- Margaret Forster's remark emphasises the dynamic nature of family relationships. Even in the calmest, most balanced of families life's still a balancing act; lots of balancing acts probably. Families have their own strategies for resolving differences, for making accepted decisions. Imagine the normal unruffled surface of a fictitious family of four being disturbed by some apparently small incident. Centre a story on this incident. Allow each character to tell their own version of events. **Write** it as if you are the confidante of each of the four.

- Anita Desai, the Indian-born novelist, talks about 'the web of family relationships'. 'Web' is an ambiguous term. Is the metaphor an accurate, illuminating descriptor of family ties? Think of an incident from your own life that reveals/ illustrates the ambiguity of the term 'web'. **Try writing** an account of the experience. Experiment by not writing it in your own autobiographical voice, but in the narrative voice of a shrewd family friend.

- Middle-class families and working-class families have their own distinctive cultures. What differences have you noticed especially in the way kids are brought up? If families figure significantly in your fiction or planned fiction then you may need to think about these distinctions. Imagine a so-called 'posh' kid coming across some kids from a run-down estate. What happens? **Write** the encounter as if it is a scene from a novel. Concentrate on getting the language and manner of speech right. A good model is Roddy Doyle's novel *Paddy Clarke. Ha. Ha. Ha.*

- Read from Anita Desai's novel *Clear Light of Day*. It's about family attachments and detachments. Look especially at the crafting of the first few pages. **Write** the opening paragraphs of an English 'family' story using Desai's work as your model.

- Read Lorrie Moore's short story 'Charades' from her collection *Birds of America*. It's Christmas and time for the family's traditional game of charades. There are eight characters divided into two teams. Read on. Take some of the ideas and techniques from this story and **start writing** one of your own based on a family event/game/celebration/outing/ party. Try a title that has the symbolic suggestiveness of Lorrie Moore's.

- Sometimes we are in disguise. We can catch glimpses of ourselves in the characters we create in our writing. If you've written fiction look at some of your stories. Do they reflect your life, bits of you? If they do, describe how. Can you draw any conclusions about writing from this? If you've written poems do they reveal anything about yourself that surprises you? Of course, sometimes, like dreams, the connections and relationship to real life are elusive and tenuous. Hunt them down. Persist. Worry the problem. All writing is worrying. **Write** about any one story/poem of yours analysing what it reveals of the writer.

Class, Queen and Country

• On the west front of cathedrals there are hundreds of statues, each in their own niche. In some cases they may be struggling out of the stone, angry at the drag of matter. These are the demons, the gargoyles, the writhing beasts. Others may feel they fit well enough and are not apparently interested in changing places. There are divinities, saints, angels, craftsmen (also called sinners), madonnas, birds, serpents, lions, devils, bishops.

There are rows and rows of them, ascensions, hierarchies of the holy and the unholy aspiring towards the summit. Each has a story out of which they have emerged and are still emerging. Each is falling into another story – the one I'm trying to tell now. And the story I'm trying to tell is about how everything is interconnected, and how one thing leads to another (contiguity) and another ad infinitum (continuity), and how we develop systems of arrangement to stop it all getting out of hand, such as cathedral façades, and plant taxonomies, and branches of science, and faculties and departments, and periodic tables, and alphabets and dictionaries, and sentences and paragraphs, and genre and grammars, and tropes and parts of speech, and catechisms and commandments. All this declining and conjugating, tabulating and enumerating imposes an order on the chaos.

So, to get a grip on the 'variousness' of things, as the poet Louis MacNeice called chaos, we need discipline, structure, form, and we need to know how to use them. That means crafting. Making. Applying this to writing I would say writing is made not born.

Back to niches. I'm turning the whole façade into a metaphor for social identity. To the medieval mind society was organised hierarchically; monarch at top, clergy, lords and ladies next, merchants in the middle, commoners at the broad base. Everyone had their place, their allotment. It was how lives were ordered, how faces fitted. Everyone was, and is, also kitted out with a survival pack of attitudes and ideas – a mindset. So, if you are a commoner, or working class as we say now, you come complete with your own self-image and images of other classes. To the bourgeoisie, the proletariat are ill-refined, unintelligent brutes. To the proletariat, the bourgeoisie are parasitic, self-interested and shallow. To both, the upper classes are louche and arrogant.

These images are stereotypes, quick-fit pictures, and like all clichés they are good shorthand for social communication. But, like clichés world-wide, they substitute an appearance of a truth for original thinking and individual distinctiveness. And, since the writer is about questing and questioning supposed truths and asserting the distinctive, then writers have to have stereotypes in their sights – all the time.

Having said all this, people do fit into types, but not exclusively. People step out of their niches often without prior notice and surprise us. So when our stereotypical character does the unexpected we have the beginning of a story. Imagine a social stereotype. **Write** a sketch of him/her. In the last paragraph your caricature becomes a character. How are you going to manage this?

- These days middle-class kids (I was thought 'posh' at school because my dad wore a suit to work!) are called Sam (Samantha) and Ben. Working-class kids are called Jason, Nathan and Crystal. Am I stereotyping people here? Is it a class marker to call your children after pop or soap stars? **Write** a stereotype profile of a person concentrating on their 'class markers'.

  Write an observational piece about someone not in your social class, showing the ways they differ from their popular and stereotypical image.

- Regionality is another identity marker. Think of the differences that supposedly exist between the Northerner and the Southerner. Simon Armitage in his book *All Points North*, half mocks half delights in the stereotypes. The North is 'where the M1 does an emergency stop . . . where England tucks its shirt into its underpants'. The South is a place of 'men in bowler hats and Union Jack underpants'. *Underpants !?* Where does the man come from? Down here we say *boxer shorts!* But that's New England, Cool Britannia. Do you think locality or regionality has had any bearing on your life? **Write** about its exact influence.

- Try and summarise what the Scottish or English or Welsh or Irish national character is like. The English are said to be dour, practical-minded Anglo-Saxons. The Welsh have hwll. They are vivacious after their Celtic ancestors. Can national characteristics really be inherited? Do they really exist? Some people say they are proud to be Cornish or Yorkshire, or whatever. What is it they are proud of? **Write** an analysis of a national character. Base it on someone you know well. Or try writing a caricature of the national persona.

- There are many Englands. Whether one dominates or we tolerate diversity, either way there's territory to be fought over. As I write, the Tory party are protesting that New Labour is destroying our essential Englishness. We are going to lose the pound. We are going to lose traditional rural pursuits like fox-hunting, a time-honoured activity at the very core of English country life. Our thatched villages are no more than rest centres. The Union is finished. The Celtic nations have their own Assemblies.

  Out of place, in a foreign country, is where you most notice Englishness, upper, middle and low caste. What are your experiences of the English abroad? What difference does it make to say we are *British*? Some people talk of the 'national psyche' as if it was something identifiable. Can you identify its main features? It's fashionable to talk of 'Cool Britannia'. Is this just the latest re-adjustment of our national identity? A marketing promotion? **Write** about your own national character. Or, out of this muddle of ideas above, shape something relevant.

- In Julian Barnes's novel *England, England* the entrepreneur, Sir Jack Pitman, has decided to cash in our national identity and sell England to the English. Realising that consumers prefer the replica to the real, he plans to convert the Isle of

Wight into a giant theme park of national identity. He instructs his Concept Developer, Jeffrey, to conduct a survey that will discover the 'Top Fifty characteristics associated with the word England'. The list includes Pubs, Robin Hood and his Merrie Men, White Cliffs of Dover, Union Jack, Gardening, Bowler Hats, Thatched Cottages, Breakfast, Emotional Frigidity, Phlegm, Marks and Spencer's, Whingeing, Flagellation and Public Schools, and much, much more. **Write** a page on any subject from this list, or any other relevant 'Top Fifty characteristics' you can think of.

- There are larger forces even than national ones that shape us. Take the words 'Germanic' or 'Aryan'. Our racial and ethnic origins powerfully validate our identity. Monstrously they are used to deny identity too. Hitler's Nationalist Socialist project for purging the race has been one of the century's most notorious experiments in social engineering. But ethnic cleansing is nothing new. In the quest for a pure racial stream in the state, Vermont passed its sterilisation law in 1931. It was an instrument for getting rid of the feeble-minded, society's 'weeds' as the director of the state eugenics programme described the native Abernaki Indians. Candidates for sterilisation were identified under the following headings: feeble-minded, subnormal, insane, alcoholic, criminalistic. If that's how society paints you no wonder you take up the pen and fight! Have you come across racism in your life? Was it petty? Unwitting? Vicious? **Write** something about it. If you want a model look up e.e.cummings' poem 'ygUDah', a brilliant double-take on racist talk.

- Read Jean Stafford's short story 'A Summer's Day' (SS2). It examines the forces in America conspiring to efface the distinctive ethnic character of its native peoples. All dominant cultures strive to erase the identity of the subject culture or at least to absorb it. Naturally, the subjected resists the assimilation, strives to retain and maintain some of its own ethnic or national distinctiveness. You may have observed these processes at work; in the education system, in the media. Imagine a small child, a refugee from a central

European country, has arrived in this country. He/she is travelling on a coach to a reception centre. Create a story out of this situation. Remember this is not a moral discourse with talking heads. It's a story of one small child first, and the larger issues second. **Write** it so that some of the account reflects what's going on inside your character's head.

- Read Grace Paley's story 'The Loudest Voice' (SS1). It's a brilliantly observed, and humorous account of the dilemmas facing New York Jewish families trying to preserve their historical identity and traditional ways of life in a predominately WASP culture. From your own experience you may recognise here the difficulties of balancing new commitments and old conformities especially if your cultural inheritance is threatened or compromised by the society around you. **Write** about these dilemmas, the compromises, the sacrifices, the resolutions. Try shaping the material into letter form, or write it up as a script. Start with an incident/chance remark/image that triggers the action and debate.

- It shocked George Orwell while he was serving in the Burma Police to discover that the Burmese thought he was pink not white, and that his hairy body repelled them, as did his strong body odour. Burmese people sweat little and are faint-haired. **Write** a description of the 'Brit' from the point of view of another ethnic or racial group.

- Shahid Iqbal is a common Asian name. The *Guardian* told the stories of five Iqbals. The first couldn't get a job in Birmingham despite his excellent qualifications. He changed his name to Richard Brown, and within days went through a successful interview. The second wouldn't change his name and said: 'I'm Asian and proud of it.' A third Iqbal had the same problems finding work. 'Would I change my name?' he asked. 'No, your name is who you are.' A fourth Iqbal also refused to changed his name. 'Changing my name would be buying into the white man's game.' A fifth Iqbal thought no one would believe him if he changed his name to Richard Brown. The Richard Brown Iqbal is now a successful businessman. As one of his clients said to him:

'You're alright for one of them, aren't you.' **Write** down your reflections on this story. Work them into a poem perhaps. Maybe use *Richard Brown* as a working title.

- Linton Kwesi Johnson is a performance poet and a black Englishman, but he's also aware of his Caribbean roots. In his early days as a writer he was influenced by the Black Panther Movement, by books like Fanon's *The Wretched of the Earth*, and by the writings of fellow blacks such as Langston Hughes, Edward Kamau Brathwaite and Aimé Césaire. Appalled by his treatment in Britain, his early impetus to write was 'an urgency to express the anger and the frustrations and the hopes and the aspirations of my generation growing up in this country under the shadow of racism.' But he, like others aware of their island roots, adopted a rasta language in some of his writing. This was language as a political instrument; a way of announcing the self and giving it strength and value through words. Do you recognise Linton Kwesi Johnson's experience in your own life? **Write** about it – the reading, the anger, the puzzlement. Have words worked for you? Do they announce who you are loud and clear?

- Language is the great marker of self and belonging. Merle Collins, another black writer, was brought up in the Caribbean on a school diet of Dickens and Austen. Thus her mind was 'colonised'. Now she acknowledges the strength of the Great Eng. Lit. Tradition, but in her writing fires a cannon of her own. She uses patois, and exploits the rhythms and patterns of ordinary speech to express the diversity of her writing identity. Anita Desai, the Indian novelist and short story writer, faces similar challenges as a 'colonised' writer brought up in the ember light of empire. Her compromise is an Anglo-Indian style that acknowledges the nativity of Indian speech while also using the lingo of a western-educated, Standard English user. One of the points I want to emphasise is the fact that, just as there is no *one* English identity, there is no *one* English language. There are many Englishes, because language thrives in diversity and difference. In fact, it is now said that Standard English and RP is just another dialect version of our lan-

guage. As writers that's something worth reminding ourselves. **Write** a piece in regional dialect.

- Tony Harrison, poet and classicist, wrote a sequence of
  poems called *The School of Eloquence*. At grammar school
  they tried to tighten his loose Yorkshire vowels and soften
  his solid consonants. The teacher didn't like his cloth-cap
  talk, and mocked his pronunciation. Eloquence is the art of
  fine speaking. Where does that leave the language of the
  street and the hearth, demotic language, the words of ordinary folk? Has your speech been mocked? Has it raised an
  eyebrow? **Write** about the occasion. If it made you angry, let
  it show, but not by shouting. Be more subtle and deadly.

- If you are interested in sport consider the part it plays in the
  construction of national identity. **Write** about this. Maybe
  you could take a sporting event as your starting point, or the
  image of the national flag.

Survival Kit

- How people think about themselves, see themselves and
  behave depends on what kind of society they are born into
  and at what kind of level they enter. Writers, most especially writers, need to understand the mechanics of social
  identity, not least because the survival pack doesn't always
  work. Sometimes the price of belonging is the loss of individual identity. The *me* gets lost in the many. How to balance the demands of one's social being and one's private
  being and resolve their frequent arguments has been the
  stuff of fiction and autobiography since pen found paper.
  Can you recall a period/episode where your private and
  public being were set on collision course? **Write** about it.

- The truth of the matter is we are all the time making adjustments and compromises and rearranging our social selves.
  I went to boarding school and I had a Birmingham accent. I
  soon changed that. Survival kit only has posh-speak available. Very soon I was like the rest of the identi-kit kids,

blazered and school-tied. In the playground I'd kick a football around, but really I was playing other games – guessing the codes, the rules of behaviour, the pecking orders.

'Rugger' was the official school sport, coarsened later to 'rugby'. Football was frowned on – too working class. Rugby encouraged team spirit, courage. Not throwing yourself willingly, eyes bolting from your sockets, into a thrash of fists and a trample of nail-sprouting boots was considered cowardice in the face of the enemy and punishable by a public, on-the-spot bollocking. What sort of survival pack were you kitted out with? **Write** about it.

- It's a commonplace to describe social behaviour in terms of games. I'm sure you've observed yourself playing games and others too. Simple ones. Elaborated ones. And ones that are highly ritualised like the mating game. **Write** about a life game. Adopt the stance of a slightly cynical observer. Not too cynical, that sours the writing. Be cynical enough to give the writing sharpness and make it tangy. Again, shaping the work as a list of instructions might suit your satirical purpose. Imagine you have conducted a field study of strange tribal behaviour among your colleagues/friends. Write up your observations in the form of an anthropological report – with recommendations!

- Of course there are lots of social groupings within the greater social order. Family is one. School is another. A gang is another. A business is another. An office is another. Select one of these groups and outline the codes and passwords entrants have to learn. **Write** about this as if you are listing a set of joining instructions. Or as if you were describing the operating instructions you might find on the inside lid of the standard issue survival kit. Or any way you like.

- Not everyone wants to be a joiner. Many people would rather be on the outside. Excluded. There are even clubs for the excluded, which kind of defeats the purpose. **Write** about the experience of exclusion. Did you choose to be an outsider or was it forced on you? Concentrate on a particular example and then perhaps draw some general conclusions from your account.

- Some writers feel that they have been excluded from the word go. Indeed from the words 'mum', 'dad', 'Britain'. What do I mean by this last sentence? Let your thinking here lead you into some writing – jottings, notes, journal entries – it doesn't matter. **Write** down something.

- Exclusion determines the way some people look at life and, therefore, the way they write. Can you think of any writer(s) where the experience of exclusion/displacement governs their work? There are some celebrated twentieth-century writers who displaced themselves. Famous escapees include Samuel Beckett and James Joyce, both of whom left Ireland to write in Paris. Each of them believed that writers in the position of the outsider are best placed to see clearly and take in a wider view. What is your own experience of leaving/departing/migrating? Maybe it's second-hand. A member of your family migrated: a grandparent from war, a parent from unemployment, a friend from a broken family? Imagine one of them telling you their story. **Write** the monologue/interview.

- Maybe, at some time in your life, you were left alone for a long period. Maybe you chose isolation. Because displacement takes many forms, it could be more psychological than physical. **Write** about displacement. Select an appropriate form for the subject such as a supposed diary or a letter to a close friend, or an address to the wall if there's no close friend.

- Edward Said, the prominent cultural critic and champion of Palestinian rights, has recently published his autobiography *Out of Place*. This title refers to his own uncertain place within his family and their ambivalent position living always on the move in Egypt, Lebanon and Palestine. He felt that his childhood home was in a place, but not *of* the place. He was an Arab, but also an American; he was a Protestant in a Muslim society; he was a minority within a Christian minority. He found all these identities conflicting and troubling as a child growing up in a wealthy, but migrant middle-eastern family. **Write** about being out of place and the adjustments that have to be made to try and get into place. What is the price of trying to belong?

- In one large sense we are all displaced, expelled from the Garden, the inheritance that is ours. We are born *in medias res* – right into the middle of things. We're halfway down the stream before we realise we're in the water. The world does not stop, waiting for us to be born before it can start up again. Some birthplaces are less des res than others however, and they force stark choices on writers.

  Nowhere is this more obvious than in Northern Ireland. Gary Mitchell is a Protestant playwright. (It's OK to say: 'a Protestant playwright' in the context of Northern Ireland. You wouldn't say: 'X, who lives in London, is a *Protestant* playwright'.) Now why is this? At school, Gary says he found out 'that the Pope was the anti-Christ, that Roman Catholics were the enemy, and that we as Protestants were in fact the chosen people.' Some identity tag!

  But when the British Government began, in his view, to distance itself from the Province in the 1980s, he and others felt let down and he started to question his loyalty to Queen and country. 'Everybody reaches a point in their life,' he says, 'where they have to make a decision – basically a question of good or evil. I decided to be good, and fortunately, what I found was writing plays. I was able to use them to continue my exploration of myself, humanity, my community, and what it means to be Protestant...'

  I think lots of us are at some kind of crisis point without realising it. Some of us feel we are at more than one crisis point at the same time, they're coming that thick and fast. It's either that, or we spend our time looking the other way hoping it will all go away. But crunch-time comes eventually. Pressure builds up. Bang! And we have to face the music. We grope for solutions hoping someone else has got one for us. But solutions are never quite resolutions, and even they can turn messy. And sometimes there's always enough critical mass left over from the first explosion to fuel the next crisis. Do you recognise this scenario? Think about the phrases underlined above. **Write** about any one of them.

- Other metaphors to describe key moments in our lives are more reassuring. 'Threshold' or 'crossroads' signify the purposeful and the positive. Consider one of these metaphors. **Write** a piece using one of them as your title. Perhaps you think these are clichéd ways of looking at/interpreting experience. OK. Choose a better title!

- So, where you're coming from makes you the writer you are. The reasons why you write may determine whether you write from the centre or the margins. But wherever you are, whatever your origins or roots, you have some critical questions to answer. They are? Where have I come from or how did I get here? What am I doing *here* or where do I stand? Am I right? Middle? Left? Nowhere? Haven't a clue? I like this last position because it's honest and because it gives writing a chance. The mind's not pre-set. It's open. Receptive even. It gives writing a space to explore, check out, test.

  You'll notice the language I've got myself into here is not monochrome. There's a political colouring to it. 'Right', 'middle', 'left' stand for conservative, conformist, radical. I'm almost suggesting all writers, 'real' writers (see chapter 4), must be committed – committed to something. Not necessarily a political position or a religious one or a moral one or a philosophic one. Perhaps especially not these kinds of commitment. The least commitment a writer should have, the minimal due, no concessions given, should be a commitment to trying to find out, to trying. I mean trying to write, everyday, just writing. Doing the act. Doing it. And I mean also trying to find out about things, you, the I, the world, the reasoning why. An undecided mind is different from a closed mind. And very different from an empty mind. If you feel you can usefully write about your writing at this point write about it. There may be little squirms of thought forming as a result of what I've said above. Look in your mind. Look *into* your mind. What's there? **Write. Just write**.

Waking in the Dark – Women Writing

- Our sexuality and gender shape us like no other. The construction of our sexual identities, which we call 'gender', how femaleness becomes woman and maleness becomes man, the script men use to become manly and masculine, the script women use to become womanly and feminine, was first the province of behavioural scientists (mainly men), and lately the concern of feminists.

Women's fate in history is neatly enclosed (feminist historians have exposed confinements of many kinds in that history) in the following story. Lenin, the Bolshevik commander, leader of the successful uprising of 1916 and architect of Communism, for a while had a French lover, a political activist and passionate supporter of the cause. Original photographs, censored and long hidden amongst Party archives, and now rediscovered, show a very beautiful woman. To prevent Lenin's image being tarnished by rumours of the affair circulating, the Soviet authorities airbrushed her image into ugliness in the belief that no one would then believe she was worthy of any man's attention, least of all, the Father of the Revolution.

The demonising (making ugly) of woman and the deifying of man has always been a perverse and discriminating pattern in western narratives. The historical record, literary texts, the institutions and practices of national and cultural life, and language itself have spoken with a predominately male voice. Women's lot has been silence, their experience mute, and muted. Until now.

At first, the voices were single, but in contemporary times they have become a chorus. First – Mary Wollstonecroft in *A Vindication of the Rights of Women* (1792). Later, Virginia Woolf in *A Room of One's Own* (1929). Then Simone de Beauvoir in *The Second Sex* (1953), Betty Friedan in *The Feminine Mystique* (1963), Germaine Greer in *The Female Eunuch* (1970), Kate Millet in *Sexual Politics* (1971), Tillie Olsen in *Silences* (1980), Dale Spender in *Man-made Language* (1980), Susan Faludi in *Backlash* (1991) and many others. For four decades now the voices of female writers have been heard exposing the oppressions of the past, asserting the experience of woman, and politicising new generations.

As Simone de Beauvoir first diagnosed, the gender identity of women is a social construct created by men defining *woman* as other or not male, and thus, less than human. A knowledge of how this came to be and continues to be – gender politics – may well be a forming and reforming influence on any young woman writer. Read one of the above books to get you thinking. In history, women have been tabooed off the male stage. Has the long history of female exclusion been echoed in your own life? **Write** about it.

- 'We are all trained to be female impersonators,' said Gloria Steinem, American feminist and critic. What do you think she means by 'impersonators'? Would you say you've been 'trained'? How 'trained'? **Write** about an aspect of your upbringing that supports Steinem's observation.

- If it's possible to talk about women being 'trained' to impersonate, what about men? Aren't they too being trained to put on other faces/voices and be someone else? **Write** a piece about men entitled *Face(s)*.

- 'All women lead a double life.' Triple or quadruple you might say. What does this mean exactly? Does it apply to men? **Write** about your 'other' lives. Choose an appropriate form.

- 'Women used to have romance parts. Now they have quest adventures.' Carolyn Heilbrun. Compare your life with that of your mother or grandmother. Have they been so different? Do the differences suggest Heilbrun is right? Interview some older women. **Write** up the interviews. Don't present them in a question/answer format. Mix physical description with comment, analysis and direct quote.

- Read Jamaica Kincaid's short piece called 'Girl' from Angela Carter's anthology *Wayward Girls and Wicked Women*. It's a non-stop tirade by a mother preparing her daughter for her social and sexual role in life. Volley after volley of do's and dont's assail the girl. They are the rules of the Cinderella game. It is still quite popular! **Write** a harangue for our times called *Boy* in which a father or mother gives advice to his/her son.

- Laddishness is a popular male identity. Always has been. Victorians called 'lads', 'roughs'. 'Blokishness' is another identity. **Write** a satirical profile/portrait of a stereotypical lad – a jack-the-lad or a one-of-the-lads lad. Title – *Lad*.

- **Write** a piece entitled *Strutting*.

- **Write** a piece entitled *Stud*.

- **Write** a piece entitled *Pulling* or *On the Pull*.

- A minor character in George Eliot's novel *Daniel Deronda* complains of the 'slavery of being a girl'. Surely in this new millennium woman's freedom has been won and sexual equality assured. Or is 'liberation' an illusion? Do the old servitudes still persist in disguised forms? Where's the evidence? **Write** a letter to a younger woman or man analysing the current state of gender politics, identifying possible areas where chauvinist attitudes and behaviour still exist, warning your recipient how the new chauvinism disguises itself, and offering advice on how to cope.

- Anne Elliott, a character in Jane Austen's novel *Persuasion*, says: 'Men . . . the pen has been in their hands.' Read some of Dale Spender's book *Man-made Language*. Read a few pages of *Womanwords* by Jane Mills. Collect some examples of man-made language from contemporary youth culture, from the street, from the clubs, from lads' mags. **Write** a short magazine article discussing the issue of women and words.

- Women writers have in the past been categorised as either bitchy or gossipy. They shriek like harpies or they're trite and trivial. But the women's movement has 'allowed' women to be angry. It has legitimised righteous anger. Read some 'angry' women's work. Read poems by Adrienne Rich, Sylvia Plath or Anne Sexton. Or read Andre Dworkin. Think of something that has made you angry as a man or as a woman, as a gay or heterosexual. **Write** about it in confessional mode as if you were recounting the episode to a close friend. Remember anger can get the better of writing and the writer, so we are talking about *controlled* anger.

There is a political point to be made here. In writing and the production of literature (all those genres and tropes) you might argue that control has always been a male restraint. Men have policed literary endeavour, setting the standards, agreeing the rules. The balance of form, the order and symmetry of sentences and paragraphs, good grammared expression have been a way of keeping literature chaste. Discipline's the word. Can you see any truth here or is this an over-reaction by exasperated women? Think about it and let rip if you want to break the bondage of conventions. But take care! Overdoing the expletives can spoil the bother.

- The women's movement has legitimised women's experience. It has made the personal acceptable in public for men and women both. Writing about the inner life, the deeper recesses is OK. You can write the body, express the erotic, flaunt your fantasies. You can write naked. Write raw. Take a look at some of Georgia O'Keefe's flower paintings. They pulse with the symbolism of female sexuality. Select one painting, for example *Canna Red and Orange*. **Write** a response. Try and use rhythms to suggest sexual energy as it intensifies or relaxes. Write a poem, or a surreal prose piece, or a psychological analysis of your chosen painting(s).

- Freud said that women daydream erotic scripts, men ambitious ones. If you think this is a true distinction between the sexes **write** a performance monologue for a male or female character. If you think Freud's remark distorts the truth write a monologue that shows this.

- According to psychologists both sexes have characteristics of the other in their make-up. **Write** a story in which a male character recognises the female side of his psyche, but cannot cope with his realisation. It might be easier to explore this theme through a monologue by himself or through one by his girlfriend or as an encounter between the man and his counsellor. But then, maybe he wouldn't go to a counsellor. That's a woman thing! Make up your mind about this guy and write in an appropriate voice and form.

- Read Kate Chopin's short story *The Awakening*. Describe an awakening of your own. Put the experience at a fictional distance by presenting it as a short story with characters other than yourself and family in a setting (place and time) unfamiliar to you in real life. **Write** in the first person.

- At the end of *The Awakening*, Edna drowns herself. She doesn't hurl herself off a bridge. She is far quieter. She puts on an old bathing costume, goes down to the beach and starts to swim out to sea. She lets the currents take her exhausted body. It is a real and symbolic death. She has struggled for independence against the stifling world of Victorian values, swum against the tide. It has exhausted her.

  The fictional fate awaiting the strong-minded woman suffocating in a dead relationship or confined within the limited perspectives of Victorian womanhood, was either suicide or madness. It often was in reality too. One of the most powerful evocations of the desperation felt by the caged wife is in Antonia White's short story set during the First World War period and entitled 'The House of Clouds' (SS1). Read this if you can. A woman is committed to an asylum after trying to drown herself. At all the critical points in her life it is a man who makes the decisions – her fiancé, her father, her priest standing in for God the Father, her doctor, her psychiatrist. In the madhouse, she passes through a series of strange and terrifying transformations. She is a horse, a snake, a bird. She is mutilated with all the wounds of the trench dead. And so on. Each of these fabled intervals in the story is a feminist parable with something to say about women's suffering. Read 'To Room 19', a short story by Doris Lessing (MBSS). **Write** a fable illustrating some aspect of women's experience of male oppression.

- One of the best-known contemporary accounts of female submission and a telling analysis of how patriarchy works with woman's collusion, is Fay Weldon's short story 'Weekend' (MBSS). Read it. Enjoy it. Have you ever observed this dutiful pattern of female forelock tugging? Is it all a matter of expectations? We do what is the expected without question. Have you noticed this behaviour in women generally

or women you know in particular? **Write** your own version
of the Fay Weldon scenario.

- **Write** an animal fable that illustrates how the power relationships work between the sexes.

- Read U. A. Fanthorpe's sardonic poem 'Not My Best Side'
(20WP). In the first two parts, women, who are the subject of
paintings by Picasso and Uccello, speak their minds, but are
shouted down in the third and last part. Choose a painting
by a male painter that depicts a woman. Look at it carefully,
trying to decide how the artist depicts/treats his subject.
Traditionally the model is female and passive, the artist
male and active, the controlling force in the relationship.
Write a story using the model/artist situation in which the
conventional relationship is reversed.

- Read Denise Lervatov's poem 'Abel's Bride' (20WP). Does
this poem put its finger on the basic differences between
men and women? Women stay in the caves beside bones?
Men go out without a mirror in their pockets? What does
Lervatov mean when she says women's 'being is a cave'?
Are men scared of women? **Write** about this possibility.

- In Virginia Woolf's short story 'Lappin and Lapinova' (SS2),
a woman and her fiancé play a game in which they pretend
to be rabbits, but when this make-believe comes up against
the realities of married life it collapses, much to the distress
of the woman. The wife feels trapped, and uses the fable to
try and explain to her husband how she feels. Lapinova has
been hunted and caught in a snare, she says. She cannot run
free anymore and play with Lappin. The husband's
response is to shrug and read the newspaper. This story
says something about the differences between men and
women. Make a list of those differences. Do this with a
friend. Look at your findings. **Write** a diatribe, lament,
prophesy based on this material.

- Read Adrienne Rich's poem 'Waking in the Dark' (20WP)
where the woman narrator walks 'the unconscious forest'
and men have sold their world to machines. The writer/
narrator despairs. She wishes she could take binoculars,

look at 'the earth, the wildwood' and see 'where the split began'. What does the phrase: 'walk the unconscious' mean? What is the 'split'? Where is the wild wood? **Write** a commentary on this and anything else in the poem.

- **Write** a spell against white male power.

- Men move on a fairly predictable path to achievement; women transform themselves only after an awakening. Has this been true of the men and women in your family? If so, tell the story. **Write** the piece as a chapter of a family history.

- 'You have to look back before you realise you've awoken or been woken.' Take a hard look at your own past. Is this true? **Write** down your thoughts as they come. Let the ideas and feelings flow. Don't try and shape them. Don't be concerned with grammatical correctness. Write free.

- **Write** an understanding, compassionate yet warts-and-all tribute/celebration of a real friend.

- Here's an intriguing idea:

  Each of us carries the imprint of a friend met along the way.
  In each the trace of each. For good or for evil
  In wisdom or in folly each stamped by each.

  Reflect upon the imprints individual friends have left in you. **Write** a piece exploring these contributions and speculate what you have given in exchange as it were.

- Read Grace Nicholls's poem 'Wha Me Mudder Do'. **Write** a poem in honour of your mother or father. The idea is to show that in the ordinary ways they have of going about raising a family, doing the washing, dressing themselves up, they express a quiet independence. Of course, if your experience is not one of admiration, qualified admiration, you won't be writing a tribute.

- In her recent book *Stiffed*, Susan Faludi claims that men are in crisis. They have lost their way. In preparing for the book she spent years interviewing men about themselves. Time and time again she heard confused sons blame their fathers for not giving them a clear idea of how to be a man. The silence of fathers was deafening. What models of maleness did you inherit? From school? From father, older brother? From mates? What do you think it means to be a man in the new millennium?

Put down some ideas. Be as honest as you can be. Don't be afraid of hurting your feelings. It may be difficult reflecting on close family relationships. Maybe more so for a man than a woman! But then isn't that part of masculinity – a stunted part of masculinity – to be anxious about feelings? **Write** a no-holds-barred, autobiographic piece. Don't worry about repetitions, mistakes, wordiness. Just avoid the clichéd. Alternatively write about a mate of yours and his patrimony.

- Imagine a male writer has written to the letters column of one of the broadsheets complaining that the women's movement has emasculated men. **Write** a letter rebutting the charge. Argue, amongst other things, that women's liberation has also been men's liberation. Of course, you may not think women have been liberated. You may think they enjoy only the illusion of freedom. In which case, this will influence your response.

- Anger and violence are not associated with women writers, but Virginia Woolf felt she had to 'kill' one particular 'woman' – the 'Angel in the House', the 'Mother by the Hearth'. These gendered images censored her writing. They had to go. What do you think she meant by these phrases? Make some notes in response. **Try writing** a sardonic contemporary piece on gender images. Use one of these Woolf phrases as your title.

- To Sylvia Plath poetry spurted like a 'blood jet'. Emily Dickinson trembled at its 'loaded gun'. Stevie Smith saw it being born 'in splinters covered in blood'. Do these painful images coincide with anything in your own writing and progress as a writer? **Try writing** about the 'birthing' of a particular work of yours and explore the difficulties and rewards of the experience.

- Your views on writing women and women writing have changed no doubt. You have cast off obsolete attitudes, assassinating angels and devils alike. Consider the evolution of your writer-image. Has it been a question of minor modifications and accommodations gradually accumulating, a slow simmer? Or has it been a matter of 'writer's rage', a sudden seismic shift in attitude and feeling? Step outside yourself and take a long hard look at the writer you see. Now **try writing** a writing biography charting the necessary and excusable assassinations. You could use this last word as your title!

- 'It's a man's world. A woman should acknowledge her hurt, her anger and her hope of "justice"; even a hope of revenge might be a good thing in her work...' said Joyce Carol Oates, the contemporary American novelist. Many women writers ignore their 'hurt(s)'. What are yours? Is this 'man's world' inhospitable to the woman writer? If you make some notes in answer to these questions you can use them to craft a more deadly reply. As a woman writer, what might you hope to avenge in your writing? What justice are you seeking? For what injuries do you want redress? For what grievances, acknowledgement? Using preliminary notes of response **try writing** a *J'accuse* piece, a fierce denunciation of some aspect of the unjust world facing the woman writer.

- 'Every woman writer has to cast off her Cinderella self and her Little Red Riding Hood habit, and become the wolf.' **Write** something wolfish just for the sake of being vulpine.

References

Armitage, S., *All Points North* (Penguin, 1999).
Austen, J., *Persuasion* (Penguin, 1998).
Barnes, J., *England, England* (Picador, 1998).
Burgess, A., *The Clockwork Orange* (Penguin, 2000).
Carter, A., *The Bloody Chamber* (Vintage, 1995).
Carter, A., *Wayward Girls and Wicked Women* (Virago, 1992).
Chopin, K., *The Awakening* (Dover, 1993).

cummings, e. e., *Selected Poems* (Faber and Faber, 1988).
de Beauvoir, S., *The Second Sex* (Vintage, 1997).
Desai, A., *Clear Light of Day* (Penguin, 1990).
Doyle, R., *Paddy Clarke. Ha. Ha. Ha.* (Vintage, 1994).
Duffy, M., *That's How It Was* (Virago, 1983).
Dworkin, A., *Life and Death* (Virago, 1997).
Eliot, G., *Daniel Deronda* (Penguin, 1990).
Faludi, S., *Backlash* (Vintage, 1993).
Faludi, S., *Stiffed: The Betrayal of the Modern Man* (Chatto & Windus, 1999).
Fanon, F., *The Wretched of the Earth* (Penguin, 1990).
Friedan, B., *The Feminine Mystique* (Penguin, 1991).
Golding, W., *The Inheritors* (Faber and Faber, 1955).
Golding, W., *Lord of the Flies* (Faber and Faber, 1996).
Greer, G., *The Female Eunuch* (Flamingo, 1971).
Harrison, T., *Selected Poems* (Penguin, 1995).
Heilbrun, C., *Writing a Woman's Life* (Woman's Press, 1988).
Hoban, R., *Riddley Walker* (Picador, 1982).
Homer, *Odyssey* (Penguin, 1991).
Kafka, F., *Metamorphosis and Other Stories* (Penguin, 1992).
Millet, K., *Sexual Politics* (Virago, 1977).
Mills, J., *Womanwords* (Virago, 1991).
Moore, L., *Birds of America* (Faber and Faber, 1998).
Nicholls, G., *Lazy Thoughts of a Lazy Woman* (Virago, 1989).
O'Keefe, G., *Georgia O'Keefe* (Phaidon, 1997).
Olsen, T., *Silences* (Virago, 1980).
Plath, S., *The Journals of Sylvia Plath* (Ballantine, 1982).
Rich, A., *Poetry and Prose* (W. W. Norton, 1993).
Said, E., *Out of Place* (Granta, 1999).
Spender, D., *Man-made Language* (Pandora, 1998).
Woolf, V., *A Room of One's Own* (Penguin, 1992).
Wollstonecroft, M., *A Vindication of the Rights of Women* (Dover, 1996).

2 | Hidden Places

The Second Self

- In Joseph Conrad's short story *The Secret Sharer*, a naval captain is ready to weigh anchor and sail his ship home. He takes the night watch to give his crew a chance to rest before the difficult return voyage begins. In the dead of night a man clambers aboard. He looks like a ghost, and he has a story to tell. He is a sailor himself, a refugee, fleeing a false accusation of murder. Members of his ship's company are hunting him down.

  The captain believes the man's story and, against his better judgement, agrees to hide him aboard. In doing this he is acting against accepted maritime practice which demands that no one shall be given passage if suspected of a crime at sea, and against the rules of the navigation company who employ him which require stowaways to be handed over to the relevant authorities.

  Shortly after the stranger is stowed away below decks the pursuers arrive. The captain persuades them only he and the crew are aboard. Reassured, the party leave. The ship casts off and moves away from its mooring. The following night, to release his secret sharer, the captain sails his ship dangerously close to shore. The nearer he gets the better the stowaway's chance of surviving the swim to safety. The man slips overboard and is gone. No one is any the wiser. The ship completes an uneventful return.

The theme of the story is the self and the other self sometimes called the alter ego. This other self is also called a *doppelgänger*. Thus an encounter with a double or *doppelgänger* is a meeting with oneself in another guise. In Conrad's story the captain meets his double and has to decide what to do with him. But double doesn't mean replica. *Doppelgängers* have a life of their own. They can be possessive tenants and dictate terms to the landlord. In *The Secret Sharer*, captain and fugitive are opposites – one, the dutiful rule-bound naval officer, the other, a renegade with a price on his head.

To understand more about this 'twin' effect you really should read Conrad's story. Try and analyse its psychological realities. On the one hand, there is the public, prescribed, scripted if you like, role of captain. He is in a position of authority and responsibility, but he behaves irresponsibly. He trusts the word of a complete stranger, endangers his ship, himself and his crew. For what? Why? It's amazing how within one person there can exist such opposite selves. **Write** about your other self. Write freely with no shape in mind. Give a name to your alter ego. Recall an event where you acted out of character driven by something you now find difficult to explain. Think back to the event. With hindsight you may be able to give a clearer account of your behaviour.

- In an interview about his autobiography *Out of Place*, Edward Said talks about the 'emergence of a second self'. He was a Protestant Arab American belonging to a small group within the minority Christian community in Muslim-dominated Lebanon. This 'mixed' identity called 'Edward' he found confusing. 'So very early on,' he says, 'I became aware of another identity. Almost a resistant one, that somehow eluded the nets and the traps and the tyrannies that one encounters as a kid growing up, which is an identity which is probably there in all of us.' **Write** about your 'resistant self' and the traps, nets, tyrannies of your development. Focus on one particular incident because this will give you more control over the material.

- Said describes how his aunt made him aware of the political situation in Jerusalem and the whole region because of the way she dedicated her life to the Palestinians living all around them. 'Reality imposed itself on me,' he writes. 'It was out of that peculiar mesh of things that this other identity emerged.' Who has had the most influence on you and the way you are? **Write** about how this influence has worked and how reality 'imposed itself' on you.

- Wilfrid Owen's poem 'Strange Meeting' (RB), describes an encounter with a mysterious brother soldier in an underground vault. Imagine meeting a forgotten you. Create a suitable setting for the meeting. **Write** a narrative poem about the event.

- In his novel *Age of Iron*, the South African writer J. M. Coetze imagines a white woman dying of cancer and being forced for the first time in her protected life to witness the racial violence of her country. After a young black activist seeking refuge in her house is killed by the security forces, an alcoholic down-and-out appears as if from nowhere and sits outside her house. His presence forces her to face up to some painful truths.

  Is he the embodiment of the county's shabby and bankrupt morality? Is he the squalid face of her own hypocrisies? Is he from the 'foul rag-and-bone shop of the heart', to quote Yeats? If you have ever come face to face with someone who made you feel accountable and who forced you to re-examine your own life **write** about the experience.

- In his latest novel, *Losing Nelson*, Barry Unsworth identifies the heroic naval captain as 'his own dark twin'. Which historical or fictional character would you choose as your twin? Maybe you could adopt the voice of some of the 'wives' in Carol Ann Duffy's collection *The World's Wife*! **Write** about your historical twin in the Duffy fashion or **try writing** a letter to a friend all about your new 'partner'.

- In both the Conrad and Owen narratives the one encountered is apparitional, a presence as much as a physical entity. Ghostly arrivals, a tap on the front door on a misty winter's night, are the stuff of supernatural fiction. The word 'ghost' derives from the Anglo-Saxon word *ghast*. We also get the word 'guest' from the same root and, of course, 'aghast' meaning 'like a ghost'. The darker, ghastly version of the alter ego theme is manifest as a psychosis in the celebrated story of *Dr Jekyll and Mr Hyde* by Robert Louis Stevenson. Many stories exploit the horror of Mr Nice and Mr Nasty co-existing in the same body. *The Picture of Dorian Gray* by Oscar Wilde explores similar disturbing territory. **Write** a modern version of the Mr(s) Nice, Mr(s) Nasty theme.

- Read Sylvia Plath's poems 'The Other' or 'Eavesdropper' – an accidental echo here of the word *doppelgänger*. Invent a next-door neighbour or eavesdropper, a less reputable version of yourself. **Write** about this character or **try writing** a poem using *The Other* as your title.

- The winning poem of the 1999 National Poetry Competition was written by Simon Rae and titled 'Believed' (*Independent on Sunday*, 26 March 2000). 'There's a missing person in everyone,' is the arresting opening line. Take this idea and **work it over and into** your own version. Read 'Believed'. In it the poet finds his missing self and goes for a walk with his new companion.

- **Write** a piece entitled *Stalker*.

- Read Tess Gallagher's poem 'Instructions to the Double' (20WP). This could be a mother's advice to her daughter, a version of Polonius's advice to Hamlet, but it's harder-edged and less moralistic. **Write** your own coming-of-age *Instructions* or *Guidance* or *Advice* or *Resolutions* to a young woman or man.

- Imagine derelict ground, an overgrown garden or a deserted park. You push open the rusted gate. You enter. It is like a place you had long forgotten. There's an overgrown pond. Some broken statuary. You interpret this fantasy as the neglected grounds of the self. Continue the fantasy. Do you recover the place? Is it recoverable? Is it worth the effort? Or do you wander round the deserted grounds surprised and maybe shocked at each turn of the path, each mossed-over relic of the past staring or ignoring you in the wilderness? **Write** about three or four pages.

- 'In the middle of the journey of our life I came by myself in a dark wood where the straight way was lost.' Dante. *The Inferno.* In his massive fresco of the *Last Judgement* in the Sistine Chapel, Michaelangelo painted his own portrait as a pelt, a skin of himself draped over Saint Bartholomew's arm. **Write** about a meeting with yourself, maybe in an altered state or form, say at a late-night party or at a conference or on the Underground. Or anywhere of your choosing.

- Read Carol Ann Duffy's poem 'Only Dreaming'. Someone has a night caller. Who is the ghostly intruder, the phantom seducer? **Write** a poem entitled *Phantom Lover.* Try and take an unexpected slant on the subject.

- The boy narrator in Edward White's novel *A Boy's Own Story* goes to see a psychiatrist. Dr O'Reilly concludes that his young patient is wrestling with his unconscious, 'an immense dark brother...a Caliban as quicksilver as Ariel...a *doppelgänger* ... determined to deny him adventure' and make him conform. The doctor has to outwit 'this brilliant tyrant'.

  But the boy himself is increasingly aware that there is another 'scattered sort of narrative' taking place within him. All the real movements of a life he says are 'gradual, then sudden...they pulse like quasars from long-dead stars to reach the vivid planet...and then something irrevocable flashes out of nowhere'. Has something irrevocable flashed in your life out of nowhere? Have you fought an inner tyrant? Remember both Paul and Tobias in the Bible had to wrestle with avenging angels. **Write** about the tyrants or the avenging angels or the irrevocabilities in your life.

- **Write** about the 'scattered narratives' emerging in your life.

- Where are you?
  How are you?
  Who are you?
  Why are you?
  When are you?

These questions are addressed to yourself. **Write** a one-sentence answer to each. Finish with an unanswered question of your own. Print both Q & A in your poem.

- I remember a teacher said something too personal about me once. Not to my face. A friend passed on the comment. 'She said you were an alcoholic,' he reported. Me? Impossible! I hardly drank. Who was this drunkard? Aggrieved, I asked the teacher why she'd reinvented me. *'Melancholic,'* she said, 'you're melancholic.' That wasn't so bad. *I* could live with that. *I* suddenly saw a pale, languishing melancholy kind of a self. *She* saw a boy taking the world too seriously and turning a position into a posture. In some school reports you wouldn't recognise yourself. Put together a self-portrait made up of all the misjudgements others have made about you. **Write** it as a poem. Remember it's someone else's *you*.

- In her poem 'Aunt Jennifer's Tigers' (20WP), Adrienne Rich weaves together traditional images of woman: the fireside spinner, the fragile creature, delicate as a bird, with 'fingers fluttering', the submissive wife whose hand is weighed down with the 'wedding band' and 'ringed with ordeals'. But another self endures in tiger-guise, powerful and independent. Aunt Jennifer's embroidered tigers may be the embodiment of her suppressed yearnings, but for Adrienne Rich herself it is the constellation Orion that represents her other self. In her poem of the same name, he is her childhood's hero, a 'cast-iron Viking, my helmed/lion-heart king in prison'. These childhood fantasies mature into a more erotic desire to be infused with his stellar burning, with the Christ-hero hanging in the sky, victim and vanquisher both. Can you think of an image that embodies your own yearnings for independence? If so, work up the idea into a poem. Rich's poems are loosely structured and present themselves as a series of vignettes. **Write** in a similar format for this piece.

- In her own, later comment on 'Orion', Adrienne Rich describes the duality in the poem as a choice between two different kinds of 'love'. On the one hand, there is the 'love' that is 'womanly, maternal and altruistic' – a love defined by the weight of culture; and on the other, there is 'love' as egotism, a force directed by men into creation and associated with achievement and ambition. Well, that commentary was written 30 years ago and things have changed. As Rich herself argued at the time, the word 'love' is in need of re-vision. In note form, write down your thoughts on how women's expectations have changed, how yours have changed. Is 'man' or the male the secret other to which all women aspire? You can only succeed if you behave like a man, they say to business-women! **Write up** your notes in a more structured form.

• It's worth reading Rich's poem 'Snapshots of a Daughter-in-Law' (20WP) because here she maps out her development as a writer and as an independent woman, and expresses her hopes for the future. In the poem, the adult woman reflects on the roles and images she has played and lived through. Taking a similar title, one that suits your role/position in the world, **write** a piece about your own progress through the variations, personifications, disguises, parts, wigs, manifestations, fashions of that category of existence named 'woman'.

Out of the Depths

• When Orpheus descends into Hades, the Underworld, to search for his dead lover, Eurydice, he charms King Pluto by plucking alluring music from his lyre. As a reward for his playing Pluto allows him to take Eurydice out of the kingdom of the dead and back to earth. On one condition. As they ascend he must not look behind to see if she is following. Only when he reaches the surface can he embrace her. The two lovers make their way slowly back from the depths of Hell. Near the surface Orpheus is unable to resist casting a backwards glance. Eurydice vanishes at his look. Orpheus, heartbroken, wanders the hills. He meets a group of Bacchanals, wild women, worshippers of the god Bacchus. They ask him to play some of his haunting music. But he's inconsolable over the loss of Eurydice and has no heart for music. He refuses. They are furious and they tear him apart.

It is customary to read such myths – journeys into dark places – as narratives of the unconscious self. Traditionally the Underworld has been regarded as the symbolic unknown in our psyches. 'Psyche' derives from the Greek word for 'breath' or 'spirit' and is also the name of the young girl in the story by Apuleius *Cupid and Psyche*. In this story, the god is Psyche's phantom lover visiting her at night. She is forbidden to look at him, but like Orpheus she cannot resist taking a peek while he sleeps. Fatally a speck of hot lamp oil drops on his shoulder as she bends over his sleeping form. He wakes, sees Psyche looking at him, and vanishes, Eurydice-like. Psyche is condemned to wander the world as a love-lost soul until Jupiter takes pity on her and unites her with her divine lover.

The story is a reverse image of the Orpheus narrative. In both there is a forbidden knowledge, temptation, a transgression, darkness, loss of happiness, aimless wanderings and suffering. Adam and Eve all over again! It is Psyche's lamp, a symbol of her intellectual as well as sexual curiosity, her desire to know, that undoes the girl. Maybe these myths are warnings against meddling in mysteries beyond our ken, against trying to find out the secret of the gods. Maybe too they reflect historical truths where rival religious cults, one devoted to Bacchus, one to Orpheus, fought for supremacy amongst the shepherds and citizens inhabiting the islands and coastlines of the Aegean.

Scholars more recently have read 'deeper', more poetic meanings into narratives of this sort. The dark and underground places are seen as the hidden springs of our creative energies. Eurydice can be regarded as Orpheus's muse, the feminine side of his nature, his imaginative and instinctive powers. In looking, either Orpheus is giving in to his desire to know and control these powers, or he has lost faith in their being there at all. Looking on the face of gods is not allowed. The lady's not for turning. There are things too dangerous for man to know. Like the knowledge of death and the illusory, vanishing nature of all things. Another moral of the story is that our creative powers need freedom to go where they will, unimpeded, unrestricted by the inquisitive, prying, keyhole-peering ego. So, writers have to go with the flow, ride the subterranean currents wherever they surge.

This is the wild view of our creative selves. It presumes that this self, feminine like Eurydice, libidinous like Cupid, has its own hiding place in the deeper recesses of the unconscious mind. A refinement of this model might add that Eurydice is the imagination; quicksilver, visionary, phantasmal, and that Cupid is the abundant mysterious energy electrifying the creative vision. Perhaps in this script Orpheus and Pysche herself represent the enquiring side of mind, the reason and the desire for understanding. This sounds like the territory of science, a word derived from the Latin *scientia*, meaning knowledge. In Greek mythology the god of derived knowledge, of method and ordered investigation, is Apollo. So, on the one hand, we have the discipline of enquiry, the conscious crafting of knowledge and action. On the other, the visionary artist, driven by the instinctual, turbulent, unpredictable powers of the deep imagination. These too are represented by the Bacchanalian women in the Orpheus story given to uninhibited dancing and frenzied singing – the original all-night clubbers. They turn on the presumptuous ego and destroy it for not succumbing to their desire.

For another celebrated example of this model read Coleridge's poem 'Kubla Khan'. Interpret the poem in the light of the above remarks and make some notes. At the end of the poem, the poet appears with 'flashing eyes' and 'floating hair'. Readers are advised to take care and 'weave a circle round him thrice'. He is a daemon (demons are minor devils and daemons are powerful spiritual forces). It's not clear whether the circle magically circumscribes the dark spirit or whether it is a dancing circle conjuring and celebrating the powers it is seeking to enclose. Whatever, it is clear the poet, like the Bacchanalian women, is possessed, enchanted, held in thrall. He is the Romantics' vision of the artist, a person possessed by some mysterious, but irresistible power who cannot escape the high destiny of his calling.

Imagine an artist as your central character. Send him on a quest in a modern version of the Orpheus myth. See Jean Valentine's poem 'Orpheus and Eurydice' (20WP) for encouragement. Salman Rushdie has also refashioned the Orpheus and Eurydice myth in his novel *The Ground Beneath Her Feet*, a modernised version of the story, in which a famous pop-singer disappears in a Mexican earthquake and is saved by her Indian lover. **Write** about four sides of a screenplay/story synopsis or write a short poem exploring a different version of this Orphic myth.

- To our modern mind, all this may seem very fanciful. But the idea of the mind being part savage, part civilised and rational, is very much behind Natalie Goldberg's book *Wild Mind*. Here she argues that writers must make contact with their wilder self if they want to write truly, if they want to reach real understanding. It's not reaching after knowledge, not seizing the apple from the tree. It is *attending* it. It is what John Keats, in one of his letters, defined as 'negative capability', the ability to wait on life, accepting 'uncertainties, mysteries, doubts, without any irritable reaching after fact and reason'. He should have warned Orpheus! Actually that's a possible idea for writing. **Write** Keats's letter to Orpheus. Or imagine any historical figure writing a letter of advice or complaint or warning to another. Conduct a correspondence.

- Imagine Casanova writing some subtly amorous pages to St Theresa. **Write** her response. The virgin and the rake!

- To Goldberg, 'wild mind' is all around us, within and without. The big sky is 'wild mind', the dark night is 'wild mind'. We have to attune to it. Its greatest enemy is 'monkey mind'. This is chatter. This is finding excuses not to write. This is preoccupation with the small print of mundane daily life. Yield to 'wild mind' says Goldberg. 'Sit down in the middle of your wild mind,' she says. 'This is about loss of control.' Sounds scary. It was.for Michèle Roberts. Writing about writing her novel *Flesh and Blood*, she admitted: 'I'm scared of all the letting go involved, the plunge into chaos, not-knowing, loss of self, in order to write.'

If this is what it takes then be prepared. This is how Goldberg describes it: 'So, finally the writer must be willing to sit at the bottom of the pit, commit herself to stay there, and let the wild animals approach, even call *them up*, then face them, and not run away.' Here is a dangerous assignment. You have to face the wild here. **Write** about something which you have always avoided, a subject or situation or event that is hard for you to write about. Don't cop out. Stay with it as long as you can. Just keep writing. Don't worry about shaping. Don't sensationalise. Write it straight. And take some comfort from Hemingway who said we should 'write hard and clear about what hurts'.

- There are other terrors awaiting the writer. Rosellen Brown writes in the hope that if she writes her stories down, 'they won't happen'. 'I am trying,' she says, 'at least to buy off the evil eye by throwing red meat at it.' What existential fears lie in wait for you? How secure is your writing self? Do you need to placate the 'dark gods' as D. H. Lawrence called them? Jot down some notes in response to these questions. **Write** up your notes.

- Michèle Roberts has tried to identify her 'deep-seated feelings of insecurity' as a writer. 'What am I afraid of?' she asks herself. 'That I shall die? That I shall jump in, give myself totally, and there'll be nothing and no one there and so I'll die?' This is the fear that made Orpheus turn round and lose his sanity. You get the impression from both Roberts and Brown that their fears run deep. Are they over-dramatising? Examine your own attitudes and feelings about the act of writing. **Write** a list of all the things about writing and the writer's life that frighten you. Group them under different headings. Now shape your ideas and bring them to life in a poem.

- Writers who run search parties for the vagrant self especially where the self is on the run, who track down the self to its hidden lairs, play a dangerous game. But then, as you have probably discovered already, writing can be a risky business. Sylvia Plath was one who fearlessly traversed the unconscious. In the poem 'Telos' from his collection *Birth-*

day Letters, Ted Hughes dramatises Plath's urgent pursuit of her demon fears.

> You burrowed for a way back out of it all.
> Down into a cellar. There in the dark
> Your eyes tight shut
> You turned your mother inside out
> Like ripping a feather-pillow...

Images of shading the eyes from the horror like a child shields itself, the tantrum destruction of the (soft) pillow-mother, the smothering/nurturing death-in-life principle, all register the psychic tremors of this woman. Read some of Plath's last poems from the group 'Ariel' in her *Collected Poems*. Selectively read from Ted Hughes's *Birthday Letters*. They may not inspire you or disturb you into writing, but like all reading they will invade your writing at some point in the future. If anything in this section touch-papers you into writing don't resist, **just write**.

- Some writers believe that we are all 'wounded' and that writers are those who are compelled to explore their pain. Of her husband's distress at their separation Edna O'Brien said: 'he's a writer so he has to explore the wounds.' Another version of this myth is that the writer needs to be a tortured spirit before he/she can write at all. Ted Hughes assumes a pathology in writing when he made this comment on his wife's suicide: 'Every work of art stems from a wound in the soul of the artist. All her creative work tells just one story: her Oedipal love of her father... If Sylvia had been able to free herself from that one wound that racked her, she might have led a normal life, perhaps felt healthy enough to stop writing.' Other writers regard this as questionable post-romantic, sub-Freudian psychology. What do you think? Taking a more balanced approach **write** a counter argument challenging this pathological view of the writer's condition.

- Helen Dunmore, poet and novelist, in a recent interview, says she writes about the lie that there is 'normal life on top'. She says: 'we all know that every moment, barely concealed beneath the smooth surface, something dark and malevolent threatens to erupt.' The threat is from within, from the emotions. 'Jealousy, sibling rivalry – the intimation that you are not loved as you should be – have the potential to destroy us.' This is a confrontational view of our hidden life. If our emotional coherence is so threatened what holds us together? Normality? Pretending to be normal? If anything strikes you about these remarks, use your writing to explore the ideas. Take your pen for a walk, let your mind wander. **Write**.

- On the other hand, William Carlos Williams, an American poet and doctor, said that medicine gave him an entry 'into the secret gardens of the self'. He was talking about the secret lives of the patients he met in his surgery and in sick rooms. Does illness make us more conscious of our real selves, I wonder? Can you answer this speculation from your own experience? **Write** about it.

- Why do you think William Carlos Williams used this image of 'gardens' to describe the territory of the self? It's a much more wholesome image than the 'black lagoon' stuff of Helen Dunmore. What are your secret gardens? What grows there? Who tends and attends it? **Write** a poem in which this 'garden' metaphor grows. Grow a poem.

- Ursula K. Le Guin, novelist and essayist, in a piece that is part fable, part allegory called 'The Writer On, and At, Her Work', describes the writer searching for 'selves in the dark forest'. She uses the image of an attic desk to describe the process of searching. First, there's a 'secret door', then a 'false panel', then a 'concealed compartment', then a spring release reveals a 'bundle of old papers', and one of them is a 'map of the forest'. This is one writer's fable. Can you invent another fable to describe your progress towards self understanding? Can you think of a fable to describe the stages you have to go through or have gone though to be a writer? **Write** two or three sides.

- Read Laura Riding's poem 'The Sad Boy' (RB). Mad mothers! Bad fathers! Drowning pools! Magic boots! Is this a profound insight into the workings of the human mind and an original take on the old nurture and nature debate? Or is it just symbollocks? **Write** a commentary of the poem.

• Sooner or later skeletons in cupboards come knocking on doors. They can be angry, bitter at being locked up and ignored for so long. Have you any experience of the 'carefully-forgotten' coming to visit, uninvited of course? Have your pigeons come home to roost, as they say? Or are the skeletons still well and truly under lock and key? **Write** about some of it.

• All fears have remedies. Some may be no more than spells to ward off evil spirits. What are your remedies for writer's angst? What cures or precautions would you prescribe the wary writer? **Write down** your advice. Cast it as a spell.

Revenants and Revelations

• Looking down the manhole cover and glimpsing the darker tunnels of the self or experiencing the disturbing 'other' beyond our normal perceptions is not necessarily terrifying. Not all visions are nightmares. At the end of Emily Dickinson's poem 'Like Rain It Sounded Till It Curved' (RB) the reader knows that something has passed through the world, something with majesty, something far larger than the human. For a moment the veil has been drawn aside.

William Wordsworth in *The Prelude* celebrated this experience of the hidden power of Nature:

And I have felt
A presence that disturbs me with the joy
Of elevated thoughts; a sense sublime
Of something far more deeply interfused,
Whose dwelling is the light of setting suns,
And the round ocean and the living air,
...A motion and a spirit, that impels
...And rolls through all things.

He also recognised the disturbing nature of this 'presence' whose exact nature he explores elsewhere in the same poem.

He writes that he was troubled by an inner darkness which he associated with a sense of 'unknown modes of being' present around him and which were symbolised by the dark cliffs looming out of Windermere Lake at night. A more recent version of this is Sylvia Plath's poem 'Crossing the Water' (RB) which carries in its title the idea of passing from one mode of existence to another and echoes the myth of Charon and his boat. **Write** about a night experience where nature seemed transformed and brooding or waiting.

- Many poems recognise apparitional moments, the sense of a sudden strangeness crossing our paths. A famous description of this is Edwin Muir's 'The Horses' (RB). **Write** a poem about a matching experience from your own life or from your imagination. It's not really about a haunting. There is no threat in this. You are a privileged witness. It is more about moments of awareness, deep but transient awareness.

- Sensing that something is lurking out there beyond the window, in the bedroom's dark corner, behind the wardrobe, under the bed is a common but disturbing childhood fear. And we have all at times been in situations where we feel something in hiding is watching us. Read Raymond Carver's poem 'Caution'. Do you recognise the experiences here? Make some notes. **Write** a poem out of this preliminary material. Try and write in the low-key, Carver style.

- Beryl Bainbridge, the novelist, has written that when she saw the film of troops 'liberating' the Belsen concentration camp in 1945 it was a transforming moment in her life. 'Everyone of us,' she writes, 'encounters a moment early or late, good or bad, when his or her snapshot of life is suddenly taken and, once exposed, obliterates all other images.' Have you encountered such moment(s) in your life? Recall the day and the events leading up to this obliterating 'snapshot'. **Write** about it.

- James Joyce, the Irish writer of modern classics such as *Dubliners* and *Ulysses*, is credited with using the term 'epiphany' to mean 'a showing' or a 'revelation'. In the traditional Christian calendar of festivals, the Epiphany commemorates the showing of the infant Christ to the

Magi, The Three Wise Men. Joyce coined the term to describe those moments when a truth illuminates a fictional character's life. So, someone will suddenly see themselves for what and who they are. In the last story of *Dubliners* called 'The Dead', Gabriel Conroy is undressing for bed. Looking up, he catches sight of his moonlit reflection in a mirror and understands in a flash the unpalatable truth about himself, long undisclosed. **Write** a short piece based on an 'epiphany' from your own life.

- The phrase, 'call them up', reminds me of conjuration, using the incantations of song and word to raise devilish powers. So we return to 'Kubla Khan' and the idea that poetic writing, writing generally, draws its magic circles to give shape and substance to what's unknown, to what's on the wild shores of our inner experience.

  In her journals and poetry, Sylvia Plath 'calls up' the dark shapes she encountered on the journey into self. She was resolved to 'write until I begin to speak to my deep self'. She knew some of the danger in this ambition and admitted that all writers have to 'break open the vaults of the dead and the skies behind'. For Plath it was a ceaseless task, this seeking after what she was and who she was deep down, and she never shirked from what shadows showed up in the searching light of her writing. Most of us are less courageous. The mind censors itself. Burying memories. Disguising and coding the real nature of experience. A. L. Kennedy describes the writer's self in her essay 'Thank You, Ceiling Rose'. She pulls no punches. Face up to yourself, be honest, don't censor. You'll find yourself out anyway, she says.

  Kennedy writes: 'Sexual weak points, everyone has them, even if they never show. All those funts and cucks, the shicks and prits that don't have the nerve to be out loud. Give them all a tug from the inside up and what do you find underneath? The ugly pantomimes and nightdreams that chose to call you home. Embarrassing, shameful, athletic, pathetic, blasphemous – some people, I swear, they have heads like a tub full of eels.' What do you think A. L. Kennedy means by 'ugly pantomimes'? **Write** a description of an 'ugly pantomime' in which you played a part.

- Elsewhere in the same essay A. L. Kennedy asked some more disturbing questions about the self. 'What if they searched your house now? Tell me there wouldn't be even one forbidden thing to find.... And if they searched your past? Envy, theft, betrayal, slithering moral digression, or something more treacherous? Too fond of the bottle, the needle, the pills? I'm asking you if you are clean?' Imagine your mind is a house with cellars and maybe secret passageways. It may, of course, be a neat suburban bungalow. Develop the metaphor. **Write** a few a pages in the form of a parable or fable.

- **Write** down what you dislike about yourself. Instead of self-address to a mirror-face transfer your remarks to a surrogate. It's a perfectly acceptable way to ease the pain of telling the self a few home truths. We do it all the time! So, invent a substitute 'you' and don't pull the punches. You could, for example, invent an irate adult voice. *Home Truths* might be a workable title. Compare your confession with judgements others have made about you.

- Now be kind to yourself and write about the likeable bits of you. Recall the favourable comments others have made about you. How do yours and theirs compare? Have they missed some of your virtues? Most people are too hard on themselves. Look after yourself. **Write** a complimentary self-portrait.

- Imagine some mysterious policeman comes to the door saying he has to make some necessary enquiries. About what exactly he will not say. In the lounge he begins to ask questions. Odd questions. Innocent at first. But personal. Probing. He seems to know a lot about the occupant. Develop as a short story. **Write** this using mainly dialogue. Or write it as a one-act play. J. B. Priestly's *An Inspector Calls* and Harold Pinter's *The Birthday Party* explore this theme.

- A warning and a reassurance! Being introspective, laying bare the shameful soul in flagellatory confessional manner may be what A. L. Kennedy seems to be advocating above. She sounds like the hellfire preacher of old terrifying the complacent into guilt and compliance. But that's her posture to power-up the truth. What she is emphasising is that honesty not hypocrisy and self-delusion are the key components of the writer's basic kit. **Write** about the most truthful, honest thing you've done in the last few days.

- And what Natalie Goldberg, author of *Wild Mind*, would say is that the self and all things past are only part of the self. 'Wild Mind' is bigger than that. It is exhilarating, self-enhancing not self-denying. It is like Blake's tiger – 'burning bright'. A consuming energy that includes the outside, the natural world too, as well as our dreams and visions. There's always a good angel to wrap wings (run rings and circles) round the bad. So forget the renegade self. Let's party. Let's celebrate. Think of something/someone you love or desire. Say why? Try a litany. Each line of a litany begins or ends with the same phrase. So you could start each line, 'I love you because...' Or, 'Love is like...' Or, 'Dancing feels like...' **Write** ten lines.

- What is it that makes you feel most alive? A hot shower? An early morning swim? Sex? Squash? Mahler's Second Symphony? Hot buttered toast? Sex? **Write** about it so that some of the aliveness comes across to the reader.

- And another thing. If the geography of the self includes all kinds of landscapes – failures and shames and pretensions, as well as brighter features – it also has strata, deposits that descend to older and older sedimentary times, to the very rudiments of existence. The first layer is the self of memory, the self we know and acknowledge and the forgotten self. There is a second layer and maybe a third.

  Angela Carter's short story 'The Tiger's Bride' from *The Bloody Chamber* is a reworking of 'Beauty and the Beast', and it takes the reader, as it were, down through successive layers of the human psyche. The beast has imprisoned the young girl in his castle and, to 'assuage her loneliness', gives her a companion. She looks like a 'soubrette from an operetta', but is, in fact, a mechanical doll. In the ideology of the story this figure represents the woman as girl, the doll, the male plaything. The bride rejects this offering. It's an insult, a typical male tactic to reduce a woman to the status of a decoration. Later she relents and decides to yield to the opportunings of the tiger-man. She prepares herself. She takes off her riding habit, all her clothes layer by layer, shift and all, until she is naked. Like King Lear's proto-man she is now ' . a bare, poor, forked thing'. Stripped of her pride and self-esteem, her ego, she goes, wrapped only in furs, down the long, draughty corridors of the castle, up the spiral stone staircase and into the den of the beast. And there she is slowly flayed as ' . . . each stroke of his tongue ripped off skin after successive skin, all the skins of a life in the world, and left behind a nascent patina of shining hairs'.

The symbolism of divesting layers of clothes and skin is obvious enough. The wrappings of self that keep it modestly protected fall away as another being emerges. I say 'another being' because what does not emerge in this tale is a reborn self. There's no moral resurrection here. The girl has disappeared. She is no longer the daughter of an aristocrat; social distinctions have evaporated. Her clothes, whereby she and we conceal our shames, have been cast aside. Her earrings melt back to their original element, water. Language that separates us from mother earth and particularises our existence returns to primal purrings. And an animal is born, something non-human.

The story takes us from the world of commerce and politics and social order and civilised arrangements into a private space and then down into a primitive region where something far more rudimentary than the dancing ego lies waiting to be born. A similar symbolic universe appears in Coleridge's poem 'Kubla Khan'. Beneath the ordered world of the city plazas and façades of Kubla's fabled city, Xanadu, there exist caverns 'measureless to man' and 'a sunless sea', Beneath man's civilised exterior run 'sunless seas', the territory of the 'old man', the reprobate Adam. Nineteenth-century silver miners in Wales called the deepest part of their mine, 'the Old Man', a recognition that in us all there are some shafts not yet plumbed. Take a mind-walk with some of these ideas as companions. Record the conversations. Take one of the ideas/images and **write it up** into a poem.

- Read Ursula Fanthorpe's poem 'Rising Damp'. She is intrigued by the fact that London's famous rivers, the Quaggy, the Fleet, the Tyburn, the Wandle and others, are now hidden under the populous streets of the city. But, phantoms of our darknesses, they return to haunt us. Do cities offer us other images of the psyche? If you can think of some, work on them. Scatter images and ideas at random on paper. **Write** a poem by working on this raw material.

- The past leaves its traces everywhere. Often they are fleeting and incomplete, but remind us of things long forgotten. Their appearance surprises. We are the forgetters. Think of something you've unearthed/dug up/discovered – old shoe, toy, letter – or seen unearthed in some archaeological dig. **Write** a poem. Try the title *Revenant*? Revenants are returners from death, from exile.

- Have you ever been trapped, in a secluded place, on your own? **Write** about it. Write it in the present tense.

- We all have secluded places of our choice. Sanctuaries. Asylums. Ports in a storm. **Write** about such a place. Gerard Manley Hopkins, the nineteenth-century Jesuit poet, described his wished-for refuge like this:

  > I have desired to go
  > Where springs not fail;
  > To fields where flies no sharp and sided hail
  > And a few lilies blow.
  > > From *Heaven-Haven* (RB)

  Describe your wished-for haven.

- Some sanctuaries are places for escape only, breathing places. Others are more recuperative. They recharge batteries. Renew the self. Raise the spirit. Is there such a vitalising place in your life? **Write** about it.

- Imagine you were given the powers of Puck to travel at the speed of light and become so small you could spy on anyone anywhere without being seen. You would be a peeping Tom Thumb. Anticipate your adventures. Plan your secret observances. Your keyhole revelations. **Write** up this pleasurable fantasy.

Walking the Wild

- One modern group of artists – notably writers and painters – who took a deep interest in the unconscious were the Surrealists. They were active in Paris in the 1920s and 30s. For them the unconscious self was the source of man's creative energies. They developed various techniques for side-stepping the censorious conscious and entering the world of the unconscious, the lower depths. One technique was automatic writing. It is not to be confused with free association where the unconscious mind leap-frogs from one thing to the next. Nor with reverie and daydreaming though all these conditions interested Andre Breton, one of the foremost of the Surrealists. No, automatic writing is a suspension of the conscious mind. What the Surrealists were really interested in was achieving altered states of being, and they developed certain meditation exercises and used hypnosis to induce such conditions.

  Try an association exercise. Select any colour. Write down the next thing that comes to mind. Let the mind leap-frog to the next image. And the next, and the next. Stop and see what you've got. Can you make a poem out of this stuff? See some of the images as doorways connecting with other events/images in your head. Allow memory to lend a hand. Take it, walk with it, and **write** the poem.

- Now sit very still. Empty your mind. This is not vacancy. This is receptivity. This is getting rid of the noise. Just be still. Breathe deeply and regularly. Focus on an object you can see. Or one in your head. Once locked on don't leave go. Hold it for some minutes. Now start talking. Say anything. Talk quickly. Keep it up for as long as you can.

  Imagine someone's talking through you. Another voice. You are just the medium. Ventriloquise. STOP. Now start writing and write fast. Go with the flow. STOP after a few minutes. Take a deep breath. Make a cup of coffee. Look at what you've got. Play with the images. One of them might strike you, light you up. Work on it. **Write** it.

- Check out some Surrealist art. Look up the work of Magritte, Dali, Arp, Leger. Choose a painting that appeals to you or mystifies or disturbs you. Take it as a starting point for a piece of writing. Don't try and describe what's in the painting. Let the painting lead you into other realms, stimulate you into creating exotic fantasies or wild impressionistic stuff. **Write** it all.

- The surrealists were interested in the irrational forces of our natures and how they could be put to good use by the conscious. In this endeavour they were influenced by the theories of Sigmund Freud, the Austrian psychoanalyst, and especially in his descriptions of how the unconscious mind worked.

> 'We are engaged,' wrote a British surrealist in 1936, 'in the exploration of the unconscious, in its conquest and final synthesis with the conscious...We propose an extension of our control over territories hitherto uncontrolled – the kingdom of the irrational within ourselves...the hidden world will become part of our common life as human beings.'
>
> (Introduction, *Surrealist Poetry in English*)

More influential than Freud was the Swiss psychoanalyst, Carl Jung. It was his notion of the 'collective unconscious' that invigorated Surrealist thinking. 'The poet,' wrote Jung in 1930, 'works rather from primal experience. The primal experience...is a vision in a dark mirror...the collective unconscious, that curious structure inherited through the generations of the preliminary psychic structures of the consciousness.'

The critic Herbert Read declared the poet had access to the secrets of mankind, 'the secrets of the self which are buried in every man alike'. These deep truths Jung termed 'archetypes', symbolic elements found in folk literatures the world over, and which included such figures as the wise old man, the devouring father, the consuming witch, the dragon and so on.

Dragons hoard treasure and protect their accumulations from treasure seekers. Jung would see this as an archetypal narrative. The treasure is the rich potential lying deep at the core of ourselves, and the dragon represents the psychic dangers threatening the questing self. All prizes have a price. But this image of the unconscious as a repository of wealth, of bright energy, so exultantly reflected in Angela Carter's The 'Tiger's Bride', should act as a corrective to the more sombre and sepulchral versions. What Surrealist writing did was to 'open the doors of the mind' and catch the unconscious in the act.

And in dreams Breton et al. believed one could catch the unconscious at work. Over a week or two, keep a dream diary. Read through the material. Use anything here as a starter for a story. Continue the free association method for a time. Take the image for a walk. The painter Paul Klee used to say when he sketched that he took 'his pencil for a walk'. Seems like an interesting way to paint a poem – take words for a walk. **Write** a dream story. Remember the Surrealists were not just interested in producing quirky images. They wanted to express hidden truths, so you need to shape your original dream material, preserving its magical freshness yet making its symbolism accessible.

- Read 'Séance' by Edouard Roditi. The archetypal stranger arrives, leaves a 'gift'. **Write** a continuation of the story preserving the Roditi style.

- Maybe some distant racial memory is stirring in John Haines's poem 'Awakening'. Imagine some 'visitor', a reminder or even a 'minder' from the primordial past, from the wrong end of time, comes into your life. Or, more likely, hovers at the edge of your life. It may be no more than a shadow. Is it animal or human? Half and half? **Write** about it, this archetypal being/thing.

- And there were drugs. In the nineteen thirties, Aldous Huxley famously tripped on peyote, the Amazonian Indian hallucinatory drug. Coleridge's poem 'Kubla Khan' was supposedly written under the influence of opium. The imagery is certainly hallucinatory, the poem highly wrought, but wrought for all that, that is made, crafted. It is a poem about the nature of writing, the poet's vision, his inner self mapped out in the imagery of palaces, ornamental gardens, caves of ice and thunderous rivers spuming in ravines. Beneath the planned and monumental symmetry of architectured life lies Nature's turbulent and anarchic engineering, the dark wild below the sunlit ordering. The same dynamics are echoed in poetry where tight verbal formations hold under wraps the hidden insurgencies of meaning.

I suppose you could say language and magic are twin impostors. Language draws circles round things, limits, defines and, at the same time, its incantations summon up the wildness in the world and turn hissing syllables into snakes. 'Kubla Khan' then, is about the nature of language and its magical origins, its capacity to spell things into being and turn them into something else. Think about this magic metaphor. **Write** a poem using the words 'magus', 'magician', 'illusionist', 'magic hat', 'wand', 'deck of cards', and so on as images to say something about words and the ways we use them. Are we just hiding one thing inside another when we communicate? Is it all a box of tricks?

- Read Raymond Carver's poem 'Artaud'. Artaud was a surrealist poet best known for his essay 'The Theatre and the Double' in which he proposed a 'direct action theatre'. Theatre's double was life itself, the vital metaphysical reality that shadows our every action. Western society, Artaud argued, was in crisis. It had moved so far from this reality that only desperate remedies, a theatre of extreme violence, could resolve the crisis and bring life and living back in harmony.

  In the poem, the poet, like a magician amongst his parchments and spells, is 'calling up old demons', the destructive and purging powers. Someone else, 'the other...watches carefully'. The 'other' is cautious and arrogant. What two parts do these characters play in the drama of writing? Is the 'other' similar to Coleridge's 'man from Porlock', the censorious intruder from the real world restraining the wilder, dangerous antics of the writer? Is the poem about the nature of poetry itself – the contesting of energy (Bacchanalian) and restraint (Apollonian)? What is the 'rustling' mentioned in the last line? How does this fit in? A bit of supernatural stage business to leave a disturbing after-taste? Think of your own writing practice. **Write** a series of reflections on the poem 'Artaud' relating it to your own understanding of writing.

- Think of a situation when words hide rather than reveal. When what is said runs opposite to the real meaning gliding away beneath the surface of the conversation. Does this sort of situation arise in your life at times? **Write** about one such occasion.

- Try a script where one character is trying to hide something from another or where both are hiding things from each other. How will the audience know these deceptions are taking place? **Write** one scene.

- Sometimes you could just scream. Some situations need an explosive force to shatter the pretence, the 'everything-is-OK-really' approach, the self-delusions paralysing the key players. After the fall-out the air is cleared. Recall such a situation in your own life. Use the material to shape a story. **Write** it from a participative narrator point-of-view and in the present tense. The narrator should be the person who blows the whistle on the whole situation.

Strip-teasing the Truth, Tabooing the Body

- According to Coleridge he was interrupted while composing 'Kubla Khan' by a 'man from Porlock' knocking on his door asking for directions. By the time the man left the poet's inspiration was gone, the fire had died. Try as he might he could write no more. Ever since, the 'man from Porlock' has come to represent all that interferes with the creative process. It is the unthinking intrusive world breaking in on the poet's reverie. It also includes interior distractions that deflect him/her from the task in hand. It is the over-censorious mind, teacher-mind, the editor, knocking on the desk with a ruler and saying: 'remember the commas', saying: 'don't forget that if you want to be a poet you have to dress in the proper manner.' From the viewpoint of the writing self you need to be honest about the devious self that tempts you away from writing. Is there a jealous self? There must be a lazy self. There must be a sexy temptress! Or maybe they are all seducers in their own way. Give each distracting self a character, a voice. **Write** a piece entitled *The Seven Temptations of . . .* (enter your own name here).

- Imagine someone from the National Anti-Writing Unit, De-Psyche Department, visits you, uninvited of course. She tries to persuade you of the error of your ways. **Write** the first part of this satirical short story/poem.

- The first hiding place is the womb. Some people say we spend much of life's endeavours trying to return to this, our first resting-place. **Write** a poem about this primal refuge.

- Read Louis MacNeice's poem 'Prayer Before Birth'. **Write** your own prayer listing the gifts that you hope life will bring the new-born and those gifts the baby will bring to the world.

- MacNeice wanted to protect the unborn baby from all the dangers of the world. Mister Death is the biggest danger. After that there's nothing to worry about. Read Elizabeth Jennings's poem 'Fragment for the Dark' (20WP). This is a prayer for self preservation. **Write** a poem called *Prayer Before Sleep* or *Prayer Before Anaesthetic/Gathering Storms/ Growing Up*, etcetera.

- Read Thom Gunn's poem 'Baby Song' (RB). **Write** your own rhyming song expressing your hopes for the baby.

- Writers have also seen death as the safest hiding place of all. No one can be found out nor found here. No one chases after you this far. Can you see any parallels between birth and death? Are they twins? The Yes and No of life? There are different kinds of deaths. Continue this line of ideas, phrases, images. When you have slowed down, stop and look back at what you've unearthed. Work on the bits and pieces. Read Josephine Miles's poem 'Conception' (20WP) for one variant on this paradox. **Write** a poem.

- Read Franz Kafka's story 'The Burrow'. **Write** a Kafkaesque parable entitled *House* or *Bridge* or *City*.

- The last refuge is silence. It is difficult to imagine the life of one suffering from Alzheimer's Disease. Bit by bit the faculties go. Read Mark Strand's poem 'Always' (EK). This is a gentle approach to a distressing subject. Read Sylvia Plath's poem 'Amnesiac'. This is a bleaker version altogether. **Write** a suitable poem on the subject.

- Rest homes are where we isolate the aged, the derelict and the dying. Both words in the phrase 'rest home' are cover-ups. Think of how our language hides the facts of ageing. Collect examples from the medical world and from ordinary usage. Give your own definitions of these. **Write** them down as a litany with a suitable refrain for each line.

- Read Carol Ann Duffy's poem 'Mouth with Soap'. Reflect on your family's use of politisms to disguise inconvenient truths. Bad words go in the sin bin. **Write** a companion poem to 'Mouth with Soap'.

- On social occasions all kinds of truth are side-stepped, circled but never looked at, felt but never touched. Think of a non-family occasion when you've sensed this pussyfooting around. Use the material to write a story. Try it as mainly dialogue in which each time the participants get near the truth they recoil, regroup, and then tiptoe back again. They never actually get there, but as the loss of nerve and successive failures accumulate, the reader begins to get at least a shadowy outline of the substance. Think of the evasive tactics we all use either to avoid the truth or skirt it. Of course, some people like to tease. Play striptease with the truth, never show all, but suggest enough to arouse interest.

  Already in this scenario there are enough characters to create your cast. The person who knows something, but wants the pleasure of having it teased out of them. The person dying to know, but restrained by a sense of propriety. The person always riding a high horse. You often get a better view of scandal and low life from a moral height! Basically we're all voyeurs! **Write** the story from the point of view of one of the group, in the first person narrative form if you wish, and in the present tense. Title? *Cover-ups*? *Voyeur*?

- Sometimes awkward/uncomfortable/painful truths are best expressed non-verbally, through gesture and facial expression, for example. Think of a scene in which the time has come to face up to the truth. **Write** the scene or scenes in dialogue, but accompany direct speech with stage directions, in brackets, describing non-verbal body language. Or write the notation/scenario for a mime of such a scene.

- Underwear is still a private matter. And clothes are for disguise as much as display. Read Lawrence Ferlinghetti's poem 'Underwear' (EK). Can you say anything about the private life of clothes, under or otherwise? Think of the come-on adverts for 'glamorous lingerie'. Think of granddad night-shirts, of nighties, shifts, pyjamas, baby dolls. And so on. **Write** a paean in praise of undies.

- Some things you keep private and hidden from prying eyes. Read Fleur Adcock's poem 'Against Coupling' (EK). Not PC! **Write** about something you'd rather the world didn't know about you. Of course, this is asking the impossible. But it can be a private act. The public doesn't need to know. And anyway, you can write sideways on like Fleur Adcock, inferring not telling it full frontally. I dare you!

- The body is full of hidden places. No-go zones. No-man's-lands. The body as an undiscovered country, a hidden landscape, is the central metaphor in Andrew Marvell's astounding poem 'Ode to His Coy Mistress'. Read it again and again and again. Now read these two poems by Grace Nicholls: 'Ode to My Bleed' and 'My Black Triangle'. **Write** a poem about some part(s) of your body. *Body Parts* might be a provocative title. *Foreign Parts* is encouragingly ambiguous. Or deploy Marvell's idea of the body as a continent and update it. Or use the metaphor of an atlas. Map out the body.

- Reputedly, John Ruskin, the Pre-Raphaelite painter, poet and art critic, was appalled when first seeing his wife's naked body on their wedding night. In her poem 'Thoughts after Ruskin' (20WP), Elma Mitchell responds to the over-refined Pre-Raphaelite sensibility by describing women's business and bodies in real terms. She challenges the image of women's porcelain prettiness, all 'lilies and roses', with an unromantic 'blood and soap' view. **Write** a 'blood and soap' portrait of a body. If you know the richly physical and honest paintings of nudes by Lucien Freud or Stanley Spencer you'll see what I mean by a 'blood and soap' portrait.

References

Apuleius, *The Golden Ass* (Wordsworth, 1996).

Brown, R., in *A Voice of One's Own*, ed. M. Pearlman & K. U. Henderson (Houghton Mifflin, 1990).

Carter, A., *The Bloody Chamber* (Vintage, 1995).

Carver, R., *A New Path to the Waterfall* (Collins, 1989).

Coetze, J. M., *Age of Iron* (Vintage, 2000).

Coleridge, S. T., *The Complete Poems* (Penguin, 1997).

Conrad, J., *The Secret Sharer* (Penguin, 1990).

Dante, A., *The Divine Comedy* (Oxford, 1998).

Duffy, C. A., *Selling Manhattan* (Anvil, 1987).

Duffy, C. A., *The World's Wife* (Picador, 1999).

Fanthorpe, U. A., *Selected Poems* (Penguin, 1989).

Goldberg, N., *Wild Mind* (Bantam, 1991).

Haines, J., in *Surrealist Poetry in English*, ed. E. Germaine (Penguin, 1978).

Hughes, T., *Birthday Letters* (Faber and Faber, 1998).

Kafka, F., *Metamorphosis and Other Stories* (Penguin, 1978).

Kennedy, A. L., 'Thank You, Ceiling Rose', *Critical Quarterly*, 37, no. 4 (1996).

Le Guin, U. K., in *The Writer on Her Work*, ed. J. Sternburg (Virago, 1992).

MacNeice, L., *The Collected Poems* (Faber and Faber, 1979).

Marvell, A., *The Complete Poems* (Penguin, 1991).

Nicholls, G., *Lazy Thoughts of a Lazy Woman* (Virago, 1989).

Pinter, H., *The Birthday Party* (Faber and Faber, 1991).

Plath, S., *Collected Poems* (Harper, 1992).

Plath, S., *Journals* (Ballantine, 1982).

Priestley, J. B., *An Inspector Calls* (Samuel French, 1948).

Roberts, M., in *New Writing 4*, ed. A.S. Byatt & A. Hollinghurst (Vintage, 1995).

Roditi, E., in *Surrealist Poetry in English*, ed. E. Germaine (Penguin, 1978).

Rushdie, S., *The Ground Beneath Her Feet* (Vintage, 2000).

Said, E. W., *Out of Place* (Granta, 1999).

Stevenson, R. L., *Dr Jekyll and Mr Hyde* (Oxford, 1991).

Unsworth, B., *Losing Nelson* (Penguin, 2000).

White, E., *A Boy's Own Story* (Picador, 1983).

Wordsworth, W., *The Prelude* (Penguin, 1995).

Wilde, O., *The Picture of Dorian Gray* (Penguin, 1994).

3 Awakenings

Reading into Writing

- In *A New Path to the Waterfall*, Raymond Carver describes how he suddenly discovered poetry. He was working as a delivery boy for a local pharmacist. He had taken a prescription to the house of an old 'gentleman', and while waiting for the owner to write out his cheque, noticed a small poetry mag on a coffee table. He leafed through the pages. He'd never seen anything like it in his life, and he 'secretly coveted' it. The old man gave him the book and suggested he might write something one day. From then on, Carver says, he was 'obsessed with the need to write something', and he savours this moment 'when the very thing I needed most in my life – call it a polestar – was casually, generously given to me. Nothing remotely approaching that moment has happened since.' Most writers can pinpoint certain 'polestar' moments in their development. Has there been one in your life? How far back can you trace your beginnings as a writer? Was it one moment of conversion or a gradual awakening? **Write** about this experience

- What is it that attracts you to or about writing? **Write** a letter to a beginner writer advising them of what to expect from the occupation. You may want to warn them about some aspects of the process as well as reassure them with descriptions of the pleasures/consolations of the craft.

- Often encounters with books set readers on the path to writing. Love of books starts on mother's knee, turns into the comfort of bedtime story-telling, and then the illicit pleasure of late-night lucubration under the bedclothes. A *lucubrum* was the candle made of wax-soaked cloth that Romans used as a reading light. **Write** about your early encounters with books and the lasting effects they have had on you.

- Did or do you have a favourite book, a prized possession? One that has become a talisman? One you would never part with? **Write** about its influence and hold over you.

- Reading, like writing, has been regarded as a lazy pleasure and as a subversive activity. Puritans have banned books; Fascists have burned them. Imagine a book on trial for 'crimes against the state and the individual'. **Write** the prosecutor's opening address outlining the case against the defendant. **Write** the summing up of the defence attorney!

- Edna O'Brien's 1960s novel *The Country Girls*, an account of sexual awakening in Ireland, offended many. The family's parish priest bought three copies in a Limerick bookshop, and, back in the village, publicly burnt all of them. Imagine one of the girls from the novel confronting the conflagratory cleric: knocking at the presbytery door perhaps, challenging him in the confessional, accosting him in the lane on the way back from benediction or evening mass. **Recreate** the scene with appropriate dialogue.

- 'Good fiction plots the downfall of the reader.' Explain this to yourself. Then convince a sceptical reader of its truth. **Write** a page of argumentative dialogue between the two of you.

- Some writers are chosen. An adult tells you how talented you are. You have a wonderful imagination they say. Great! You are now a writer. It has been decreed. You have permission. Many beginner writers aren't so fortunate. They don't have a 'patron'. Indeed many start by writing 'against the grain', by being closet writers. No one has approved. Their 'habit' has been dismissed as self-indulgent, as a distraction from the real business of living. It's all yearning, no earning. Have you had to struggle for recognition and 'permission'? **Write** about it.

- Here's how to kill the reading and writing habit. David Briers writes about his 'initiation into the world of literature'. His mother took him to a second-hand bookshop to make his first purchase. The bookseller had a pile of volumes supporting his three-legged stool. The young David Briers wanted the one at the bottom, and threw a tantrum when it was refused. He was told to choose another one, and in his rage, pointed his little finger at random. 'And thus,' he says, 'I started my library with *Teach Yourself Swahili.*' What a telling tale about mutilation and masochism! I once saw a notice in a school library which said: 'Do not touch the books after dinner'!!! Books are barbed-wired round with do-nots. Do not bend the corners. Do not write in the margins. Do not bend the spine. Wash your hands first. How were you initiated into literature? Was this 'book thing' all prohibition and taboo? **Write** about this side of your reading biography. **Write up** the experience as a book blurb or as a publicity leaflet.

- In his book *A History of Reading*, Alberto Manguel points out that reading is a cumulative activity. Each new reading builds on whatever the reader has read before. While reading one book some readers 'recall, compare, conjure up emotions from other, previous readings'. It is a 'delicate form of adultery' according to Martinez Estrada, an Argentinian writer. All readers are serial adulterers then, but some are addicts as well. I am not referring to the compulsive reader. By 'addict', I imply there is such a thing as 'narcotic' literature. Such books lull the reader into an opiate dream. When they come down from the high of the read they discover they can remember nothing of the book at all. The senses have been dulled, the brain drugged. Real reading is more like adultery – risky, exciting, desirous, pleasurable, rebellious, revealing. It awakens, revitalises. The other type of reading dulls and kills off the vital signs. Is there a book that you have read as an adult that has had a startling effect on you? Describe your first meeting, first kiss, your illicit assignations, the love notes, the promises, consummations, the parting. **Write** the account. Possible title – *Love Letters*.

- You could just as well take the narcotic image above to describe the hook of a book. In this case **write** an account of a book you have enjoyed as if it was a 'trip'. Maybe use diary form to trace the trip, the highs and lows, the encounters with pushers, the search for treatment, the therapies. And so on.

- Despite these racy views of the book, some writers have accorded them an almost sacred role. Here is what Edna O'Brien wrote in the *New York Times Book Review*. 'Books are the Grail for what is deepest, more mysterious and least expressible within ourselves: they are our soul's skeleton. If we were to forget that, it would prefigure how false and feelingless we could become.' Are writers so heroic? These remarks suggest they have a vocation, a calling – to search for the 'deepest ... the least expressible'. Is this all too grand, even grandiose? Or are books a saving grace in a world of barbarians, predators and ogres that chain up the innocent? Can books save the world? **Write** a piece showing how books save the world.

- Here's another 'big' view of writing from Alberto Manguel. 'Since the earliest vestiges of prehistoric civilisation,' he claims, 'human society had tried to overcome the obstacles to geography, the finality of death, the erosion of oblivion. With a single act – the incision of a figure on a clay tablet – that first anonymous writer suddenly succeeded in all these seemingly impossible feats.' So writing makes us immortal! I suppose a text could be some lasting monument. Anything we write and publish joins the procession winding its way through history and into the future. Our biological drive to perpetuate ourselves is reflected in cultural behaviour too. At least, that's what a behavioural geneticist would say. Artistic creation in his view is just another survival strategy amongst all the others that drive our evolutionary momentum. Do you think we are programmed to write? Are we hard-wired for signs and literary codes? These are tough questions. What arguments would you use to support the contention that writing is an evolutionary necessity and/or a survival strategy? **Write** them down.

- The first signs of writing appeared in Mesopotamia (modern Iraq), and probably derived from the city of Babylon about 6000 years ago. The first 'books' were tablets inscribed with cuneiform, a written language of wedge-shaped marks pressed into the tablet clay. Scroll 'books' or papyri, developed in Egypt, gradually replaced the heavy tablet form. They were made by pressing together the split ends of a reed-like plant called *papyrus*, the origin of our word 'paper'. By 2000 BC scrolls started to give way to the codex, a bundle of leaves sewn and bound together, for which parchment (treated animal skin) became the preferred writing medium. A codex could be folded and made handy-size. It was portable, durable and easily stored. Scrolls were unwieldy, had only one writing surface, and needed a large unrolling and reading space. Codices had pages that could be flipped, and access (reading) was far easier. Today's computer 'page' has returned to the scroll's limited format. It's much easier to get a sense of the whole text from a codex than from the flat monitor face where you have to scroll from screen-page to screen-page, and are limited to a single dimension up-down viewing.

  In the twelfth century the Italians developed 'real' paper, and in 1455 came the breakthrough that revolutionised the word – Johannes Gutenberg invented the type press and published the first printed book: *The Gutenberg Bible*. Reading material could be produced quickly and in vast quantities and cheaply. The production of a quarto-sized bible (12 by 16 inches) in vellum required the skins of over two hundred sheep!

  Computer technology and the Internet have produced a new alliance that threatens the existence of the book. Books will yield to electronic information management systems. Or so they say. For the latest on the print versus pixel fight read a book: *Gutenberg Elegies* by Sven Birkerts. **Write** a defence of the book. Take an upbeat view. Birkerts thinks that the book and writing itself is doomed in the seductive digital world of gameboys, e-mail, voice recognition software, VR, multi-channel TV, DVD and interactive video.

- But just think. In 1995 over one third of a million books were added to the Library of Congress. Yes, think. We may have *too many* books! In the business jargon, we have 'overchoice'. **Write** a satirical proposal outlining your plans for a book cull, explaining your motives and the advantages to be gained. Remember, it may be kinder to guillotine than burn your victims. And there are moral issues here. Which books go to slaughter first? Airport novels or Booker Prize winners? Philosophic treatises or softporn mags?

- Writers and readers live in what Fay Weldon calls: 'creative complicity'. Alberto Manguel expands on this collaboration. He speculates on the earliest known beginnings of writing – marks on clay tablets, cuneiform: 'The writer is a maker of messages, the creator of signs, but these signs and messages required a magus who could decipher them, recognise their meaning, give them a voice. Writing requires a reader.' Paradoxically, the arrival of a reader heralds the death of the writer. The writer creates the reader who takes over his text and gives it meaning, and she can only do this after the writer has killed himself off. Only when a readerly eye contacts the marks on the page, magics them into images, does the text come alive. If then, writers and readers are creative partners, what does writing learn from reading? To be a real writer you should be a real reader. **Write** a list of ten ways in which reading aids/nourishes writing and/or the writer.

- In her autobiography *Once in a House on Fire*, Andrea Ashworth writes about her teenage obsession with the horror fiction of Stephen King and James Herbert. 'They sent cheap, flat shudders' through her. The books she grew into were the 'fancy-cover classics', posh books that her stepfather scorned and scorned her for. They appealed to Andrea because 'They touched on deep, disturbing things too, but they lifted you up, towards a sort of light, instead of dragging you down into darkness.' Have your reading habits and reading interests changed over the years? Is the pleasure from reading popular novels 'cheap and flat'? How would you distinguish the experience of reading popular novels from reading literary novels, and both categories from reading the classics of English Literature? **Try writing** about a book that has sent 'flat shudders' through you and one that has 'lifted' you. Draw some tentative conclusions about the varied pleasures different types of book offer.

- Some writers have dismissed popular fiction as 'narcotic'. You overdose on sensation, travel in a daze, and after the come-down, remember nothing of the experience. After too many reads they leave the brain progressively soggy. Fair comment? After she had been reading *Tess* or *Great Expectations*, Andrea 'went about feeling crammed with passion and a murky sense of something brewing. Some brilliant storm.' Think of the fall-out from books you have read. Did they cram you with passion, brew some brilliant storm about you? Imagine telling a sceptical friend of the effects and **write up** the dialogue between the two of you. OR imagine there's such a thing as the *Emma*-syndrome, a bundle of mysterious symptoms associated with reading Jane Austen. Your concerned but unsympathetic parents take you to see the doctor. They fear you are imbibing dangerous substances. Imagine sitting in the waiting room rehearsing what you are going to say in the consultation. Using the first person point of view, **write up** this scene and the following one in the doctor's surgery as if they were part of a novel.

- Weldon's catchphrase for National Reading Week 1999 was: 'Turn the page and turn your life.' Has a book ever saved or 'turned' your life? **Write** about this sensational event or imagine it happening.

Weavers and Hunters

- Ursula K. Le Guin says that for a long time she was unaware that her writing 'was controlled and constrained by the judgements and assumptions which I thought were my own, but which were the internalised ideology of the male supremicist society'. You may think in this new millennial, post-feminist world that you are a free, independent thinking writer. Are you? Or have you too been invaded by the ideology of male supremicism? Can you escape its power? **Write** a self-appraisal of yourself as an invaded writer. Suggested title: *Body-snatching.*

- You may have noticed that in this chapter so far, I have been referring to readers as female and writers as male. Look at any book about reading, encyclopaedias and anthologies of literature, and you will see a cover depicting a woman, sitting or lying down reading, neither in a contemporary setting nor in contemporary dress. Is this because reading is a passive, recreational activity and, therefore, feminine? It keeps women quiet? Are we back with the old gender stereotypes – the silent and silenced woman, decorative and decorous? On the other hand, women do seem to read more or are more actively interested in reading than men. A recent survey of reading clubs found that women outnumber men by a ratio of nine to one. How do you explain this statistic? There must be cultural as well as psychological reasons. Writing's a man thing? Of course! Writing is an active process in which something is made. Men are the makers. Writing is a man-made thing! **Write** an article exploring the underlying gender assumptions about books and reading and writing.

- Until recently women's challenge to the male prerogative in literature has been muted and sporadic and full of subterfuge. Some nineteenth-century women novelists wrote under male pseudonyms. As pseudo-men they improved their chances of acceptance by the male literary establishment. The idea that women were permitted only to read and write romantic fiction is as old as first-century Greece. In eleventh-century Japan, Confucian scholars decreed that male literature was about heroic, philosophic and public themes; female literature about the trivial, the domestic and the intimate. In response, Heian women developed their own writing version of the special language they were allowed to speak. This became known as 'women's writing', and since it was restricted to the female hand it became, for their masters, highly erotic, a peephole into the private lives of women.

In Heian culture, writing mirrored women's own lives and created a literature of their own characterised by acute observation and understandings. In one famous Heian diary the courtly lady hoped that her journal 'might even be able to answer the question: is this an appropriate life for a well-born lady?'

Marginalised, confined to 'small-talk' in the woman's place, and thus 'proving' they only had heads for trivia, women writers in all cultures have had to be resourceful and wily. They've had to mimic men (that shows they cannot be original and are flatterers and dissemblers by nature), write primarily in the romance mode (which shows an unhealthy preoccupation with the unstable and unbalanced side of life) and describe private worlds (which, by bringing them to public attention, shows a lack of propriety and a want of taste). History has its revenge, of course. Women have fought back, and history has had its satisfactory small ironies. I like the fact that despite successive millennia of male dominance the first named writer was a woman: Princess Enheduanna, born around 2300 BC, daughter of King Sargon 1 of Akkad, high priestess of the god of the moon, Nanna, and composer of a series of songs in honour of Inanna, goddess of love and war. **Write** a poem in her honour or one dedicated to her.

- Yes, things have certainly changed. Writing, which in the nineteenth century confirmed women's limited role has, in the twentieth, destroyed or redefined those roles and begun to answer the question posed a thousand years ago by the writer of the *Fleeting Journal* quoted above: 'Is this an appropriate life?' Do you see any evidence that old attitudes to women writers and readers still survive? Who reads books at school? Boys or girls? Who uses the school library? Who write stories in the classroom? Whose are pinned up for display? **Write** about it.

- The question of whether men and women write differently has teased many contemporary critics and writers. Amy Tan, the American novelist, has written: 'Men pan the whole scene...but the sense of intimacy is not there... when men close in their observations are cerebral – in men the mind is connected to the brain. In women, the mind is connected to the heart.' **Write** a letter to Amy rebutting this analysis. Draw support from your reading or your writing.

- Maybe women and men have different attitudes to writing. Henry James described his creative struggles in epic, biblical terms when he wrote that he 'wrestled with the Lord'. Margaret Oliphant, a contemporary of James, describes her writing regime and herself 'sat at the corner of the family table with my writing-book, with everything going on as if I had been making a shirt instead of writing a book'. Norman Mailer, an American commentator and novelist, regarded by many as a roughhouse chauvinist, has re-established testosterone as the dynamic constituent of the writing persona. 'The one thing a writer needs,' he proclaims, 'is balls.' That leaves women with the option of sex change or shut up.
    Ursula K. Le Guin's woman writer is a fisherwoman; an image borrowed from Virginia Woolf's paper entitled 'Professions for a Woman'. Woolf sees the female writer as a meditative figure, 'like a fisherwoman, sitting on the bank of a lake with her fishing rod held over its water...She is not thinking; she is not reasoning; she is not constructing a plot; she is letting her imagination down into the depths of her unconsciousness while she sat above holding on by a thin but quite necessary thread of reason.' How do you see the male or female writer? **Write** a profile, poetic or satiric, of one of these two. **Write** a fable that explores the dilemmas and difficulties that face woman writers.

- Le Guin has also characterised women as 'weavers' and men as 'hunters'. Are these useful distinctions to apply to writers? For a feminist writer this is a surprising twinning. It seems to perpetuate gender stereotypes and roles. Penelope, Odysseus' wife, was the perennial shuttle queen, weaving her tapestry by day and unweaving it by night, a subterfuge to stall her suitors. She had promised them that she would choose a suitable husband from their ranks once the cloth was finished. Le Guin takes the Woolf image and develops it into a feminist political parable. Does the fisherwoman catch a huge silver fish? Does the fish talk? What does it say? Develop the Penelope story as a myth of writing. Or think of another more apt narrative. Steal from the vast hoard of past stories – anecdotes, fables, legends, myths, allegories, parables, folk and fairytales. And so on. **Write** a two-page parable about writing.

- At first women belong to the unborn. They have to give birth twice; once to their children and once to themselves. Does this make sense to you? In what ways? **Write** about it.

- Books have a visual life too. They are pictured on posters, covers, videos and illustrations. Books are promiscuous. They spawn other texts in their own image. They are gossips. They tell tales about themselves and others, hiding their second-hand scandals in the discourse of academic and critical writing. Books are for life not just for reading. **Write** a story or poem entitled *The Secret Lives of Books*. **Write** the autobiography of a book.

- One endlessly inventive book that explores the reading experience is Italo Calvino's classic *If on a Winter's Night a Traveller* .... In this novel the reader is a central character seemingly enacting the text, making it up as he goes along, being both subject and object, simultaneously maker and made. It all emphasises the playful and invented nature of the fictive process. The illusion is that the text exists in real time, happening as it were under our very noses, unfurling as we read. It's like looking at ourselves on CCTV.

  Calvino's novel rewards endless readings, offers endless readings. It is multi-textual. Not only does it spin one plot out of another like a continuous Scheherazade, but it lures the not unwilling reader into filling the seductive gaps with her own fictions and converting the non sequiturs into sequiturs. This book has more to say about writing and reading than a library of analysis and theoretical study. Buy it, read it and treasure it. Imagine the text you're writing starts to talk to you. **Write** the first page, unless it threatens to commit suicide, in which case you have to be very tactful. Don't let it see you reaching for the phone otherwise all trust will be lost and anything could happen. Play with ideas here. See what comes up.

Writing Positions

- 'A man may write at any time,' wrote Doctor Samuel Johnson in 1750, 'if he will set himself doggedly to it.' There's a real writer. 'The one thing a writer has to have is a pencil and some paper,' wrote Le Guin. No mention of genius. In fact the genuine thing ain't genius at all, it's attitude. As the Doctor supposedly said, genius is 10 per cent inspiration, 90 per cent perspiration. The word 'genius' derives from the Latin word meaning 'to generate'. In other words, at the root, 'genius', when we rub off the fancy shine it acquired in the late eighteenth century, simply means 'to produce' or 'to make'.

  As Raymond Chandler said of marriage: '3 per cent of people are in love; the rest of us just work at it.' Almost the same with writing. We're all in love with it and we just work at it. I like the remark by the artist, Kathe Kollwitz, quoted by Tillie Olsen in her book *Silences*. Kollwitz says she works 'the way a cow grazes'. Nothing idyllic here. Bucolic perhaps. Is the cow image accurate? Does it describe your own practice in any way? Bovinely self-absorbed? Chewing the cud? Just getting on with it? It's a disappointing metaphor if you believe in writing as a high art. Chew on the cud of these ideas. **Write** something.

- In the sixteenth century, the word 'genius' meant the distinctive spirit of a place, the defining quality of a person. Today we are more likely to talk of a 'writer's voice' than their defining 'genius'. But if it is the individual voice that determines our genius we're all potential geniuses. And real ones, if we write in an individual fashion and not in the fashion of others. More of this later.

You can be a real writer or a sham writer. There are writers who work at what they have. There are writers who give up. And those who talk about it, but never start. The first is a real writer, the second is a realist, the third is a sham writer. And there are writers who are intimidated by other writers, especially dead ones. After all, we stand now in the millennial dusk under the long shadow cast by the 'great' writers of the English Literary Tradition stretching far back from Dickens to Wordsworth to Milton and Shakespeare. Their achievements, long canonised by the educational system, can make our efforts seem diminutive. Step out of the shadows. Are you a real writer? **Write** an honest assessment of yourself as a writer. Or sum up your own ideas on the differences between sham and real writers. First draft your notes. **Write** them up as a magazine article.

- Some writers oversell writing. It's a vocation they say, not a business. You've got to be special, they say. Writers are born not made. Not true. Nobody is born writing. That's a 'messiah' myth. Though present research suggests that humans are born with an innate capacity for language they still have to learn the rules, play with words, put on the style.

  Writing's not a gift; it's a craft. Raymond Chandler understood this. He wrote the classic Philip Marlowe detective stories and was a Hollywood script-writer. He wrote in one of his letters that writing was a question of learning. You learnt the art. But not by being taught. You taught yourself – by practice. By finding good models and imitating them. That's how Shakespeare learnt. He went to grammar school and studied rhetoric, a subject that included the practice of *imitatio* – writing in the manner of the great ones of the past: practising by copying and perspiring for the art. This is why I've suggested so many texts for you to read. In an age that overvalues individuality, it may seem a form of dependence, even subservience. And in an age that is seduced by progress and technical novelty, it may seem defeatist to return to the past for exemplars of good practice. But all writers have found their mentors in the literature of earlier times. **Write** about a writer who has been your guide and friend, who has influenced your work.

- Allegedly, Hemingway rewrote the first paragraph of *The Sun Also Rises* forty times. That's not inspiration, that's perspiration. It's not genius, it's attitude. Inspiration is like the hovering bird in Genesis disturbing the void into being. It burns as tongues of fire in the New Testament inspiring Christ's disciples into prophecy and eloquence. Today, it is seen more prosaically as a bright mental light or flash. Bird, fire or flare it is the force driving an artist (in this metaphor he/she is unable to resist) into glittering, enthralled expression. Like the 'Kubla Khan' dancer already discussed. But inspiration cannot be relied upon. Perspiration can. Does 'inspiration' play any part in your writing? Think of examples when you were 'inspired'. What were the circumstances? Did something just come? A bolt from the blue? Some writers say you just need a 'trigger' to set you off writing, a spark that bursts memories into life. How is it for you? **Write** an account of one moment of inspiration. Backtrack and try and see if it had any hidden or forgotten source in your memory.

- Sometimes writers say they don't feel inspired. It's not worth trying. They are suffering from Writer's Block. WB may be a problem, but only a broken hand actually stops you writing. You'll be waiting forever waiting for inspiration. It is just a delaying tactic, a way of blaming something else. Behind this excuse lurks the misshapen image of the Romantic poet moonstruck in his garret waiting for the muse to visit. William Stafford, the American poet, when asked what he did about WB said: 'Nothing, I just lower my sights.' Have you suffered from genuine WB? **Write** about it describing the symptoms, your attempts at a cure and your explanation of its cause(s).

- Many writers struggle with their craft. One of the most searching explorations of the writing experience is to be found in Sylvia Plath's *Journals*. Her entry for 26 September 1959 reads: 'Must get into deep stories where all experience becomes usable to me. Tell from one person's point of view; start with self and extend outwards: then my life would be fascinating, not a glassed-in cage. If only I could break through into one story.... if only I could get it real.' **Write** a week's entries in your own writer's journal. Concentrate on the writing experience. Come back to the material and, out of the jagged and improvised pieces, write an edited version.

- Assuming that 'inspiration' comes unbidden is to misunderstand the nature of the phenomenon. I think writers go to inspiration; inspiration doesn't come to them. We need to rewrite the old magic formula of breath and light and fire. What I mean by 'going to inspiration' is this: in writing we are looking at ways into experience, stored and veined as it is within ourselves and our language. Inspiration is like the miner's candle of old. We hold it spluttering our way into the darknesses; sometimes brilliantly illuminating, other times laying its flame so low we are left groping. But we are holding it, and we can nurture it, and we can blow it and breathe it into brilliance again.

  Word-exercises, that is breathing exercises ('inspiration' if you like), warm us up for writing. The effort of writing itself is a kind of friction; from it, writing smokes then bursts into life under the pressure of thought and the search for the right words. **Write** about your experience of writing. Are you a binge writer, sustaining a session for uninterrupted hours? Are you a fast writer or is writing for you like pulling teeth, each word resistant to the last tug? Some writers like to write in a muddle: paper, books everywhere. Is this a regression to the comfort of childhood messes? A defiance of maternal orderliness? Others need order and the reassurance that only a row of post-its can give. Do you handwrite? Some writers prefer this to word-processing. Why?

- In her poem 'Writing Positions' from her collection *Electroplating the Baby*, Jo Shapcott describes the ambivalence of her self-chosen writing spot. She's as happy writing at 'a desk, a kitchen table, or on the sofa' as anywhere else. But wherever she plants herself, and however high grows her 'barricades of books, stockades of paper', the outside world and its green light 'floods in' till there is finally no 'hiding place'. Are you a nomad writer always wandering away from the threatening expanses of the blank page? Are you a control freak who has to sharpen ten pencils each time you want to write in case you run out of lead? **Write** about your 'writing positions' or your 'hiding places'.

- Don Paterson, the Scottish poet, recognises the positive value of writing rituals. Pay attention to these 'prefaces' to writing, he argues, because they 'serve to put you in a receptive frame of mind'. For him libraries are 'useless' places to compose. MacDonalds are good; noisy cafés the best. What puts you in 'receptive frame of mind'? Music? A walk in the country? A cup of dark, aromatic Costa Rican coffee? One of my former students needed to drive very fast down a stretch of the local motorway before she could work up enough charge to start writing. How do you get up a head of steam? **Write** about it. Local heroes used to pump themselves up before battle by ritual boasting, inflating their exploits, talking up their prowess, adopting threatening postures. **Try composing** a writer's boast, a self-motivating chant or haka for the worried and the tentative.

- **Write** a piece entitled *Writing Postures*.

- Read Natalia Ginsburg's account of her writing life in Janet Sternburg's book *The Writer on her Work*. She describes how her youthful ideas about writing changed, and changed radically. **Write** an account of one radical change in your writing.

- The phrase 'I'm waiting for inspiration' is a code for many things, only some of which are mentioned above. Another translation of the code is this: 'I'm not ready to write. I think I am a writer but I'm not sure.' This is a genuine problem of identity and self-belief. Everyone else is so much better, you think. So much more confident. **Write** a statement to your psychiatrist outlining your 'problem' with writing and writers.

- New writers are often inhibited by the notion of originality. They believe that creative writing has to be 'original', which is why the semi-mystical notion of inspiration still holds sway. If we are not 'original', so it goes, we are worthless in the same way that a reproduction of a Picasso is worthless next to the original. Some writers feel that to be a real writer you have to be novel, innovative, experimental, different. This perception leads the unwary into phoney writing; stuff that's trendy, obscure, pretentious, bizarre and overly self-conscious. Real writers see through these pretences early on and quickly go in search of their own voice. And real writers get scared doing this. But real writers still do it. **Write** about the occasion when you tried to impress someone with what you now recognise was pretentious writing.

- Again, some people think writing has to be visceral, raw. Real fiction has to be set on squalid housing estates or the city's mean streets. So it is assumed. Gritty realism is OK. A reviewer of Peter Reading's recently published *Collected Poems* described his material as 'scabrous and shocking...a world of extreme urban distress; of homeless alcoholics, appalled "oldies" and brutalised youth'. Most people 'know' this world from television soap and docu-soap, and some know it for real. So, is it legit for *anyone* to write about the downside, or does a writer have to be in the front-line before he/she has a right to be heard? Truth has to be witnessed before it can be recorded? Imagine someone accusing a writer-friend of yours of not facing up to the real world, of turning a blind eye to the economic, racial and social injustice that surrounds us all. Writers have to be political first and personal second. A writer's first duty is to right wrongs, declares the accuser. **Write** a stinging riposte on behalf of your friend, challenging the assumptions about writing that underlie these charges.

- When Yeats writes about the 'masterful images' of literature in his poem 'The Circus Animals' Desertion', he recognises that their mastery grew out of less than noble beginnings. They emerge, not in the lofty sentiments and the poetic utterances of the past, but in:

> A mound of refuse or the sweepings of a street,
> Old kettles, old bottles and a broken can,
> Old iron, old bones, old rags, that raving slut
> Who keeps the till. Now that my ladder's gone,
> I must lie down where all the ladders start
> In the foul rag and bone shop of the heart.

Is this an invitation to write about the bleaker side of life, the 'lower depths' as Gogol, the Russian writer, described the world of the destitute and dispossessed? Or does every writer have to acknowledge that underneath our heart warmth there lurk scowling and distasteful truths? Is the descent into this foulness what distinguishes real writers from the sham? The real confront it; the sham evade it? Yeats was re-evaluating his ideas about writing and writing practice in this poem. **Try and write** a re-evaluation of your own work. Do you think you should broaden the subject matter of your writing? Experiment more? Are you for real or for the quiet writing life? How do you relate to the world out there, to social exclusion, yob culture, dumbing down, declining standards of public behaviour, trash media, fat cats, welfare dependency, racial violence, jingoism, misogyny, urban dereliction, environmental spoliation, et cetera? It's enough to make you stick with flowers and sunsets! Use a phrase like *Flowers and Sunsets* as a satiric title for your piece.

- Of course, writers' conversations with themselves never end. There are no answers; only a bit of territory temporarily gained on Truth's slippery slope, as John Donne might have said. For this and other reasons, Yeats wrote of the poet's endless 'quarrel with himself'. **Write** a duologue where the two sides of yourself 'quarrel' over writing behaviour. Or **write** their exchange of letters in which the correspondents argue over a writing matter of pressing importance. In both these scenarios try and create distinctive voices with their own style of expression. One 'voice' may be excitable and given to extravagant gestures; the other may be calculating and reticent but tend to talk jargon.

- 'Kitchen sink drama' was a term coined in the sixties to describe plays that dealt with themes of domestic violence, poverty and 'exclusion'. The writers in that decade of plenty were dismissed by critics as 'angry young men', as new boys on the block sounding off in order to establish some street cred. When is writing 'gritty realism' unacceptable and just another form of sham? **Write** a two-paragraph response in 'gritty realist' mode.

- There is a belief that the working class is nearer the quick of living than, say, the middle class, whose affluence and values cushion them from 'reality'. Is there any evidence for this notion? Is this another spin on Northern grit versus Southern comfort? Is it yet another myth about truth and truthfulness in writing, about the real thing and faking it? **Write** down your thoughts on these questions. Out of these notes **compose** an article for a writing magazine. Title – *Faking It!*

- Imagine you have been asked to give the keynote address at a writer's conference. You decide to challenge the prevailing fashion of in-your-face fiction, and you give five reasons why every writer should keep their head in the sand. Entitle the speech *Ostrich Attitudes* and **write** the first two pages.

- Read some book reviews and/or author interviews from the broadsheets and collect some examples of common misconceptions/myths about writing. Alternatively, over a period of time, listen to the comments and judgements made in your writing class. Identify the misunderstandings, delusions or dubious assumptions made about writing. Note them down. **Write** a piece stereotyping these ideas. Each false view of the writer, for instance, you could identify as a separate syndrome. So, there might be the 'Chatterton' syndrome to describe the overly Romantic view of the writer as the wounded genius, named after the poet, Thomas Chatterton, who died young and penniless in a garret. You could write a profile of the 'Messiah' syndrome, or the 'Hemingway' syndrome, or the *Hello* magazine syndrome, or the Doctor Freud syndrome. And so on. You could also write about the 'Daffodil' school of writing, the 'Bottom-of-the-barrel' school of writing, the 'Path. Lab.' school of writing, the 'Tesco' school of writing, et cetera. Make up your own titles.

- In her reflections on the writing life entitled 'Avoid the Spinning Plates', A. L. Kennedy takes issue with the Byronic myth of the writer as the brooding genius. She's tired of being asked if her childhood was unhappy, if her parents were wicked, if she ever came close to suicide. The assump-

tion at the heart of all these questions is that creativity stems
from 'mental anguish or . . . the vivid recreation of hideous
torments past'. 'People in torment don't write fiction,' she
says dryly. *After* torment they might write, but not *in* torment. Kennedy has a more positive view of creation. She
accepts that the writing life starts with 'dark beginnings',
with low self-esteem and confidence, but says it warms to
'assurance and joy'. It travels from the fearful to the familiar.

To create is to be generous, she says. 'A writer has a daily
opportunity to unveil worlds, to explore them as no one else
has and then to give them to others.' Fine. Writer as saviour
and therapist. She seems to divide writers into two camps.
Some begin in recovery, writing away their pain. Some are
inspired by an excess of 'love or exhilaration'. She belongs
to the joy club: 'Because, even in the worst cases, writing can
bring a positive result out of a negative situation, because it
allows me to articulate the quiddity of my life, because it
can spring simply from delight in existence, ability and the
sensation of language. I feel I can say for me writing is
generally very much more about joy than pain.' **Write**
about a situation in your life where writing worked a positive out of a negative.

- Think of one thing that has recently 'delighted' you. It may
be a momentary image, like sunlight burning an anemone
petal deep red or a line recalled from a poem or a sudden
memory. **Write** a delighting poem. Use words with verve.
Goose-pimple the reader with sound effects both lush and
lemon-sharp, and sinewy rhythms. Read Gerard Manley
Hopkins's poem 'Spring' (RB). By the last line the world
has arrived fresh as the first day of Genesis.

The Vision Thing

- Are you a wannabe writer still doing warm-up exercises
wondering how to start or even whether to start at all? Well,
you can't learn to swim without getting in the water. Forget

about being a writer if it means being clever, trendy, wordy, preachy. Better try being a not-writer. Which means forget about the weight of your office, the seriousness of your calling and JUST WRITE. We are haunted by the ghostly taboos of our past. A teacher may have said never start a sentence with the conjunctions 'and' or 'but', and never end one with a preposition. You've never forgotten the commandments. The rubrics appear like demons as soon as you pick up pen, and they look over our writing shoulder all the time, checking, censoring. The incubus of the classroom sits on our back and hisses: 'Do not misspell simple words. Do not forget full stops, commas and semi-colons and speech marks, especially speech marks.' **Write** about the devils on your writing shoulder.

• There are other devils – those we make ourselves. Natalie Goldberg identifies 'monkey mind' as the biggest threat to real writing. 'Monkey mind' skips on the surface and avoids going deep into things. 'Monkey mind' makes lists and substitutes busy-ness for the business of writing. 'Monkey mind' does the cleaning, pays bills, invents 'necessary' work. 'Monkey mind' wags an admonitory finger. 'Monkey mind' dismisses first thoughts and tells us writing etiquette, correct spelling, precise punctuation come first. 'Monkey mind' substitutes show for substance. 'Monkey mind' disconnects the mind from itself, from the vital depths, from 'wild mind'.

What tricks does your 'monkey mind' play? Read Raymond Carver's autobiographic story 'One More', from his collection *A New Path to the Waterfall*. A man (Carver) decides to 'clear his decks first' before writing the poem that has 'held him in his grip after a restless night'. By the end of the day he's caught up with his correspondence, paid bills, blabbed on the phone, got his life in order. A man like that, says the accusatory author, ought to have his poems 'eaten by mice'. A man like that 'doesn't deserve poems'. **Write** about the ways you avoid and evade writing? The guilts, the temporising, the false apprehensions, the self-deluding tactics, the self-victimising, the false modesties.

- It is common to talk about 'the burden of writing', 'the weight on the shoulder'. In her *Journals*, Sylvia Plath describes how she found the responsibility of trying to nurse an injured bird back to life quite disabling. For a few days it was touch and go. Was she curing or killing it? Was it best to put it out of its misery? How? How awful! The bird died, but another was born – the Panic Bird. It was the thing that visited her, weighed her down and stopped her writing. What animal represents your writing fears? **Write** a curse against it.

- The 'impostor syndrome', as the American novelist Charles Baxter remarked, is the biggest problem facing any new writer. Before you can write a novel or short story you have to *pretend* to be a novelist or short story writer. You start as nobody and never quite lose the feeling that you are a great pretender, a fraud. Do you feel you are just playing at it? Is it just a game for you? An idle amusement? Has your feeling about writing changed? 'Let's pretend' is at the heart of writing. So maybe the roles of pretender, fraudster, licensed fool are part of the writer's costume wardrobe. Some robes are thrust upon us; some come with the job. What role do you play as writer? Read Robert Coover's story 'Hat Act'. Has it anything to say about the writer and the position she finds herself in? The title of this story is revealing. Mull it over. **Write** about these ideas. Try the Coover format using another metaphor, appropriate to writing, as the core of the narrative.

- Much of this book so far has been about facing up – to yourself. It's like there's a big bully outside the door and you've got to go out and be brave. But he's only there while the door is shut. Open it, and he disappears. As a writer, always open the door. And keep it open. These last two exercises are about exorcising a few ghosts. A bell, book and candle job. Don't get me wrong. Ghosts are to be taken seriously too. But some are not worth the candle. The thing is to face the real ones.

  Real writers face the truth. They open doors to do that. They cross thresholds and take the consequences. This is another way of saying that writing is not a vocation, but an adventure, a search, a quest. The truth of the business is that we don't know what we want to say until we say it. Adrienne Rich puts it like this: 'Writing is discovering what you don't know you know.' All this suggests that we must let go. An adventure means we agree to let things get out of control. James Hill says: 'ideas we don't know we have, have us.' Thus writing can be seen as a form of possession. Facing up to the truth is, paradoxically, facing up to the not-known. If we start writing by thinking we've got some T-R-U-T-H to communicate to the world we become prophets, messiahs, preachers, not writers. One critic has called this concern with TRUTH, 'elephantine' art. The artist starts with a big idea, an abstraction, a great theme, a MESSAGE. Ezra Pound recognised the self-importance of the big-idea approach and advised all writers to avoid the 'cosmic'. Whenever you get an attack of the cosmics, go and do the ironing.

If you've got a message, send a telegram. The truth is, truth is elusive. It is for this reason that writers strive for it. They seek 'the the' in life as Wallace Stevens puts it. The first thing to accept is that we can neither seize nor size the TRUTH. It may be the guiding light, but its starlight is years away. And receding. It's just too mega.

The thing is to start with *your* truth. How *you* see it. This is the essence. Raymond Carver again. In his essay 'On Writing', he distinguishes between talent, which most writers have, and vision, which he describes as 'a unique and exact way of looking at things, and finding the right context for expressing that way of looking'. Similarly, elsewhere he says: 'Writers carry news from their world to ours.' Carver is saying a number of things about writing here. Tease out the implications of these two statements. **Write** a commentary or meditation on the ideas.

- The former hoodlum turned successful crime writer, Edward Bunker, has written about how he came to writing. It's a salutary tale. Imprisoned for armed robbery, he was encouraged to write. His first books were 'absolute fucking crap'. But he persisted. A New York publisher saw his manuscripts, said the stuff was unpublishable, but told him to keep trying. He did. Year after year. In desperation he decided to write in the first person. He cut out every spare word, every loose sentence, every unnecessary description. He cut and cut. 'And suddenly,' he said, 'I found my own voice.' Do you think you have you found your 'voice' yet? Are you seeking, trying and trying like Edward Bunker? If not, then he has shown a possible path to success. Try, try, try is the message. Survey the last few months of your writing life and note the advances and retreats, the desolations and consolations. **Write** a brief writer's dairy covering this period.

- Bunker has crucial things to say about developing your work once you feel you've hit your true note. He describes his writing style as 'slow and relentless'. He writes and rewrites endlessly looking always for a 'core of honesty' which he believes exists at the heart of all good literature. His ambition is to get his readers to understand the 'criminal mind and the way people can be sucked into dark places and dark ways of life'.

  Bunker has lead an extraordinary life (recorded in his autobiography *Mr Blue*), and has material enough there for a library of stories. Some novice writers feel that life should feed literature and that those with a dramatic, adventured life are at an advantage. Not true. The criminal mind may be particularly interesting, but all minds are fascinating, seething as they do with impotent passions and unfulfilled hatreds, frozen terrors and melting hopes. As Edith Wharton said, all stories are about 'soul drama', 'the inner workings of people's lives'. Act out yourself, or invent your altered egos, and voice their workings and awakenings. Consider the behaviour of someone you know well. Disentangle their motives for behaving as they do, and distinguish the ostensible from the real. **Write** three pages revealing the inside story of your subject. The idea here is not to show how devious and hypocritical people can be (they are all the time of course), but to show the complexities and contradictions in the way we act and think and feel. It's amazing how virtuous vices can be and how vicious virtue in the wrong minds. When does pride become pig-headedness, self-belief – arrogance? When does love become possessiveness; thrift – miserliness; enterprise – avarice? Where do you start? There's so much to say.

- Alfred Adler, the Austrian psychologist and associate of Sigmund Freud, believed that all relationships are based on power and the desire to assert the self. Does your own experience support this view of human behaviour? Choose any relationship you have watched over the years and analyse it in Adlerian terms making the necessary notes as you think along. Now **try writing** a scene from a play in which the Adlerian traits of the situation are explored. Here's a possible scenario. A 70–year-old widow has been partially incapacitated by a stroke. She fears her children may neglect her. She's nurtured them all her life; now it's their turn to support her. One of her married daughters takes her home from the hospital and plans to spend a few days there to help the mother 'get on her feet again'. Start the play from this point.

- There are some things that impede a writer's unique way of seeing. Here are three bad counsellors. Flattery (flattering the reader) is the first. Abasement is a second (to flatter we have to demean the self). Ventriloquism is a third. **Write** and explain how these three work. There are other darker counsellors waiting in the wings should the lesser ones fail. Who are they? How do they disguise themselves?

- We can all see, but do we look? When Raymond Carver talks about an *'exact* way of looking', he is talking about trained eyes habituated to accurate observation and the cultivated ability of not just looking carefully *at*, but looking *into* things. That's what vision means – going beyond the *surface* into the hidden life of things. This is what Primo Levi, the great Italian writer, described as the writer's essential quality. It is 'a mental habit of correctness and concision, the constant desire not to stop at the surface of things'. 'Fundamental accuracy of statement is the one sole morality of writing,' said Ezra Pound. Suppose a friend reveals a secret to you. Something she has done. You are astonished.

It is so out of character. **Write** the scene bearing in mind that what you are trying to achieve is accuracy and depth.

- In her essay on Marcel Proust included in her book *The Writing of Fiction*, Edith Wharton, the author of the classic novel *The Age of Innocence*, says the good writer has 'this faculty of penetrating into a chosen subject and bringing to light its inherent properties'. Wharton goes on to warn the apprentice writer in these words: 'The reluctance to look deeply enough into a subject leads to the indolent habit of decorating its surface.' Verbal vanity and self-display and indolence! More bad counsellors to be added to the disreputable entourage described above. Take a piece of your own writing which is 'decorative' and 'surface'. **Rewrite** it so it loses its false glitter and gets nearer the 'inherent qualities' of the subject.

- This in-looking power that Edith Wharton describes can be fostered. Commentators like Natalie Goldberg use specific meditation to get below the surface and into the real nature of things. Other writers have been more mundane. They talk about 'mulling things over', letting the mind 'take its course'. When the American playwright Arthur Miller started *Death of a Salesman*, he first built a log cabin. Then he sat down and waited – 'letting things happen'. Edith Wharton offers more sound advice to the novelist: 'If, when once drawn to a subject, he would let it grow slowly in his mind instead of hunting about for arbitrary combinations of circumstance, his tale would have the warm scent and flavour of a fruit ripened in the sun instead of the insipidity of one forced in the hot-house.' Ripen your writing.
    Raymond Chandler felt much the same way: 'A good story cannot be devised,' he said. 'It has to be distilled.' William Stafford, an American poet, had influential ideas about writing. In his famous essay 'On Writing', he says the writer should 'attend' the world, should like a bystander watch, and, in a state of receptivity, take for his material what passes by. What swam by he thought swam *in*. By looking and waiting the extraordinariness of the ordinary becomes apparent. Read some of his poetry. Also poems by

William Carlos Williams. Look at, I mean really look at, an object – pebble, flower, old shoe, piece of broken glass – and write about it. Reflect on it. Walk your mind around it. If you get impatient because it's not answering to your gaze, then get tough. Interrogate it. Don't take No for an answer. **Write** a poem in which you feel you've got to the heart of the subject.

- The bystander role is applauded by other writers too. Rosella Brown, a contemporary American novelist, is more proactive in her stance on writing than William Stafford, but points in the same direction. She quotes with approval the photographer Walker Evans's advice to the artist: 'Stare. It is the only way to educate your eye. Stare, pry, listen, eavesdrop. Die knowing something. You are not here long.' The last word is from Carver once more: 'At the risk of appearing foolish, a writer sometimes needs to be able to just stand and gape at this or that thing – a sunset or an old shoe – in absolute and simple amazement.' **Write** about an ordinary domestic object in amazement.

- Over the radio, I've just heard Richard Dawkins, the celebrated evolutionist, advising listeners to go out and enjoy the beauties of a meadow in sunlight. His latest book *Unweaving the Rainbow* is a rebuttal of the notion that scientists by *explaining* the world are destroying its mystery and beauty. He takes his title from Keats who complained in his poem *Lamia* (1819) that Newtonian physics had reduced the beauty of the rainbow to mere prismatics. Scientists like artists do go behind and below the surface and get into the heart of things. But it's not like going behind the surface glitter of a stage set and finding the dull and disappointing clutter of scaffolding, cables, spilt paint and pallets. The spiral helix is a wonder to marvel at. Imagine the sub-world of an object, the microscopic views of the internal structure of matter. **Write** a piece from a sub-surface view.

- The Stafford approach does seem passive. But, like the insectivorous plant, it is playing a waiting game with life. Once the images fly by and into the mind the system goes into overdrive. More of this later. No, writers may attend, but they also contend. Writers are driven, or good writers are, by a desire to know, by a curiosity. Henry James advised young writers to be 'someone on whom nothing is lost'. Be *open* to the world. Barry Lopez, essayist and travel writer who wrote the marvellous *Arctic Dreams*, said in his book of autobiographical essays *About This Life*, that writers should develop a 'patient eye'. I like that phrase: 'a patient eye'. Annie Proulx, author of *The Shipping News* and more recently *Close Range*, sees writers as diggers, collectors of unconsidered trifles, road drifters, second-hand bookshop browsers whose first rule is – never take the high street when there's a side road. 'Stop often,' she says, 'get out, and listen, walk around, see what you can see. What you see are signs.... the personal messages. We live in a world of signs.' Our job as writers is to read them. **Write** about your digging.

An Axe for the Frozen Sea Within

- Writers who stay on the surface are there because they have nothing worth saying. They substitute surface froth (verbal flash, sententiae) for substantial expression. Fancy-dress stuff. Developing *ways of looking* is basic to the writer's craft. Having *something to say* is just as crucial. The second is subsumed in the first. John Gardner, whose book on writing fiction is still one of the best around, says: 'A writer's materials are what he cares about.' Kurt Vonnegut, who wrote *Slaughter House Five*, another must-read, offered the same perceptive advice to all writers when he wrote: 'Find a subject you care about.'

  Barry Lopez tells the story about a fellow plane passenger asking him what instruction he would give to his daughter who wanted to be a writer. After suggesting she read and study grammar he said: 'If she wishes to write well, she will have to *become someone*. She will have to discover her beliefs, and then speak to us from within those beliefs. If her prose doesn't come from out of her belief, she will only be passing on information. Help her discover what she means.' I have not come across a better statement of the writer's life than this. It's what this book is all about. 'Tell her to leave town,' was the final piece of advice Lopez gave to the father. **Write** to the daughter explaining what this last remark means.

- We are back with the mantra: 'Find yourself, find your subject.' Fortunately writing is good at finding. Ask yourself what you care about, what you truly believe in, or to use Joyce Carol Oates's phrase, what your 'forbidden passions' are. She says you've got to be passionate as a writer and be prepared to 'rage'.

  Make a list of everything you care about. Make a list of what you believe in. What would you defend with your life? What would you most hate to lose? **Write down** as much as you can. Now shape it into a credo using the list as a simple structuring device. Or **write** a rage poem.

- Do you, for instance, believe in telling the truth? In honesty? **Write** about an episode in your life when your resolve to be honest was either put to the test or found to be misplaced altruism.

- Imagine you have been arrested as a participant in an ANTI-CAPITALISM protest march that got out of hand. The police want a statement. Your appalled parents want you to be circumspect in what you say, want you to play down your role, want you not to incriminate yourself, et cetera, et cetera. What are their motives? **Write** down the final statement.

- Read Denise Lervatov's poem 'Matins' (20WP). Each section is a reflection on the idea of 'The authentic!' Domestic routines like feeding children and getting them to school mingle with images from memory and symbolic narrative sequences. At one point she holds:

  the new-laid
  egg whose speckled shell
  the poet fondles and must break
  if he will be nourished.

  Towards the end of the poem she imagines 'the authentic' rolling like a stone below the waves. She asks a 'little horse, beloved' to tell her:

how to follow the iron ball,
... to the place where I must kill you and you step out
of your bones and flystrewn meat
tall, smiling, renewed,
formed in your own likeness.

I think this is a revealing poem about the nature of
writing, and covers many of the ideas I've been exploring
in this book. What is the poem saying? Any idea? Matins is
the service of morning prayers performed by monks each
day as part of the Divine Office. The word derives from
Matuta, the Roman goddess of dawn. Is the poem a prayer?
Have you come across some of these metaphors or symbols
before? For instance, the 'iron ball' metaphor connects with
a similar one in 'Ode to His Coy Mistress' by Andrew
Marvell. **Write** a commentary on 'Matins'.

- The injunction to write about 'forbidden passions' suggests
  writing is an illicit, subversive affair. Joyce Carol Oates
  offers some examples of writers who wrote about such
  things: Eugene O'Neill and Sylvia Plath, who raged
  against their fathers; Hemingway, who raged against his
  mother all his life; Anne Sexton, who struggled against the
  'seductive Angel of Death'; Edgar Allen Poe, haunted by the
  fear of madness. It seems many writers are haunted by the
  'black dog' of depression, and fear of failure! Not all
  are haunted for a lifetime, though mothers and fathers, the
  twin maypoles round which our lives and ideas dance
  and intertwine, never leave us. **Write** about a 'forbidden
  passion'.

- **Write** a poem in the form of a shopping list or Christmas
  present list itemising all the things you are hoping for. All
  the things you want to be lies. All the things you want to be
  true. All the dreams you never want to fade.

- 'It's a man's world. A woman should acknowledge her hurt,
  her anger and her hope of "justice"; even a hope for revenge
  might be good thing in her work...' Joyce Carol Oates.
  Write about your hurt, anger and hope.

- Time to reflect and take stock after this rush of ideas and advice. **Write** a job description for the writer. One line for every role and responsibility.

- Lervatov's poem above is sustained by past writers; the vigour of Marvell's recycled image propels it. All writers plunder the past for verbal treasure. How could it be otherwise! We drink from the same well of language! We walk paths others have trodden safe for us. No, the relationship between our 'father' writers and ourselves is well defined. I should say relationships. Our connections with past performers are clear but complex and contradictory. One man's borrowings are others' texts burgled. Plagiarism blights the hand that feeds it, and a writer may just as well imitate antecedents to flatter and/or celebrate achievement. Though we may be intimidated by it, we can't cast the past aside.

  We can't cast readers aside either. They are the writer's life-blood. That being so, writers need to care for them. And here's the rub. We write the texts of ourselves and give them, as A. L. Kennedy explains, generously to the reader. What if the reader does not want our gift? Well, we can be snotty too and say tough, see if I care. Or we could offer inducements. We could write so compellingly; so subtly manage our storying that the reader finds our work irresistible, wondrous. The writer as illusionist. We could go downmarket; offer volume not quality. We could make her groggy with violence, tingle her with free textual sex, and warm her after the plot peaks with a cosy chocolatey conclusion. Writer as salesperson! Pitching it right on the Freudian button, the text letting her pleasure herself. Flattery? Yes. Placation? Yes. Book as libation. Imagine books as characters in a play. There's Aga Saga, the airport novel. There's the slim petite Novella, the rosy-eyed romance; Grit Real wiv a ring frew his ??? Put them in a focus group or a pub or on the Booker Prize selection panel. **Write** up the conversation.

- Paul Celine, the Romanian poet, described his poems as 'messages in bottles'. This is richly ambiguous metaphor. It circumscribes crucial aspects of the reader/writer relationship. **Write** down some notes on the ramifications of this trope.

- Casting your writings on the water does illustrate the chancing and chancy nature of the reader/writer relationship. Even so, the writer has to think about his/her audience and adjust voice and style to suit anticipated readerships. Writers are surrogate readers. All this is commonsense. What is also obvious is that writers have to be their own readers. Writers read themselves. They have to read from inside their fiction, like moles. They have to understand structure and style, point of view, character and plot; scene arrangement, theme, and the narrative contours of their whole fictional world. Thus every real writer is a critical reader; no reader is more so.

   Edith Wharton, in *The Writing of Fiction*, is very clear about the importance of the thinking writer, the one who critically reflects on his or her work. She thought writers should interrogate their writing, ask questions, seek answers. 'Is it useless,' she asks, 'to try for a clear view of the meaning and method of one's art? Surely not. If no art can be quite pent-up in the rules deduced from it, neither can it be fully realised itself unless those who practise it attempt to take its measure and reason out its processes.' Can you think of other ways of representing the reader/writer relationship? Is it a marriage? Is it consumerist as I suggest above? **Write** a poem describing your ideal reader, appearance, habits, possessions, et cetera.

- One of the most forthright and uncompromising statements about reading came from the Czech writer Franz Kafka. Writing to a friend in 1904 he asserts:

   We ought to read only books that bite and sting us. If the book we are reading doesn't shake us awake like a blow to the skull, why bother reading it in the first place? So that it can make us happy, as you put it? Good God, we'd be just as happy if we had no books at all; books that make us happy we could, in a pinch, also write ourselves. What we need are books that hit us like a most painful misfortune, like the death of someone we loved more than we love ourselves, that make us feel as though we had been banished to the woods, far from any human presence, like a suicide. A book must be the axe for the frozen sea within us.

(Ernst Pawel, *The Nightmare of Reason.*
A Life of Franz Kafka)

Most writers would prefer to awaken their readers more gently. Disturb maybe, disrupt possibly, arrest even, but they draw the line at blows to the skull and axes. What do you think Kafka means by 'the frozen sea within us'? Are readers so resistant to the text or the imagination that only extreme measures can succeed in breaking the caskets of ice? Perhaps a gentle thaw would suffice? The poet W. H. Auden said: 'We don't read books: books read us.' Is the text a Peeping Tom, spying on us readers? A mind-snatcher? **Write** a journal entry reflecting on these ideas and images.

- For Kafka, the reading/writing relationship is not fraternal and well-mannered. The tranquil posture of the reading act, supine and restful, belies the darker purposes of the infiltrator writer, her treasonous intent. Such a writer is the old-fashioned zealot type angry for change, laying siege to the reader. Kafka is not referring to writers with a political agenda, feminist, anti-racist, anti-totalitarian, et cetera, but to a broad writerly commitment – a *belief in one's own vision* and a desire, even compulsion, to *communicate that vision*.

  So when Joan Didion says: 'I write entirely to find out what I am thinking, what I want and what I fear,' she may be writing herself into being, opening herself up to herself, but she is being disingenuous when she says self-knowledge is her *entire* reason for writing. I like the ambiguity of Didion's word 'find out'. It means to 'investigate', but carries with it the reluctant yielding of secrets as implied in the phrase – 'being found out'. There seems to be an eternal conflict between the side of us that seeks the truth and is willing to risk exposure (publication?) of it and for it, and the side that wants not 'to be found out'.

  I think writing is about *defining* the self as much as about exploring the self. Exploring suggests there is a fixed entity to discover. What we get is versions of self. Partly because language, our means of enquiry and expression, is all signs and not the actuality, and is therefore slippery and unreliable. Partly too, because the self has a built-in immobiliser or decoy system that evades self description, and partly, because nothing stands still, the self is always a moving target aiming at itself. What writing does is *invent* working selves, stand-ins awaiting the arrival of the real one – sometime, maybe, whenever, if.

If Didion is articulating the broad purpose of writing it appears in a variety of versions. Some writers have an avowedly political purpose. Linton Kwesi Johnson writes as the representative voice of a disenfranchised people: 'documenting the experience of my generation... of black people, ordinary folk'. Anita Desai's novel *In Custody* was written to protest against the Hindu drive to extinguish Islamic history. In a recent interview she explained her position: 'I am not trying to idealise or romanticise the Mughal past. There's a lot that's decadent, as well as beautiful. But it's wrong to pretend it never existed. It's reinventing history books in order to obliterate traces of the past that I want to make a stand against.' Torchbearer! Witness! Two roles for the writer. Shaman? Jeremiah? Thersites? Imagine each of these roles as 'characters' appearing in a play. Each one introduces himself/herself/itself in a short speech to the audience. There is some rivalry between them! **Write** the three speeches with the occasional heckling.

- Clive Barker says he wants his work to reach out to the world, to infect his readers with the teenage fervour he still feels himself. Writer as missionary here? For him, the alternative to writing 'is probably going crazy'. He explains his compulsion so: 'The business of writing helps me think more clearly. There's something therapeutic about it. I have a fierce sense of purpose when I'm writing...' As therapy, writing supposedly works as release, exorcising demons even. Or it may be compensatory. For Ted Hughes it was expiatory, an endless attempt at disposing of devils. The terrible 'wrestling-with-angels' view of writing is best exhibited in Hughes's poem 'The God' from *Birthday Letters*. Here the driving force is an angry and demanding divinity, and, like the terrible biblical Moloch, it demands its blood sacrifices. Again the image of the 'wounded' writer bearing an impossible burden is a retro version of the tortured Romantic. Is writing therapeutic for you? Is it compulsive? A necessary evil which, like a habit, needs fixing? **Write** about it.

- 'Writing is playing with the body of the mother,' wrote Roland Barthes. Can you make any sense of this strange observation? **Write** a fantasy using a phrase from this remark as your title. It should read as a myth about writing.

- 'Writers lie in wait for readers.' **Write** two paragraphs each one showing a different way in which this statement is true.

- 'Writing is not a gift from; it is a present to.' **Write** an explanation.

- Walt Whitman, recycling the old image of the book as destiny, declared: 'Nature is a living book and has to be deciphered.' And Barry Lopez, writing in the introduction to his autobiography *About This Life*, echoes Whitman when he says that writing is about 'the endless deciphering of what we are up to'. Gertrude Stein thought that the writer was a watcher seeking in the world clues to the 'real' reality that lay under the conventional and misleading cover. She saw mediation and reflection as the gateways to understanding. **Write** a poem entitled *Watcher*.

- Read Louis Simpson's poem 'Things' (OBV). It is about some of the issues I've been discussing above. The material poet meets a visionary stranger; the world of ordinary things confronts the 'spiritual world'. After some discussion, they acknowledge that 'things have a third substance', and because of this, they agree that ' . . . there be a perpetual coming and going' between their two houses. Can you make sense of Simpson's conclusion? Decipher the poem. **Write** your interpretation.

- In *The Writing of Fiction*, Edith Wharton comments on the mimetic view of art in these words: 'The mind of a creative artist is a mirror, and a work of art the reflection of life in it. The mirror, indeed, is the artist's mind, with all his experiences reflected in it; but the work of art, from the smallest to the greatest, should be something *projected*, not reflected . . . something on which his mirrored experiences . . . are to be turned for its full illumination.' **Write** a poem or very short story in which a mirror is a threshold. **Write** a poem or very short story in which a mirror begins to take over the life of its owner.

- In 'Things', Simpson's persona says that the simplest articles of household use, such as 'a chair, a dish . . . in the pure state are mysterious'. **Write** about the 'mystery' of a household object. 'It is possible,' wrote Raymond Carver, 'to endow those things – a chair, a window curtain, a fork, a stone, a woman's earring – with immense, even startling power.' See if you can do it. Read William Carlos Williams's short poem 'The Red Wheelbarrow'. The first lines read: 'so much depends/upon/a red wheel/barrow . . . ' What depends on it?

- The poet Michael Longley has written: 'Nothing remains ordinary if you look at it long enough. Anyone's back garden can become a gold mine.' He gives as an example two homely images: snow settling on coals, white on black, cold on fire, and a blackbird that appeared one day in the garden with a fleck of white feather on its plumage. Out of these two images and their blacks and whites he crafts a poem. Look at your own literal and metaphorical back yard. Can you turn it into a 'gold mine'? Just to prove Longley's point, look at your unregarded household world. Look long enough to turn the mundane into the miraculous, the familiar into the fantastical. **Write** a mini-collection of six short poems that grows out of house or garden.

- To the material world the writer's preoccupation with 'other worlds' looks like old-fashioned dilettantism. Most people take a utilitarian view of writing. What does it do? Of what practical use is it? Can it make a difference? The questions come nearest to being accusations when asked of verse writing. In some cultures the poet has performed a sacred office. He/she is soothsayer, prophet, guardian of knowledge, keeper of the mysteries. Not any more.

In his book *The Redress of Poetry*, Seamus Heaney has sought not so much to recover the poet's lost cultic powers, but to position him/her more centrally and sensibly within the contemporary political and cultural frame. In a world looking for action and a voice for the voiceless, arguments mirroring back bright images of the reader's own life to verify and uplift do not appeal. What Heaney proposes is a poetry that counterbalances the bias of 'actuality' as it leans towards extremes. As a regime becomes more oppressive the writer becomes more counteractive, and in redressing the balance, leads minds towards a new moral equilibrium. In her book *Gravity and Grace*, Simone Weill wrote: 'Obedience to the force of gravity. The greatest sin'. Is Weill referring to a writer's public responsibilities? What does she mean here? What responsibilities has a writer? What more does a writer do but write? 'Every writer should be an anarchist, committed to nothing.' **Write** a speech or manifesto justifying this position.

- George Orwell wrote a famous essay entitled 'Inside the Whale' where he accused Henry Miller of hiding away from the realities of Fascism and political oppression. **Write** Miller's reply in the form of a letter entitled *Dear George*.

References

Ashworth, A., *Once in a House on Fire* (Picador, 1998).
Birkerts, S., *The Gutenberg Elegies* (Faber and Faber, 1996).
Bunker, E., *Mr Blue* (No Exit, 1999).
Calvino, I., *If on a Winter's Night a Traveller...* (Minerva, 1992).
Carver, R., *A New Path to the Waterfall* (Collins, 1990).
Coover, R., *Pricksongs and Descants* (Putnam, 1998).
Dawkins, R., *Unweaving the Rainbow* (Penguin, 1999).
Didion, J., 'Why I Write', in *The Writer on Her Work*, ed. J. Sternburg (Virago, 1992).
Gardner, J., *On Becoming a Novelist* (Norton, 1999).
Heaney, S., *The Redress of Poetry* (Faber and Faber, 1995).
Hemingway, E., *Fiesta: The Sun Also Rises* (Arrow, 1994).

Hughes, T., *Birthday Letters* (Faber and Faber, 1998).

Keats, J., *Selected Poems* (Penguin, 1999).

Kennedy, A. L., 'Avoid the Spinning Plates', *Critical Quarterly*, 37, no. 4 (1996).

Lopez, B., *About This Life* (Harvill, 1998).

Manguel, A., *A History of Reading* (Flamingo, 1996).

Oates, C. J., 'To a Young Writer', in *Letters to a Fiction Writer*, ed. F. Busch (W. W. Norton, 1999).

O'Brien, E., *The Country Girls* (Penguin, 1960).

Olsen, T., *Silences* (Virago, 1980).

Orwell, G., *Essays, Journalism and Letters*, Vol. 2 (Penguin, 1970).

Plath, S., *Journals* (Ballantine, 1982).

Proulx, E. A., *Shipping News* (Fourth Estate, 1994).

Proulx, E. A., *Close Range* (Fourth Estate, 2000).

Reading, P., *Collected Poems* (Bloodaxe, 1998).

Shapcott, J., *Electroplating the Baby* (Bloodaxe, 1988).

Stafford, W., *Crossing Unmarked Snow* (Univ. of Michigan, 1997).

Sternburg, J., *The Writer on Her Work* (Virago, 1992).

Yeats, W. B., *The Collected Poems* (Picador, 1990).

Vonnegut, K., *Slaughterhouse Five* (Vintage, 1991).

Wharton, E., *The Writing of Fiction* (Touchstone, 1997).

Weill, S., *Gravity and Grace* (Routledge, 1987).

Williams, Carlos W., *Selected Poems* (Penguin, 1976).

Woolf, V., 'Professions for a Woman', in *The Pargitters*, ed. M. Leaska (Hogarth Press, 1977).

SECTION 2
WRITING THE SELF

4 The Well of Memory

Remembrance of Things Past

- The film-maker Louis Bunuel wrote in his memoirs: 'You have to begin to lose your memory, if only bits and pieces, to realise that memory is what makes our lives. Life without memory is no life at all... Our memory is our coherence, our reason, our feeling, even our action. Without it we are nothing.' To lose memory means that in some fundamental way we lose ourselves. Conversely to recover and call back memory is one way we have of establishing and finding ourselves.

  Memory is the mirror of self, and nothing illustrates this more clearly than the examples of people who have suffered memory loss. In his celebrated book *The Man Who Mistook his Wife for a Hat*, the neurologist Oliver Sachs explores the significance of Bunuel's words. One of his patients, whom he refers to as 'The Lost Mariner', is suffering from retrograde amnesia. He is a 48-year-old ex-naval rating who thinks he is still 19 and living in 1945. All his memory has been eradicated back to that date and fixed there. Each hour, each day, each week, adds nothing to that time. He can remember nothing recent, nothing of present time beyond the last few seconds, the last few sentences. He is fixed in the mid-forties. He thinks Truman is still President, and when shown a mirror is appalled at his premature ageing.

  Sachs sums up the dilemma of the 'The Lost Mariner': 'He is, as it were, isolated in a single moment of being, with a moat or lacuna of forgetting all around him...he is man without a past (or future), stuck in a constantly changing, meaningless moment.' How can he help his patient? Sachs is at a loss. Then one day, he goes into the hospital chapel and sees the 'Mariner' taking Communion. So intent and absorbed and stilled is the man in this moment that the doctor realises he has found some coherence in a life otherwise fractured and unconnected. Sachs recalls the words of another great neurologist, A. R. Luria: 'A man does not consist of memory alone. He has feeling, will, sensibilities, moral being...'

Elsewhere in the book, Oliver Sachs considers an even more disturbing case of amnesia. A patient comes to him who forgets everything instantly, who has to constantly invent and reinvent identities for himself. Within five minutes of the consultation beginning he has addressed the doctor as 15 different people, and, in the same space of time, has himself become a grocer, a delicatessen-owner and a car mechanic. He has to make himself and his world up every moment, and thereby fix himself in time. But each new self fails to hold, dissolves into forgetfulness, and he is forced to try again and again and again. But no permanent self emerges from these endless inventions.

This case makes Sachs consider the very nature of identity. Each one of us, he writes, has an inner narrative, a life-story. Each one of us '*is* a biography which is constructed continually, unconsciously, by, through, and in us. To be ourselves,' he argues, 'we must *have* ourselves – possess, if need be repossess, our life stories. We must recollect the inner drama, the narrative of ourselves. A man needs such a narrative...to maintain his identity, his self.'

Perhaps writers do not need to be reminded of the importance of memory for their trade. Imagine that instead of a stream of memories flowing behind you there is only a blank wall. Well, you could write on the wall, graffiti a past of sorts. Read some of Oliver Sachs' extraordinary book. Despite the sometimes distressing material it is both compassionate and consoling, full of triumphs and resolutions. It's worth thinking about the ideas here and exploring them a little further in your journal. Use some of these journal ideas to **write** a 'comment and analysis' piece on *Memory*.

- The Canadian writer Carol Shields says we wake up every morning and reinvent ourselves. We accessorise ourselves. What does she mean exactly? She thinks mobile phones are the newest identity tag. **Write** a poem about accessorising the self.

- Norman MacCaig, in his poem 'In My Mind' (OBV), imagines his persona going 'back ways' in time. He is in a townscape, sniffing alleys, hurling rooftops, lassoing from the tops of spires 'two counties in an eye-blink...' Nothing deters him. He is a master magician, an 'honorary citizen', who has the power to walk through walls and 'burn as traffic lights'. BUT, then he comes to 'that terrible cul-de-sac', and his confidence collapses. He turns away. **Write** about a persistent memory. How does it arrive? Unexpectedly knocking? In disguise, slyly emerging? MacCaig uses the image of the wanderer, the free spirit, as his recollective self. How do you see your backwards travelling self?

- The self as time-traveller free to roam the past is a more fanciful than truthful image of the relationship between memory and the present. Taha Hussein, the author of *An Egyptian Childhood*, says: 'The memory of man plays tricks when he tries to recall events of his childhood; for it depicts some incidents as clearly as though they had happened a short time before. Whereas it blots out others as though they had never passed within his ken.' Recall a distant incident from your past, one that is as clear as if it happened yesterday. **Write** down this latest version of it. Can you say why it is so clear and recent-seeming?

- In his poem 'The Phantom Horsewoman', Thomas Hardy describes himself as the 'careworn' man, and sees his dead wife as a young rider. The image of her is 'drawn rose-bright'. He, on the other hand, 'withers daily'. The memory is everywhere: 'In his brain, day, night...' Do you have a single 'rose-bright' memory permanently switched on? Try **writing** about it.

- So is memory an unreliable friend? Or does it seek to protect us from discomforting passages in our past lives by hiding them, losing them, disguising them? From your own experience how would you say memory operates? Watcher, jailer, censor? Think of some recurrent memories. Do they always reappear in the same guise? **Write** about the nature of memory.

- Is memory like a car model, every relaunch it gets a facelift? Do we fictionalise memories, a bit of additional trim here, some upholstery cut there? Take a simple memory and fictionalise it; tweak it here and there for effect; freshen it up with some new material; stitch in another memory. **Write** a new model version.

- Is writing a mere assemblage, a bricolage of memories? A ragbag in the end, just distracting us by its illusory order? Read Raymond Carver's piece 'His Bathrobe Pockets Stuffed with Notes'. The poem catalogues images as inconsequential as notes stuffed into an old jacket or 'messages' pinned to a kitchen notice-board. **Write** your own impromptu list of mental messages ('Notes') from the past. Is there any cohesion to the piece? Can a haphazard accumulation of 'notes' say anything about our lives, our existences?

- **Write** a poem on one of these titles: *Telegrams from Yesterday* OR *Telegrams I Should Have Sent*.

- In *Travels with Charley*, John Steinbeck describes how he sets out to revisit places of his past and rediscover the America he has, over the years, lost touch with. One of his images lingers in my mind/memory; he describes one small unremarkable town as 'the sort of place that gets lost in the crease of a map'. Wonderful!

  He visits his home town not seen for years, and realises the uneasiness his friends feel at his reappearance is connected with 'the pattern of remembrance'. To his old pals he is now a 'ghost'. His arrival has 'muddied his memory'. When he had gone away all those years earlier he died in the sense he became 'fixed and unchangeable' to his friends. 'You can't go home again,' he reflects, 'because home has ceased to exist except in the mothballs of memory.' Have you been trapped in other people's memories? Is 'trapped' a suitable metaphor? Can you think of a better one, one you could stir up a bit of writing with? If not, **write** a poem entitled *Mothballed*.

• Before he leaves his native town, Steinbeck climbs Fremont's Peak, the highest point for miles around and a favoured playground from his past. 'This solitary stone peak,' he writes, 'overlooks the whole of my childhood and youth.' Is there any place/location that dominates and 'overlooks' your past? **Write** about it and a single significant event that happened there.

• 'Childhood is the bank balance of the writer,' wrote Graham Greene. Has it been for you? If it has, **write** a short commentary explaining how it has bank-rolled your writing.

• As he looks down from Fremont's summit, Steinbeck remembers a story about his father whom he recalls burning the name of a girl he loved into the bark of one of the oak trees in the valley. As the years passed the bark grew over the burn and covered it. Years later, a man driving a wedge into the same tree uncovered the hidden message and sent the piece of wood to the son. I like this story because of what it says about memory. **Write** a poem using the patterns of covering and uncovering, or erasing and revealing as the underlying motif. Think of the inexorable erasures of the sea; its soft effacements, for instance. Think of bark scabbing things slowly.

• The last words of Steinbeck's chapter read: 'We hurried away from the permanent and changeless past where my father was always burning his name with his love.' **Write** about a part of your changeless past that is precious to you.

• Marcel Proust in *Remembrance of Things Past*, has written an ironic comment on his own writing achievement: 'It is a labour in vain to try to recapture it [*the past*]: all the efforts of our intellect are useless. The past is hidden somewhere outside its own domain in some material object (in the sensation which that material object will give us) which we never suspected. And it depends on chance whether or not we come upon it before we die.'

The Irish writer Brian Moore was long exiled from his native Belfast. From his occasional visits to the city he realised, like Steinbeck, that places change, memory holds firm. The city, 'with a carapace of flyover' and 'a new notoriety as a theatre of war', was unrecognisable from the city of his childhood. Moore records that while holidaying in Connemara he came across an overgrown graveyard, and one of the headstones startled him into remembrance. The stone, he said, was his Proustian 'material object'. Looking at the stone his mind was filled with 'a jumbled kaleido-scope of images fond, frightening, surprising and sad': his 'pet canary singing'; the 'shrill electric bell' summoning him to Latin classes; 'the swish of the rattan cane; holding the hand of his nurse; hearing the squeal of a pig about to be slaughtered...'

Holden Caulfield, the sardonic narrator in J. D. Salinger's novel *The Catcher in the Rye*, has to write a composition for one of his room-mates. It is supposed to be about a 'room or a house'. This doesn't appeal so he writes about his brother Allie's 'baseball mitt'. Allie is dead, but out of the flood of memories released by this familiar object Holden writes a moving tribute to his lost brother. Salinger starts up this episode with a brief physical description of the mitt. Is there any object in your life that holds pent-up memories for you? **Try writing** about a 'memory-rich' object, starting descriptively, but writing from the third person point of view.

- Read *The Memory Box* by Margaret Forster. In this novel a grown-up daughter learns about her long dead mother through objects left in a 'Memory Box'. Imagine or recall the contents of a 'Memory Box'. What do these possessions reveal about their owner? Write a piece entitled *Memory Box*.

- Or let your mind relax. Wait for the memories to rise or drift past. Imagine they are like a series of side-shows you are passing, or that you are afloat and the scenes/objects idle past you. Now, as I write these words, the image of two lovers is coming into my mind. They appear in a painting by Chagall. They are hanging in the night sky, slowly swirling with animals and crosses and mirrors. Some of these are props I'm adding to the canvas. I think this is because by emphasis and analogue I am trying to describe that strong sense of release the painting gives me. In the floating reds and blues I see ordinary objects, which are miraculously loosened from their bonds, go gravityless. **Write** about the tug of memories each one pulling the next out of the dark.

- Julian Barnes's character Martha Cochrane, from his novel *England, England*, reflects on the unreliability of memory. 'There's always a memory just behind your first memory, and you can't quite get at it.' All first memories she thinks are lies. But what is at first contrived can become 'unprocessed memory' to use Martha's phrase. It's like lighting a bonfire. The artifice of sulphur ignites the fire first. After that it feeds on itself. Try and get in recall mode. See if you can get through to the unprocessed, often the forgotten past. Maybe these memories are dulled and imprecise. They need the patina of time and the mental dust brushing aside so they can come up shiny from the concentrated effort of recollection. Martha never trusted memories that entered her head squeaky bright from the very start. Dingy, cobwebby ones she liked. **Write** a meditation on your cobwebby memories.

- 'Memory is mirrors set in parallel.' Julian Barnes. **Write** a piece that confirms the truth of this metaphor.

- In his celebrated investigation into the sources and origins of Coleridge's poetry, *The Road to Xanadu*, John Livingstone Lowes travels back through the poet's reading trying to isolate the seminal instance of creation. For instance, in 'The Rime of the Ancient Mariner', Coleridge uses the phrase: 'they moved in tracks of shining light' to describe the water snakes following in the wake of the ghost ship. Lowes tracks this image of phosphorescent water, first, to the poet's reading of Joseph's Priestley's 800-page scientific treatise on *Optics*, then to the fifth volume of *The Philosphical Transactions of the Royal Society*, then to the *Letters from Mis-*

sionary Jesuits and, finally, to the *Voyage to the Pacific Ocean* by Captain James Cooke.

He concludes from these monumental researches that a person's reading fills the unconscious memory with a million images. Lowes cites Henry James's remark to explain the process. James, when a plot for his novel *The American* was suggested to him, said he 'dropped it for the time into the deep well of unconscious cerebration'.

Cerebration describes the processes of thinking, of shaping, reshaping and synthesising. For both Lowes and James there was an automatic creator or creative process working below the surface transforming the raw stuff of memory. Lowes talks about: 'images and impressions even in the sleepy drench of our forgetful pools'. These 'fragments sink incessantly below the surface, fuse, assimilate and coalesce,' he argues. Later he says the writer uses 'conscious energy and drags the deeps for their hidden treasure'.

You will recognise this description of the relationship between memory and the writer from some of the explorations above. Lowes believed that in the unconscious memory – the lagoons of the mind – images merged into complex associations or new 'life-forms' which could never be disengaged. Such associations could be brought to the surface wilfully by a powerful act of concentration, or accidentally when a sensation (smell, visual image, sound) acted as the lure.

Proust went as far as to suggest that each of these memory complexes is *tagged*. A simple sense memory, the tag, can release the whole 'flood of remembrance'. He recalls a crucial moment when the taste of a small sponge cake, called a *petite madeleine*, dipped in tea, suddenly brought back memories of his childhood days so powerfully he felt he'd moved into another realm of consciousness. He decides to try and recover the feeling. Can you recall having a *'petite madeleine'* type experience where a simple sense impression produced, and still does produce, an overwhelming sense of the past coming alive? **Write** about the sensation and the subsequent surge of fresh memories.

- As Proust tried to repeat the 'madeleine' moment he hesitated. 'What an abyss of uncertainty,' he wrote, 'whenever the mind feels that some part of it has strayed beyond its own borders; when it, the seeker, is at once the dark region through which it must go seeking, where all its equipment will avail it nothing.' He puts before his mind's eye the little cake. Concentrates on its image, eyes closed. He feels something 'leaving its resting place... something that has been embedded like an anchor at a great depth... mounting slowly'.

  Eventually the past surfaces, and Proust can discern in its rise 'the echo of great spaces traversed'. He concludes from the experience that as time scatters memories, 'smell and taste remain poised a long time... ready to remind us... and bear unfaltering, in the tiny and almost impalpable drop of their essence, the vast structure of recollection.'

  For Proust's beautiful exploration of memory read the last three or four pages of 'Overture', the first chapter of *Swann's Way*, Book One of *A la Recherche*. Close your eyes. Conjure up a favourite smell/taste/feel and associated memories. What ghostly people are beginning to arrive on the stage of your memory? **Write** a Proustian account of how your memory seems to work. Does the oceanic depths analogy apply to the way your memories travel and arrive? Is memory like a raised wreck that brings up a treasure hoard?

Bogs, Gardens and Houses

- I'm not sure every piece of writing needs a refining nudge, but I like Seamus Heaney's description of how his poem 'Bogland' came into being. The phrase, 'We have no prairies', had drifted into his head at bedtime, and he says it 'loosened a fall of images'. A brilliant phrase. It has the suddenness of poetry. We recall the danger of long-stored, cobwebby cases, old tennis-rackets, dusty books tumbling at a careless touch.

  At the time of writing Heaney was reading about the expanses of the American West. It was the idea of frontiers and pioneering that pulled the rug on the poem. Ireland has no western plains, but it does have bogs; deep verticals in place of broad horizontals. So writing out of personal memory the writer frames a myth of collective memory and consciousness. Bogland figures as both the poet's memory and the nation's history.

Commenting on the genesis of the work, Heaney says it grew out of 'something lying beneath the floor of memory'. Only months afterwards when he suddenly recalled childhood warnings about going into the bog did he realise it was these prohibitions that lay under the flags of memory. Afraid children might fall into the bogpools of old workings (turburies) and get drowned, older people used to say that there was no bottom to the bog-holes. Thus the idea of the limitless depths of the past and of memory seeped into the poem. Can you recall adult warnings from your childhood? The 'bogeyman', for instance? The word is a corruption of 'Bonaparte', the Hitler of his time, who was the night-stalker waiting to snatch unwary, over-wakeful children. Use one of these spectres as a starting idea for **writing** a poem.

- It would seem that we can command memory, bid it appear like a boat from over the waters. It is our craft. But what we cannot bid is the current to take us and the winds that guide us. These we have to go with. We can steer the poem, drop anchor occasionally and patiently sit out becalming passages. **Write** a poem using the boat/water image. Start with a particular experience. First, cast the line, play out the words, feel the tug on the lines, bring the first ripples into sight, watch the fin cut open the surface, then slowly draw the flashing fish ashore.

- One of the most celebrated of modern fictional openings begins with these words: 'The past is another country. They do things differently there.' L. P. Hartley. *The Go-Between*. These two sentences could be read as a synopsis for the whole of Marcel Proust's monumental seven-volume novel. For him the past was another reality. Glimpses are all we can hope to get of that country. Imagine Hartley's novel has been destroyed. All copies. Only this first sentence remains. Like a literary archaeologist you decide to reconstruct the

beginning of the book, intelligently guessing from the opening line what the rest of the paragraph might have been like.
Write five sentences of your reconstructed opening.

• For Carol Ann Duffy the past is also a foreign field. 'What
country do we come from?' she asks in her poem 'Home-
sick'. Like others before her she thinks the soul longs for
some primal innocence. It strains for 'the first sound, what
we heard once...' What are these intimations? The faint,
faint echoes of what? Do they reach us from some unim-
aginable time and distance? **Write** something on the theme
of longing or yearning or exile.

• The metaphors we use to describe the past multiply. 'City',
'country', 'boat', 'angling', 'bog-pools'. Writers have meta-
phorised the past. The word 'house' has been a frequent
poetic construction raising the past on its little plot of
words. An intriguing working of this metaphor is to be
found in John Glenday's poem 'The Empire of Lights' (FB).
'In the House of the Past,' he writes, 'we move backwards/
from room to room, forever closing doors...' Imagine walking deeper and deeper into the past. **Write** about the journey.
Maybe it starts as a casual stroll but as the landscape
changes...?

• A house is so rich a figurative object, because it has rooms
and windows, cellars and attics, floorboards and cupboards, passageways and thresholds, mirrors and stair-
ways, chests and overgrown gardens, all desirable facts for
furnishing a poem. With dusting and digging, damps and
dimming candles, cobwebs and pale faces at windows it's
hard to avoid clichés. **Write** a piece about a house you know
and the secrets living on the premises.

• Jane Cooper has written a mysterious three-part poem
called 'Dispossessions' (20WP). In the house of memory
things have a voice of their own, and make mysterious
and sudden interventions in the life of the owner. So, why
keep souvenirs asks the poet, when the past invites itself
and keeps calling on us? We lodge in empty houses,
'husks...seeking the unborn/in a worn-out photograph,
hoping to break free/even of our violent and faithful

lives'. What do you think Cooper means by these words? **Write** a commentary on them.

- Perhaps Jane Cooper is saying it is self-deluding to think we own the past, own memory. Memories may not possess us, but they have dispossessed us, taken over the house. In the third and final section of the poem she quotes Rainer Maria Rilke's novel *The Notebooks of Malte Laurids Brigge*, and concludes that to have memories is not enough: 'they/must turn to blood inside you.'

  How are memories to be turned to blood? What exactly does this last phrase mean? **Write** some notes in answer. Use them to shape a poem. Or **rework** the 'house/memory' partnership into a poem about memory. Recall Pip's visit to Miss Haversham, the 'withered bride', in Dickens's novel *Great Expectations*. The old woman, 'shrunk to skin and bone', still dressed in her yellowing wedding gown, lives amidst the decaying remnants of her life, in the arrested moment when she was jilted at the altar. While he plays cards with the old lady Pip notices the earthy paperiness of her dress, and senses that at a touch she would fall to powder like some ancient corpse suddenly brought to light. Any possibilities here for **writing**?

- Michèle Roberts has used the phrase, 'the garden of memory', and in a recent interview about her book *My Favourite Plant*, Jamaica Kincaid has said: 'a garden is a metaphor for everything.' 'It is,' she continued, 'a metaphor for raising children, for possession and dispossession. We all began in a garden, in paradise, and had to leave it ... The garden has within it the original story of envy – we had everything and it just wasn't enough. And the original story of disappointment.' It's interesting that the 'garden' image is a woman's coinage. Does this motif appeal because of its nurturing associations? Gardens are tended. Or is it that they mix the wild and the tamed? Or that gardens are secret places, naturalised wildernesses, where it is possible to return to a truer sense of being? Are there ancient echoes here of our original paradisal origin? Or is the garden a metaphor for childhood: for growth, vitality, exuberance and freedom? **Write** a poem called *Garden*.

- Marge Piercy, an American novelist and poet, has written that women live more in the past than men. Is memory like a garden; a consolatory place for women; a refuge perhaps? Consider the idea of the past as a sanctuary, as seclusion, as an escape. Make notes in your journal. **Try writing** a story about a 'memory recluse' or someone who is absorbed in cultivating a garden or someone who is over-reliant on the past.

- The word 'reminiscence' suggests memory offers compensations. It echoes with an end-of-the-day, an after-the-meal, an over-a-pint sharing of moments. The consolation of walking worn paths once more. What are the consolatory memories told and retold in your family? **Write** about them as if you were an outside observer and commentator.

- A more complex consolation is explored in Hugh MacDiarmid's poem 'Crystal Like Blood' (PBBPI). The poet-narrator's wife has died. Geology and the technology of mineral extraction provide the unlikely analogies comforting him in his loss – that, and the ancient device of the 'treadmill' memory. The poem is an elaborate conceit, its two threads knotted in the last verse. Douglas Dunn, the Scottish poet, wrote a moving sequence of poems called *Elegies* in memory of his wife. Read a sample. Or read some of Thomas Hardy's anguished love poems in his '1913' collection, such as 'At Castle Boterel', 'Beeny Cliff', 'The Going'. **Write** an elegy to someone you knew and loved.

Peep-holing the Past

- Memory abets loss. Negotiates with the now. How? **Write** about the now, the how and the afternow.

- In Ciaran Carson's poem 'Calvin Klein's Obsession' (EK), smell is the invitation. The poem is a paean to the pungencies and perfumeries of his past. It is irresistible in its particulars. **Write** a similar rhapsody to your olfactoried memories.

- Read the opening pages of Carson's autobiographic book *The Star Factory*. Here he is peep-holing the past, recovering pinhole pictures of his childhood. It's magic writing. Miniaturised and particularised so precisely. It starts with a memory of his dad sitting in the dark of an outside lavatory. He is talking to his son who remembers the periodic red glow of the cigarette in his father's mouth. Take a strong image from your childhood. **Write** it and see what other memories it calls to light.

- D. H. Lawrence, in his poem 'Piano' (RB), recalls how the voice of a woman singing 'takes him back down the vista of years' to a time when he and his family used to sing in the parlour, and when he used to sit under his mother's piano in the 'boom of the tingling strings'. For the poet the song of the past is 'insidious'. It lures like the siren song lured Homer's Odysseus and crew to shipwreck and death. The poet sees his 'manhood is cast down...in the flood of remembrance', and he weeps 'like a child for the past'. Is remembrance so powerful, so alluring? Can it destroy? **Write** a story based on a homecoming where the past insists on being present and spoiling the party.

- It is often the senses that trigger strong memories. Take smell. **Write** about the memories that smell resurrects. Try in your writing to capture the vividness and power of the memory. Hold the image, scrutinise the picture. Search for the right, the exact words. Avoid all-purpose, quick-fix adjectives like 'rich', 'wonderful', 'marvellous', 'vivid'. And so on. Be exact. Be particular.

- Read Seamus Heaney's poem 'The Skunk'. Sitting on a veranda in the warm Californian night the writer is reminded of his absent wife. The tang of the eucalyptus 'spells' her presence. In the aftermath of a taste of wine he inhales her. Think of someone you love. In their absence what 'spells' them, what conjures up their intimacies? It doesn't have to be *Arôme de Paris* and roses. A skunk seems an unlikely emissary of love. **Write** a poem about the loved body.

- As the poet writes his love letter, the word 'wife' comes timidly to mind. He broaches the word, uneasy about its reception. 'Wife' is like 'a stored cask'. What do you think

Heaney implies in this phrase? Think carefully about the associations of both words, their echoes and resonances. Are there any words that you approach tentatively? Skirt round? Still need to, or want to get to know better? Are there words you couldn't do without? What depths do they sound in your life? What are their reverberations? Maybe it's a name. Maybe it's a word rich with sexual colouring. **Write** about it. A song perhaps! Or write a lament for a word that's lost its power for you. **Write** a sensuous poem. Under your skilful, searching touches it might turn erotic.

- The passing instance of our lives is gone before we know it. But writing can freeze the moment and thereby catch its significance. Thomas Hardy, in his poem *The Self-Unseeing* (RB), imagines his older self visiting the ruins of his childhood home. He suddenly 'sees' his mother sitting in her fireside chair absorbed by the flame-light, and his father, bowing the fiddle, standing beside her engrossed in his playing. The young Hardy, taken up by the music, is absorbed in his dancing. It's a happy memory. But the last line reads: 'Yet we were looking away.' Only recollection can validate the past.

  Is our habit of making a history of ourselves a consolation? A reaffirmation? A celebration? A compensation? Recall a time you returned to a place that held fond memories for you. **Write** about the occasion, and say why it was so important to return. Were you disappointed by what you found? Nonplussed? What did you learn?

- Imagine there's a gap in your past. You want to find the lost part. You meet Memory on your wanderings. You have some questions to ask? Set the encounter in a suitable location. **Write** a story centred on this unexpected meeting. And forget old men with long beards. Be different. Make Memory a surprise figure.

- Imagine you are a fugitive from memories. But you know they are pursuing you. Like the poet-traveller in Norman MacCaig's poem 'In My Mind' (OBV), you avoid certain danger areas. You seem to have escaped your minders/ stalkers and then . . . you are seen. The hunt begins. **Write** a short story based on this scenario using the 'chase' as a motif round which the narrative circles.

- In the same poem, McCaig, the poet-traveller, also imagines himself as a ghost, able to vanish through walls. Imagine your present adult self is an invisible presence at a past family occasion. You are a helpless spectator until you discover a way of influencing events. **Write** about what happens.

- All writers are pilgrims to the past. Think of the purposefulness of a pilgrimage. Think of the pilgrim mentality. What does the image say about the writer's mission? Extend the image into a full-blown allegory. The writer with staff, setting out, a mix of hopes and anxieties. **Write** the first short chapter.

- Stephen Poliakoff, in writing his play *Remember This*, was intrigued by the fact that video tape, the medium for recording events and therefore a facsimile of memory, has started to disintegrate with the passing of time. The chemistry of degeneration has begun. Poliakoff sees this degradation of image as a metaphor of our collective loss of memory over such catastrophes as Kosovo and Rwanda. 'Our memories are short-term these days,' he says, 'because we are so obsessed with the present and insecure about the future. The past has never seemed less important to those controlling the present.' Do you agree with this last sentence? I thought reinventing the past was a national occupation! Or is collective amnesia a desirable 'coping strategy', as the therapists say? No? Yes? Make out a case for burying the past. **Write** as a futurologist.

- Control the present? Can anyone do that? I would have thought institutional control freaks would see the way to control the present was in controlling the past. Can you think of any examples of this happening? In his satiric novel *England, England*, Julian Barnes imagines a wealthy businessman has turned the Isle of Wight into a heritage park, a virtual Olde Englande. Imagine a machine that 'preserves' parts of the past and which allows users limited access. **Write** a short story based on this idea.

- Imagine a new encephalographic headset that can reassemble fragments of an individual's memories into cephaloramas or cephs, coherent narrative nets. **Write** a story based on this idea.

- Read Beckett's play *Krapp's Last Tape* and **write** a Last Tape of your own.

- In his poem 'The Otter', Seamus Heaney exults in the procreative power of memory. The animal of the title seems more present and palpable remembered than the one seen on the Tuscan river bank. Just how do the memory of the thing and the thing itself relate? Is one just a mirror image of the other? What have words to do with this relationship? From the menagerie of your mind pluck an animal. It's a copy of the real. A copy cat? **Write** about it.

- One of the most perceptive explorations of how memory and the past shape the present and the poet is to be found in Seamus Heaney's essay 'Feeling into Words'. He deploys the metaphors of 'digging' and 'flowing' to explain something of how memory and the imagination work in concert. Digging turns over the rich clod, the Irish turf, the bog of the unconscious, as the writer searches the dark self for 'truth' or illumination. But digging is not an accident; it is wilful labour. And as Heaney puts it, his spade is the pen. He tracks down his spade image to early childhood sayings and playground chants, to a childhood landscape of smallholdings and rural ways. To the rhythms inhaled from his reading and so on. Take one of your poems. Think yourself into its undergrowth. Dig down to its roots. How did it start? Where did the images/ideas come from? What was their source? Trace the origins back and back as far as you can. **Write** an account of its genesis.

- In Greek myths, the gods sent the three winged Furies to punish transgressors and torment the guilty. They were also called Eumenides, the kindly ones; an ironic and expiatory title. Imagine that the Eumenides, or a modern version of them, arrive at your house banging on the door and demanding entry. They have your records. They show a history of reprehensible behaviour. There's a doorstep argument. They are going to do something about your past. **Write** the scenario as a one-act play.

Landscape and Oblivion

- For a prolonged and profoundly poetic meditation on memory and longing read Anne Michaels's novel *Fugitive Pieces*. At one point, the narrator recognises that nature has its memories too. A tree's rings read ancient weathers, seasons of suns and rains. Genes are scrawled with ancestral graffiti. Oceanic sediments carry the stories of distant catastrophes and the tumult of continents. Palaeontology and geology and genetics and astrophysics offer intriguing images for writers interested in the concept of perpetual memory. Some scientific terms are irredeemably poetic. 'Strata', 'sediments', 'donor', 'extinction', 'tectonic', 'crust', 'crinoid', 'mother lode', 'magma', 'unctuous'. Research the language of one of these sciences and use some of the words in **writing** a poem about earth's memories.

- Geologies, weatherings, depositions, erosions, inundations are the metaphoric contours of Michaels's book. The geological past has long memories and severe compression techniques. An aeon thins to a pencil line of in-rock carbon. K2 extinctions hardly leave a bric-à-brac of bones. In 'Slate' (PBPBI), a poem by the Irish writer Richard Murphy, the poet speculates on the history of the house slate he has found in a nettle-bed. He colours in its history. But not its early wanderings as fluvia, nor its more settled period during the Silurian depositions, nor its mid-life crises of upendings and about-facings, nor its final settlements and beddings. Read Gillian Clarke's poetic meditation 'Chalk Pebble' (PBPBI). Contemplate the memories locked in some ancient object/material landscape. **Write** about it. Let your ideas settle slowly into a poem.

- 'The whole landscape a manuscript/We had lost the skill to read.' All around him, says the Northern Irish poet John

Montague in his elegiac poem 'A Lost Tradition' (FB), are the 'shards' of the past. The poet draws attention to our generation's forgetfulness, and breathes a little life into history, press gangs a few ghosts to raise Ulster's pride. The Welsh poet R. S. Thomas is far more reproachful about the decline of Welsh culture and 'nationhood'. Read his two poems 'Welsh Landscape' and 'Reservoirs' (PBPBI). Think of the past embedded in the particulars of your neighbourhood: names of topographical features, pubs, streets, memorials; local legends; customs; geographies; public buildings; geology. Take any idea from this paragraph and work it up into a piece of writing. **Write** a side.

- In her poem 'Forget It' (FB), Kathleen Jamie examines the relationship between Scottish history, the Gorbals slums, the old Clearances, the new demolitions, and the present. She questions the value of 'tarmacking' over the past, bulldozing the tenements. The child has a historical imagination and a desire to know the secrets of the 'long driech, now demolished street' of Scotland. The mother, however, has real memories of the bad days – the shaming times of want and destitution – and she'd rather slam the door on the past. Can we, should we slam the door on the past? What is the point of preserving and recovering it? What part does writing play in this process? **Write** down your ideas.

- Maybe one answer comes from Jamaica Kincaid who feels that forgetting is a form of complacency, a submission, a willingness to turn a blind eye to the discomforting past, and a partiality for the quiet life. Writing needs a pinch of anxiety, a bit of risk. Those who prettify the past and paint it out in anodyne theme-park colours are not engaging with the actual; they are playing safe. **Write** a satiric view of a heritage site or historic recreation. Or invent a suitable target for your satiric barbs. Be cutting. Be risky.

- The poet A. Alvarez has talked about the 'anaesthetic of familiarity' and the need to resist the view that the past is a never-changing, wished-for haven. **Write** about the dangers of nostalgia and the problems of fabricating the past.

- Our public past always turns to triumph; our private to tribulation. Select some evidence to support this antithesis. **Start a piece of writing** with this first sentence and complete a page.

- In *The Man Who Mistook his Wife for a Hat* Oliver Sachs describes the case of one of his elderly female patients. As the result of a mild stroke she is assailed by childhood memories so vivid and real it is as if the past has become her present. After a few months, the sequences become less frequent and less powerful till they fade altogether. The patient regrets their passing. In opening the door to her lost and forgotten past she feels her life has acquired a richer meaning. We need to recapture childhood memories so we can 'ground our lives', says Sachs.

  Has recall and reminiscence in whatever form – family talk, autobiography – had the comforting effect of 'grounding' your life? Use the words *Grounded* or *Grounding* or *Ground* as titles and lead-ins for a poem on this subject. As preparation for the **writing** jot down ideas, phrases, images, and out of this speculative mix shape your poem.

- Is there a particular place for you where the past is very much alive? Somewhere you can sense the lingering ghosts? **Write** about it. Imagine the ghosts whispering, murmuring, gossiping even. Include some of their breathless converse in your writing.

- Mnemosyne, the Greek goddess of memory, was the mother of the Muses, the nine deities who presided over the arts and the sciences. Thus, for the Greeks, memory was the source of knowledge. Imagine a character who is memoryless. Describe him/her waking up. Try and avoid the obvious. For instance, don't start by saying: 'She opened her eyes. Where am I, she wondered?' **Write** a page or two.

- **Write** up a sequence of extracts from the diary of an amnesiac.

- Whether our inability to remember things is a minor fault of the circuitry or a major breakdown in the system, it seems recall is always less than perfect. We don't seem to own the rights on our own past. Read Mark Strand's poem 'Always' (EK). It's about 'the great forgetters'. My mother invented a new word. She called the bit that kept forgetting, her 'forgettery'. **Write** a poem using this word for your title.

- Watching the onset of Alzheimer's and its ravages is as distressful as it gets. John Bayley has written a moving testament to his wife, the writer Iris Murdoch, a victim of the disease, in a book called *Iris*. Have you witnessed Alzheimer's effects? Can you **write** about it?

- Media controversy over recovered memory syndrome has highlighted the illusory nature of mental processes. What we want to happen, we invent, and live with the narrative so long it becomes a familiar truth. What we want to avoid, we erase. It never happened. Memory and imagination are rival sisters here. Have you got a cluster of ambiguous memories where sifting truth from fiction is difficult? What have been your reasons for fictionalising? Motives can be evasive; they slip into hiding too! Find them. Be honest. **Write** a report to yourself after a thorough examination of the patient.

- As travellers in the past we are all uninvited guests at the feast. Use this metaphor as a starting point for **writing** a poem.

- Read Norman MacCaig's poem 'Summer Farm' (PBPBI). From the wonderful opening image of zigzag straws 'like tame lightning' hanging on hedges, the poem drifts to a less material, more metaphysical dimension. Just as the hen picks at nothing, and the grasshopper leaps and 'finds himself in space', so the poet finds himself not lying on the hillside any more but dangling in a no-where, 'Self under self, a pile of selves ... Threaded on time'. These little cut-outs of himself suddenly transpose to a giant scale, and he is lifting 'the farm like a lid' of a box. Inside he sees 'Farm within farm, and in the centre, me'.

  The laws of physics and the time–space continuum do not apply in the terrain of memory. Continuity is not the narrative logic there. Replication is. MacCaig's child-self recurs and recurs. Is the self and/or selves always at the centre? Is memory best described as a box inside a box inside a box?

This poem is like the flight of a grasshopper. It stays rooted in the real world. The insect is vividly, physically present in the phrase 'plated face'. Like the insect the poem leaps into space, and is surprised that it finds itself in the middle of ideas, but ideas precisely articulated in physical image again. The leaping between the material and the immaterial is done as effortlessly by the poet as it is by the grasshopper. Recall an early memory of yourself. Jot down notes. **Write** about chasing an elusive memory.

- 'On the ice a woman skating/jacket sudden/red against the white...' This clean exact image fills the writer's eye at the beginning of Margaret Attwood's poem 'Woman Skating' (20WP). In the second section, a plain-speak voice denies the clean vision, and remarks prosaically that her mother at this very moment is beside a rink surrounded on all sides by buildings and dirty banks of snow. The third section returns to the red-jacketed skater whom the poet recognises as a figure indeed, a timeless circling miniature. 'Over all 1 place/a glass bell', she concludes.

  The poem seems to be saying something about memory and the daughter/mother relationship. In preserving this purified mother image, in glassing it in, maybe the daughter is freezing out the parent, and anaesthetising the maternal in herself. What images do you have of your father or mother? What object/activity do you associate with either one? **Write** about the mother-object or father-object. In this poem, Attwood's 'real' voice intrudes on her 'poetic' voice. Try using two voices in your piece.

References

Barnes, J., *England, England* (Picador, 1998).
Bayley, J., *Iris* (Abacus, 1999).
Beckett, S., *Krapp's Last Tape* (Grove, 1960).
Carson, C., *The Star Factory* (Granta, 1997).
Carver, R., *A New Path to the Waterfall* (Collins, 1990).
Coleridge, S. T., *The Complete Poems* (Penguin, 1997).
Dunn, D., *Elegies* (Faber and Faber, 1985).

Dickens, C., *Great Expectations* (Penguin, 1996).
Duffy, C. A., *Selling Manhattan* (Anvil, 1987).
Forster, M., *The Memory Box* (Penguin, 2000).
Hardy, T., *Selected Poems* (Penguin, 1986).
Hartley. L. P., *The Go-Between* (Penguin, 1997).
Heaney, S., *New Selected Poems 1966–1987* (Faber and Faber, 1990).
Hussein, T., *An Egyptian Childhood* (The American University in Cairo Press, 1992).
Kincaid, J., *My Favourite Plant* (Vintage, 1999).
Lowes, J. L., *The Road to Xanadu* (Picador, 1978).
Michaels, A., *Fugitive Pieces* (Bloomsbury, 1997).
Poliakoff, S., *Remember This* (Methuen, 1999).
Proust, M., *Swann's Way* (Penguin, 1957).
Rilke, M. R., *The Notebooks of Matte Laurids Brigge* (W. W. Norton, 1992).
Sachs, O., *The Man Who Mistook his Wife for a Hat* (Picador, 1995).
Salinger, J. D., *The Catcher in the Rye* (Penguin, 1994).
Steinbeck, J., *Travels with Charley* (Arrow, 1997).

5 | Childhood

Trailing Clouds of Glory

- Play the game of reveries. Use the mind to travel your own Internet. If you choose a time without distraction – sitting in a waiting room, curled up before a catnap, lying in the mental dusk before sleep, drifting through a long journey – then reverie comes on automatically and the images spool and fold into each other.

  A pin lies on my desk; then, suddenly, I think of catching butterflies as a boy, and pinning tortoiseshells and red admirals to white display cards. I see my lepidopterist companion, my freckle-faced cousin, in his baggy shorts and braces and ginger hair spiky at odds with itself and his billowing white net. Over a week or two, record your own loops of memories. Select one or two to develop into a snapshot of the past – a whole album if you like. But keep each shot short, impressionistic. **Write** a page.

- Childhood is an important metaphor for any writer. Picasso said that he spent all his time at art school trying to paint like an adult, and all his life trying to paint like a child. What was he getting at here? William Blake's cycle of poems, *Songs of Innocence and Experience*, explores the concept and nature of childhood. **Write** some notes about the relationship between the notion of childhood and the idea of creativity.

- The reviewer of Oonja Kempadoo's novel *Buxton Spice* praises the way the author 'captures brilliantly the child's kaleidoscopic powers of observation'. Read the first three short chapters. To the child narrator everything is new and fascinating, even the chrome bean grinder full of 'glistening cream-coloured fat beans with black belly buttons' and the fat white hookworms squiggling like swollen sausages in the pig mud and the toy fish in the brook like 'see-through flashes' and ... and ... The same intense life of sensation and awareness is described forcefully by Laurie Lee on the first page of *Cider with Rosie*. **Write** a similar evocation of an early childhood moment when things seemed particularly vivid and intense.

- Here's a sentence from Maureen Duffy's *That's How It Was*:

  Mr Munnings, who worked in the garage opposite our front-room window – there were thousands of snap-dragons that hot, dry summer in the garden under the window, I pulled them off their plump green calyxes – grew like weeds they did my mother said so it was alright – and pushed my fingers down their gaping throats – Mr Munnings had hanged himself.

  What does this long digressive sentence say about the child's way of looking at things? Look at how gossip and homely idiom rub shoulders with technical termino-logy. Look at the digressions that interrupt the expected narrative of the sentence. Look at the sensuous thrill in the language of 'plump green calyxes'. Look at the hier-archies of events – pulling weeds located next to the image of a man hanging. And the image of a hanging man next to pushing fingers down 'their gaping throats'. **Write** about a childhood event as if you were six years old. James Joyce writes from the baby's point of view in the daring opening to his autobiographical novel *A Portrait of the Artist as a Young Man*. You could even go back to infant experiences. See *Hideous Kinky* by Esther Freud for a model of how to write from a young child's point of view.

- If any one poem catches the rhapsody of childhood it is Dylan Thomas's poem 'Fern Hill' (SB). The child is lord.

The world is as it was in the beginning, at the first light – paradisal. The carefree boy is 'prince of the apple towns', and, while he rides to sleep, 'the owls are bearing the farm away'. **Write** about the delirium of being a child. Write hosannas to childhood times. Concentrate on a particular incident or a golden time in your life.

- Another celebratory poem is Patrick Kavanagh's 'A Christmas Childhood' (PBPBI). It is written in quatrains of alternate rhyming lines. **Try writing** a joyous poem, in rhyming quatrains, about a 'good time' from the past. If you do not feel confident about rhyming technique, try starting with just two lines, and rhyme say lines 1 and 3. What you must avoid is 'trotting' rhythm or doggerel. You can break the dominance of rhyme by sometimes ending a sentence midline instead of coinciding it with the rhymed line end. If you vary sentence length like this, the reader will follow the sense not the sound, and will hear rhyme as a musical note, and not as the clang of a town-hall clock.

  The best way to develop an ear for rhyme and musical sound is to read more and more poetry, and examine carefully how accomplished writers achieve their effects. You could begin with Kavanagh's poem. Hardly any of the lines in the first three verses are end-stopped. Each line runs on through the rhyming syllables with a natural-seeming vigour despite the formal restraints of verse form and metre. Perhaps you can work out the other techniques the poet uses to create an air of freedom and energy, so appropriate to his subject.

- Read Seamus Heaney's poem 'The Railway Children' for a view of the innocent, self-delighting world of the child. He recalls that as children they climbed up the slopes of the railway cutting till they were eye-level with the 'white cups of the telegraph poles'. They looked down the length of the sagging wires and thought words travelled down them in 'the shiny pouches of raindrops'.

  Recall some of the imaginative misconceptions of childhood. Someone recently confessed to me that as a child they thought nuns ran on castors not legs, and that they wheeled and turned on elaborate machinery hidden within their voluminous skirts. Share and swop similar myths with workshop partners or friends. Make an interesting inventory and **compose** a simple list poem, or autobiographic piece.

- Like all children, the characters in Roddy Doyle's *Paddy Clarke Ha Ha Ha* enjoy a variety of street and playground games. Whooping on their wild pony bikes round disused industrial sites as 'Red Indians' leading the charging buffalo, Paddy and his mates exhaust their summer evenings. Think about the carefree games of your early childhood and **write** about them, giving the reader brief but strong images of the characters involved.

- Here's a classic sentence from James Joyce's story 'Araby' where he is writing about children playing in the street as evening falls:

  > The career of our play brought us through the dark muddy lanes behind the houses, where we ran the gauntlet of the rough tribes from the cottages, to the back doors of the dark dripping gardens where the odours arose from the ash-pits, to the dark odorous stables where a coachman smoothed and combed the horse or shook music from the buckled harness.
  >
  > (*Dubliners*)

  Write a commentary on the crafting of this passage. Consider the sound effects, the pace and the length, and the sensory language. The next sentence in the story is nothing like this one. Why not?

- After reading about Brother Damien, the leper priest, Paddy Clarke decides he'll re-enact scenes from life in the leper colony. In his back garden he collects his younger brother and some of his friends. Paddy is to be Damien, the rest lepers. Read the scene from the beginning of Roddy Doyle's novel *Paddy Clarke. Ha. Ha. Ha.* It is hilarious. **Write** a *Ha Ha* account of a 'let's pretend' moment from childhood.

- 'The Centaur' by May Swenson (20WP) is a poem in which the writer sees herself as a young girl once again playing in the summer fields, making her pretend horse out of a willow stick and riding it. The girl becomes the horse, so intimate is the identification between horse-stick and she. Is the poem saying something about the power and nature of the imagination? Is it about animality and female sexuality? Check out the sexual imagery in the poem. Once she comes home and enters the house, the wild and exuberant is behind her, and she returns to the ordered world of restraining manners and adults. In the kitchen, a different woman's world, her mother says she must tie back her hair and straighten her dress. That's how girls should look. Recall a similar experience of intoxicating and absorbing play where, in hindsight, you recognise much deeper feelings at work, and **try writing** about it.

Shades of the Prison-house

- There are some very pessimistic views of children and childhood in literature. Wordsworth brooded on the loss of youthful joys and saw 'shades of the prison-house begin to close/Upon the growing boy'. William Golding, in his well-known fable *Lord of the Flies*, traces the descent of a band of schoolboys into tribal savagery and barbarity. **Write** about a shady side of childhood.

- Louis MacNeice, in his poem 'Autobiography' (RB), identifies a moment in his childhood when the prison-house shades visited and closed in on him. He writes in rhyming couplets each tagged with a haunting refrain. **Write** a ballad or song in rhyming couplets entitled *Autobiography*.

- Kevin is Paddy's 'best friend'. He is delighted when his teacher, Mr Hennessy, separates some of the trouble-makers in his class and lets Kevin and himself sit together. However, later the rivalry running just below the surface of this relationship eventually destroys the friendship. **Write** an account of a 'best friend' relationship. Be sensitive to both the attractions and drawbacks of the experience.

- Raymond is the narrator's best friend in Ian McEwan's short story 'Homemade'. But Raymond is older and more street-wise. So is Wendy, Andrea Ashworth's friend in *Once in a House on Fire*. Wendy is thrown out of school for her outrageous behaviour: swearing at the nuns, wearing nose studs, bunking off. She leads Andrea towards boys and kissing and shoplifting. If there was such a wayward friend in your life **write** about them. Did you secretly admire their defiance of convention, their self-confidence, or what?

- At her new secondary school Andrea has to fight her corner and get accepted. All newcomers are tested by the resident group. Some have elaborate initiation rituals, other groups are more subtle in the way they suss you out. New kids on the block have to learn the 'passwords', prove themselves, pay their dues. For instance, Andrea learns to 'cuss in different colours' in the playground, and then talk a different language in the classroom. She learns to punch her weight and stand up for herself. Such are the ways and the rules that govern existence and survival in school.

  Recall your experience of being the 'new kid' – the testing, the running of gauntlets, the name-calling, the put-downs, the politics of playground allegiances, the forfeits. Read Chapter 8 of *Once in a House on Fire*. The bite and tightness of the writing is something to be emulated. **Write** three short passages based on incidents from your own schooldays when you were just learning the art of fitting in. Model your writing on Andrea Ashworth's style and narrative 'nugget' approach.

- Many children invent imaginary companions or animate favourite toys. In the novel *A Boy's Own Story*, Edmund White's central character is so afraid of his taunting elder sister he invents safer, 'imaginary playmates'. He creates three of them: Cottage Cheese, a sensible, bossy girl but an ally; Georgie-Porgie, a dimwit whom they could protect; Tom-Thumb-Thumb, a disobedient trouble-maker always running away and living in the wild wood. The young boy invents elaborate and reassuring narratives for his threesome thereby giving shape and substance to his own wishes and dreams.

  The more equivocal side to this fantasy cloning is depicted in Elizabeth Bartlett's poem 'Charlotte, Her Book' (20WP).

Here Charlotte, the imagined brat kid, is fostered out by her mad mother, and finally disposed of in a car accident. For the narrator in White's novel his fantasy friends began to fade when he saw a marionette version of *Sleeping Beauty*, and realised only the figures on stage were 'lit within' and that his 'imaginary playmates were insubstantial' and that the people who surrounded him 'were opaque'. Can you remember the fictional companions of your childhood or recall observing the play of younger children with their invented 'friends'? When did the hold of these fictions begin to wane? Look at this 'evidence' and explore what lies behind this behaviour of inventing imaginary friends. **Write up** your ideas as autobiographical notes, or as an essay/article. See too *Claudia*, a novel by Susan Wicks in which prudence invents an imaginary friend called Claudia.

- In Charles Dickens's novel of the same name, Nicolas Nickleby arrives at the notorious Dotheboys Hall as the new tutor. He is appalled at the bullying and mistreatment of the pupils. Matters come to a head in Chapter 13 when the brutal Squeers tries to thrash Smike, a 'backward' boy in his late teens, for absconding. Nicholas intervenes and beats both Squeers and his wife. Then he and Smike flee the school. Think of the petty tyrants, the 'little Hitlers', you have come across in your time. If such a person had injured you it would be satisfying to use writing as a way of fantasising your long-delayed revenge. But writing has other fish to fry. Revenge is easy, and understanding difficult to maintain in the face of painful or angry memory. **Try writing** about an encounter with a Mr or Mrs Squeers type from a neutral point-of-view where you get inside your subject and develop a critical sympathy for him or her.

- Two chapters in Seamus Deane's *Reading in the Dark* are set in school classrooms. One is a maths lesson, the other a religious instruction lesson. On both occasions, the teacher dominates his class, inviting, even luring, pupils into challenge, and then demolishing them or backing them into impossible corners. His power is exercised through language, and is irresistible. For another view of the politics of the classroom read the opening chapter of Bruce Robinson's novel *The Peculiar*

Memories of Thomas Penman. How did your teachers exercise power and control in your school? Was authority abused? Choose a particular lesson. **Write** about what happened.

- In James Joyce's autobiographic novel *A Portrait of the Artist as a Young Man*, the young Stephen Dedalus is sitting in Fr. Arnall's Latin class unable to read and write because he has broken his glasses. Quietly, the Prefect of Studies enters the room. He is looking for 'idlers'. He finds Fleming, a 'lazy idle loafer', and thrashes his hands with his pandybat. He comes to Stephen. 'Break your glasses? I know that trick,' says the Prefect. 'Lazy idle little loafer,' he explodes. 'Out with your hand.' The injustice and the brutality! **Write** about an injustice based on an incident from your school-days. Either write it as straight autobiography, or transpose the experience into fiction as Joyce has.

- 'In the little world in which children have their existence...there is nothing so finely perceived and finely felt as injustice,' writes Charles Dickens in *Great Expectations*. He is writing apropos of Pip who has been humiliated by the disdainful Estella. She sneers at his uncouthness, his ignorance of genteel manners, his use of the vulgar term 'jacks' to describe the playing card politely known as a 'knave'. **Write** about childhood humiliations. Pip kicks the garden wall and tears at his hair in frustration and distress. How did you cope?

- At boarding school I was caned frequently. The names of those to be 'tanned' or 'flogged' were 'announced' every day in the refectory by the Prefect of Discipline after the evening meal. Sixth-form prefects regularly and indiscriminately sent the naïve and the nasty for a 'flogging'.
    At the prescribed hour the punished were to line up out side the Prefect's room. One by one each was called in to face the same questions: Why have you been sent? Why did you do it? Whatever the answer the culprit was then told: 'Step to the chair, bend over the back, place hands flat on seat, spread legs.' Thwack. Thwack. Thwack. Thwack. The bamboo cane left hard purpling ridges on the buttocks. There was a punitive tariff. Four strokes for minor offences like talking

in ranks, hiding in the lavs during cold breaks instead of going outside, having hands in pockets. Six for fighting, talking in dorms after lights-out, not wearing school ties, skipping rugby practice. Eight for smoking; ten, if caught a second time. Twelve for a third, or for being found drinking in a local pub. This was ritual humiliation. Have you experienced anything like it? **Try writing** about it.

- His family's on welfare and his gran's on gin, but Timothy, a 'blitz of a boy', takes it all in his stride. In Charles Causley's ballad 'Timothy Winters' (RB), the schoolboy suffering from what the authorities now call 'social deprivation' is impervious to neglect and education in equal measure.

  Whereas Timothy W is an innocent, the character of Timothy Gedge from William Trevor's novel *The Children of Dynmouth* is only superficially similar. He comes from a broken family, is the despair of his teachers, and spends most of his time spying on people around the town. He's an ambiguous figure, insensitive to people's suffering and yet, like a disreputable conscience, he calls on people to drop their hypocrisies and face the truth he brings. Create an 'outsider' character loosely based on someone you have known. **Write** a ballad about him/her. Or **write** a fictional scene set in a classroom and/or school toilets in which your character is a figure of dissent.

- Anne Sexton reveals the dark contradictions of child abuse in her poem 'Red Roses' (EK). The title is ironic, and the poem echoes with innocent deceptions and the mother's damning denials and heartless casuistry. Language has betrayed innocence and, like the hidden bruises, the pain throbs just beneath the casual idiom of the poem's surface talk. Recall an image of a saddened child, a poster by the Salvation Army or a photograph of refugees or an ad by the Children's Society or the NSPCC. **Can you write** a controlled protest against the injustice before you?

- Dylan Thomas has written a disturbing and hallucinatory story called 'The Burning Baby' (MBSS). The horror of child abuse and murder presses inexorably on the reader. If you feel you can handle strong material **write** about dark deeds or family secrets. Pope Brock, an American writer, discovered from an aunt's deathbed confession that there was a secret history of murder, incest and adultery in his family. He was astonished and his book *Indiana Gothic* is based on these revelations.

- In the second chapter of Bruce Robinson's *The Peculiar Memories of Thomas Penman*, young Thomas is on his way home from school and calls at his granddad's house. He finds no one at home, and so he wanders through the house going from room to room looking through the accumulations of the owner's life. He finds stuffed animals, old bus timetables, wind-up toy cars, Edwardian pornographic photographs, spineless books, tins of hard pastilles and so on.

As a young person did you ever come across rooms holding the detritus of a life? The young narrator in Joyce's story 'Araby' sees in his garden the discarded possessions of the former tenant, a priest. Joyce's inventory of these remnants is calculated, and the titles of the books left to mildew and dampen in the grass are not innocent. What is a priest doing with historical romance on his shelves? Perhaps the mix of books – pious, devotional literature sprawled next to political memoir – and their neglected state says something about Irish attitudes to culture and bookish learning. Perhaps the wild disordered garden is intended as a quiet echo of the spiritual emptiness of Irish Catholicism and its troubled relationship with Irish nationhood.

The story is about romantic disillusionment and the destruction of dreams. Possibly Joyce is establishing his symbolic co-ordinates in the story. The garden representing innocence, our primal state, is now a shambles of the broken and the wasted, and acts as a foretelling, a warning to the young boy smitten by the girl living in the house opposite that his romantic hopes are to be scattered in the bleak conclusion to the story. **Write** a story based on your own experience of viewing or going through the possessions of someone absent. You may have 'visited' the house of a friend or relative furtively in the past and got a sneak view of their private life. The story may be inspired by a visit to a historic home or museum and seeing an unknown's personal belongings on display.

To illuminate character and theme, in your opening paragraphs, use the Joycean technique of remembered images. For instance, a broken-stringed guitar may hint at a person's frustrated creative life or the loss and decline of creative powers. The titles of books or sheets of music may reveal not just the temperament of the owner, but they could also represent little verbal anchorages settling the story into deeper waters like Joyce does in 'Araby'.

- Stuart Hall, the writer and cultural critic, was born in Jamaica. His mother had ambitions for him. She wanted him to like the whites and buy into a colonial culture which she felt was superior to anything Jamaica had to offer. As he grew up he found it increasingly difficult to accept Anglo-Jamaican values. It meant betraying his native culture, and so he decided to turn his back on home and emigrate to England. Have you had a similar experience? Was a path mapped out for you? Did it make you feel increasingly uncomfortable? Did you turn your back on it, step off and strike out on your own? **Write** about the experience, the forces that kept you on the straight and narrow, the forces that urged you off it.

- **Write** about your favourite teacher.

- Read Ciaran Carson's poem 'Slate Street School' (FB). He writes about the tedium of rote learning in the days of imperial measurements. The chanting of the multiplication tables seems to act as a conjuration for the miracle of falling snow, and the children watch it wondrously. Think of a time in your schooldays when tedium gave way to the wondrous or the dramatic. **Write** an account of the incident. Notice how Carson's poem starts with a dull roll call of schoolday memories, a list as mechanical as the litanies of mathematics. Then, in the second verse, the language rises into loftiness of expression and the ringing voice of the avenging angel. In your writing try stylistic variation for effect.

On the Edge of Innocence

- In his well-known poem 'Death of a Naturalist', Seamus Heaney describes how his schoolboy self collected jampotfuls of the 'warm thick slobber' of frog-spawn and watched the dots burst into 'nimble swimming tadpoles'. Miss Walls, his class teacher, talks about mammy frogs and daddy frogs and little eggs. One day he goes through the hedge and meets the real thing – 'gross-bellied frogs... that slap and plop with obscene threats... poised like mud grenades, their blunt heads farting'. Sickened he runs away. The field is a dangerous place! When did your cosy childhood images run slap-bang into the real thing? **Write** about such a time. Absorb the powerful sensory language of Heaney's poem. Try and mimic in your own work this same ability to capture the physicality of living things.

- Edward Thomas's poem 'The Mill-Pond' (RB) has a watery connection with Heaney's 'Death of a Naturalist' and a shared theme. Here Thomas recalls sitting beside a mill-pond as a boy dangling his feet in the foaming waters. A storm is brewing, and its boom can be heard in the plunging waters of the mill-race. A girl in white appears and warns him to 'Take care'. He is angry at first at her intervention, but as he crouches to shelter from the sudden storm-burst he realises the girl is in fact 'beautiful and kind'. And in his memory she is always so. The poem appears to be about a moment of realisation, a 'threshold experience'. The gloomy pond, the warning thunder, the white girl! What do these images portend? And why are they, after so many years, still fresh and indelible? If you have a similar haunting memory that seems now to have been a turning point of some kind **write** about it.

- Another moment of insight is described in Frances Cornford's poem 'Childhood' (20WP). The writer recalls the time when she saw an old family friend groping blindly for her fallen necklace beads. The child on the stair secretly observing events through the banisters. **Write** about a childhood incident secretly observed; one which showed adults in a less-than-flattering light.

- Heaney concludes a later poem 'Personal Helicon' with the apologia: 'I rhyme/To see myself, to set the darkness echoing'. Out of the childhood memories of his fascination with wells, ditches and old pumps with buckets, he fashions a poem about writing. **Write** about some of your early fascinations. Maybe this recollection and recovery will lead you into some larger truth. Heaney's recollections are fringed with fear. In one shallow well he draws up 'long roots from the soft mulch', and sees his own white face hovering in the dark stirred water below. On another occasion he says a 'rat slapped across my reflection'. Does fear or apprehension attend your memories?

- Read the opening four pages of *I Know Why the Caged Bird Sings* by Maya Angelou. Here is a rich mix of contrarities. The exultation of childhood dreams is shot through with more sombre moments of uneasy self-consciousness. Maya believes that one day she will wake up white, wear beautiful dresses and enjoy the adulation of the world at large. But on Easter Sunday morning the dress that on Friday made her look like a 'movie star' is a bitter disappointment, its lavender taffeta dull as a 'white woman's once-was-purple throwaway'. Maya wants to wake up from her 'ugly black dream'. She thinks some cruel fairy stepmother has 'turned her into a too-big Negro girl, with nappy black hair, broad feet and a space between her teeth that would hold a number-two pencil'.

  Maya's story is about how she fought for and asserted her black identity in the face of economic deprivation and cultural exclusion and disdain. The incident of the hand-me-down dress symbolised her earliest sense of difference and disadvantage. Have you any early memories in which you now recognise echoes of your later struggles for self-assertion and independence? Do they centre on one or two events/images, like the faded dress and Maya's clumsy escape from the Easter Sunday Service and the 'silly church'? **Write** a four-page re-creation of such memories in the manner of Maya Angelou's account quoted above. It is possible that, with hindsight, incidents that in early childhood were innocent of significance take on, under pressure from adult recollection, the force of the symbolic. The faded cloth now becomes for Maya Angelou a significant metaphor for the impoverished destiny that white America handed down to its black peoples.

- Andrea Ashworth, in her autobiography *Once in a House on Fire*, describes how she used to sneak out at night and visit the better-off areas near her neighbourhood. She would tip-toe up drives where there were no lights on, lift letter-box flaps, and sniff the posh interior smells: lamb dinner caught in the carpet; expensive wallpaper. How different from her own home! It's like not being invited to the party. You're on the outside looking in. **Write** about a time in childhood when you felt particularly excluded.

- W. B. Yeats, the Irish poet, wrote that there is 'for the lucky man one picture that is the image of his secret life'. In a recent interview Edna O'Brien, who quotes this Yeats observation, says her secret picture 'is the vision of Christ; sallow-faced, dark-eyed, a gravity'. Do you have such a primal image and how does it embody your 'secret life'? **Write** an account of the portrait hanging in your psychic gallery.

- 'The child-self does not die. It stays in the cupboard.' Can you think of an occasion when your child-self has come out of the closet and started behaving badly? Maybe you've seen other child-selves taking over their grown-up versions. Make some notes about regressive behaviour. Why do adults play the child again? **Write** a piece on this subject.

- The child-self is not the same as your self as a child. Imagine the voice of the child-self whispering to you from inside the cupboard. **Write** a dialogue-poem between yourself and the hidden one.

- The line between adult and child behaviour is often uncertain. Children can be mature beyond their years – disturbingly so in the case of Thomas Hardy's Old Father Time, the prematurely aged boy in *Jude the Obscure*. There's something unnerving about a knowing child. Or an *idiot savant*.

Write about the knowingness of children or a particular child of your acquaintance.

- For a sketch of the early years of childhood read 'The Drowned City' section of Anna Michaels's novel *Fugitive Pieces*. 'The memories we elude catch up to us, overtake us like shadow.' Jakob recalls a childhood incident. He has hidden a half-eaten apple in the garbage. His father finds it and is angered at the waste of food. This memory leads to a chain of childhood vignettes. The opening chapter of *England, England* by Julian Barnes is a rich evocation of childhood and early schooling. Recall some early memories and **write** your own chain of vignettes.

- 'Every last body on this earth has a particular notion of paradise...' writes Daisy, the child narrator, in Carol Shields's novel *The Stone Diaries*, a history of the Stone family, distaff side. In this story the mother's paradise is to eat and most especially to cook. In Chapter 1 there is a wonderful description of Mercy Goodwill in the oven-hot kitchen going about her recipes and relishes. **Write** a closely observed, loving portrait of someone enjoying their 'particular notion of paradise'.

- Read Les Murray's poem of praise to the bean called 'The Broad Bean Sermon' (EK). How the 'frown-shaped, bird-shouldered, boat-keeled ones' multiply in joyous profusion! Their love of life is infectious. **Write** about an ordinary domestic activity that delights.

- Seamus Deane's novel *Reading in the Dark* is about family secrets and hauntings from the past. *Reading the Dark* would be a more obvious title given that in the novel the past is exposed story by painful story. Tell some stories about your past. In one incident the novel's narrator has a row with his father, and in revenge cuts down all the family rose bushes with a pickaxe. **Write** about a family row, the immediate cause and the deeper turbulence in the situation.

- There's a family row. A boy refuses to wear braces for school. His mother insists. The father is drawn into the argument. It ends in violence and seething silence. These are the bare bones of Raymond Carver's story 'Suspenders'. Typical of rows it soon gets out of all proportion. Also typically, it's not really about suspenders at all. They are just the cover for something else far deeper and unresolvable. Rows are often the same row. **Write** about a repeated row.

- Stories of adult betrayals, forbidden places, sinister threats roll like storms on the horizons of the children in Deane's novel. One day the father takes his two sons to see 'The Field of the Disappeared'. The souls of drowned sailors whose bodies were never recovered and those not given a Christian burial gather there thrice-a-year, to cry like birds. Any living person entering the field dies; anyone who hears the wailing birds has to run home, shut all windows and doors to protect the house. Does this fable find an echo in your own experiences? **Write** about it.

- In Deane's novel, Crazy Joe is another oddity in the boys' lives. A 'wise' madman. He accosts boys in libraries and talks about 'carnal knowledge', tells stories about the phantom witch-woman seducing mad Larry in a dark lane, and with each tale shoots out his false teeth and rubbers his lips round the last words.

  James Joyce, in his story 'Encounter' from *Dubliners*, tells of another unsettling meeting between two lads playing truant and a mysterious man in a field. Both boys lose a little bit of innocence that day. An even darker experience lies behind Ian McEwan's collection of short stories *First Love, Last Rites*. **Write** a story about a Crazy Joe character you met as a child. Write in the third person. Read too Dylan Thomas's poem 'Hunchback in the Park' for another approach.

- Kathleen Jamie's poem 'Mother-May-I' (NP) is about innocence playing at the edge of forbidden knowledge. Beyond the council estate, behind the dump is the wood where 'hitchhikers rot' and men leave 'tight, rolled up dirty magazines'. The girl in the poem wants her mother's permission to play Man-hunt! Remember playing kids' games! Some were less innocent than others! **Write** about the edge of innocence.

- Carol Ann Duffy writes about children on the cusp of innocence and experience in her poem 'In Mrs Tilscher's Class' (FB). It reads as if it has come out of the poet's personal memories, and is a melange of remembered smells and visual images. In the end the child narrator runs out of school 'impatient to be grown,/As the sky split open into a thunderstorm'. Can you remember such impatience? Such a threatening storm? **Write** your own poem on this topic.

- Helen Dunmore, poet and novelist, used the vivid phrase: 'the electric storm of puberty' to describe early adolescence. In your view is this an accurate description? Recall some supporting evidence from your own experience and **write** a piece using one of the words from Dunmore's phrase as a title.

The Facts of Life

- In the chapter, 'The Facts of Life', from *Reading in the Dark*, Father Nugent instructs our hesitant hero on the biological rudiments of sex. Relieved to escape the suffocating atmosphere of the master's study the boy dashes from the school building eager to catch a glimpse of Irene McKay, the girl of his dreams. **Write** a relevant chapter from your own life-story, taking Seamus Deane's title.

- In his poem 'A Picture of a Girl in a Bikini' (PBPBI), Hugo Williams describes how he is called into the headmaster's study to explain why he has a copy of 'Man Junior' under his mattress. In the last line of the poem the headmaster asks: 'What is the meaning of this?' **Write** down *your* answer to the question. Or continue the scene in the study as if it was from a novel.

- **Write** a piece under the title *Caught Out*.

- In Ian McEwan's story 'Homemade' printed in the collection entitled *First Love, Last Rites*, the teenager narrator contrives a 'desolate coupling' with his young sister. It is all the fault of his friend Raymond because his ribald talk of the legendary Lulu Smith, a local lass with a reputedly inexhaustible appetite for sex, has overexcited him. Listening to Raymond and the randy talk of adults around them as they sit in a local café the narrator feels he is in 'yet another furlined chamber of that vast, gloomy and delectable mansion, adulthood...' Write about a time when the prospect of adulthood seemed attractive.

- In *Once in a House on Fire*, Andrea Ashworth writes that her teenage period was a time 'when she was waiting for her life to start'. **Try writing** about a similar time in your own life. Maybe you are still waiting for lift-off! You could frame the experience into a short story. If you want a model, James Joyce's story 'Eveline' explores this subject. Start with some image that resonates with the central theme of 'lost opportunity' or 'settling for second best'. The Joyce story opens with an image of Eveline sitting in a window seat watching the evening closing down the avenue, the smell of dusty cretonne curtains in her 'nostrils'. It's interesting to speculate why Joyce used the word 'nostrils' and not the more conventional, 'nose'.

- There was a time in her early life when Ashworth felt she was 'buried alive', 'locked inside herself'. Is this true of any part of your own life? Start digging down into the past. Make some notes and let one thing lead to another until you have unearthed some surprising memories. Use this material to **write** about the experience, and show how you unlocked self from self.

- On the other hand, your life may have taken off in the past, but you feel it is now parked. Consider a character whose life has come to a stop. **Write** a 'Talking Head' TV script in which your character slowly comes to realise their life is stagnating.

- For another view of joyless coition see Janice Galloway's story 'David' printed in her collection *Blood*. Two women teachers join school-leavers Colin and Marie, Sam and David to celebrate. David's parents are out for the night so they decide to go to his house for drinks. The story is written in the dispassionate tones of one of the teachers. Use the same detached voice to **write** a story about a young woman seducing a young man.

- The welter of imagery that sometimes thickens and distorts sexual experiences surfaces in Ian McEwan's title story from his collection *First Love, Last Rites*. Rivers ooze, eels and rats slither through the narrative mesh. **Write** about some aspect of the body and sex.

- Read Chapter 17 of Margaret Attwood's novel *Cat's Eye* where the four girls are talking about bodies and 'things'. When they try to explain to themselves where babies come from it's a choice between 'juice' entering through the belly button and God making them. The girls side with God. The thought of boys putting a tongue in their mouths disgusts them. Recall your own naïveties about 'bodily functions'. Write two pages of dialogue in which a group of young girls talk about growing up and 'things'.

- Martha Cochrane, a central figure in Julian Barnes's novel *England, England*, composes a Brief History of Sexuality, her history. It is a pithy piece, and is divided into such headings as: Innocent Discovery, Technical Advance, Socialisation of the Impulse, Paradox of the Impulse, Pursuit of the Ideal, Funfair, Pursuit of Separateness. Create your own headings for a Brief Sexual History. It may not be brief. It may be a long epic tale stretching from keyhole to capitulation, from onanism to orgasm. **Write** a paragraph for each section.

- You could create Brief Histories for other aspects of your life. Invent some suitable topics and **write** about any one.

- In Laurie Lee's acclaimed book *Cider with Rosie*, rites of passage are celebrated in the chapter called 'First Bite of the Apple'. Laurie knew that if you gave brazen Bet a wine gum 'she'd show ya, if ya want'. But it was Rosie Burdock who took young Laurie in hand after he had 'breathed the first faint musks of sex', and lured him with her 'cidrous kisses'. See the hilarious episode in Chapter 8 of Frank McCourt's *Angela's Ashes*. Here the hunchback boy, Quasimodo, agrees to take a shilling each from Frank and his friends for a chance to shin up his back drainpipe and watch the naked Dooley sisters at their weekly Friday wash. **Write** a rite of passage chapter. Write it from the viewpoint of the opposite sex.

- When it was first published in 1960 Edna O'Brien's novel *The Country Girls* scandalised Ireland. The book was about sexual awakening in a repressive culture, and was immediately banned by the Irish censor.

    Things have changed. Now, it is claimed that this and other early novels by O'Brien changed the fate of Irish womanhood, and a recent survey placed *The Country Girls* in the top twenty best-selling Irish books of the century. After deliberately getting themselves expelled from convent school the two country girls, Cait and Baba, find jobs, independence and sexual freedom in the city of Dublin. Baba is the wild one of the two. It was her idea to write something 'dirty' on a holy picture in the convent chapel and leave it signed with both their names for the nuns to find. In Dublin she vows she's 'going to blow up this town'. She arranges a night out with two older men, but the encounter turns squalid when one of them, clumsy with drink, tries to seduce Cait. What Cait really wants is 'Romance. Love and things...' Think of your own experiences of romantic hopes and consequent disillusions. **Write** a story in which a fictionalised self and best friend go out on a blind date.

- Read James Joyce's story 'Eveline'. What happens to romantic notions when reality intrudes? In this story, an elder daughter caring for her drunken and brutish widower father suddenly has a rare opportunity to escape her domestic servitude by marrying her sailor admirer and emigrating to start a new life in Argentina. What part does romance play in our lives? Can the romantic be reconciled with the real? **Write** about an occasion in your life or a fictional character's life when the two were irreconcilable or when they were reconciled.

- At the end of *The Country Girls* Cait meets up with Mr Gentleman again. He is a neighbour and close acquaintance from back home. French by birth, he is a distinguished, grey-haired solicitor who develops an ardent relationship with the adolescent Cait. She responds to his chaste but tender approaches, flattered that she is the centre of an older man's affections. **Write** a story about a 'relationship' between an older person and a younger person. Cait and Mr Gentleman are loving and gentle with each other though the faint shadow of his austere wife dims their brightness a little. He invites his young country girl to go to Vienna with him in order 'to get this out of our systems'. Read the last three chapters of the book.

- At the end of her first volume of autobiography *I Know Why the Caged Bird Sings* Maya Angelou is 16 and worried about whether she is a lesbian or not. Her mother puts her right about the facts of her physiology, and is reassuring on the issue of her sexual identity. 'I wanted to be a woman,' she writes and 'what I needed was boyfriend.' But she is not one of the 'pretty' ones. Plain girls are virtuous she notes wryly, because they have no opportunity to be otherwise. They 'shield themselves with the aura of unavailableness (for which in time they begin to take credit) largely as a defense tactic.'

  Maya feels she cannot hide behind 'a curtain of voluntary goodness', because she is driven by two unrelenting forces: 'the uneasy suspicion that I might not be a normal female, and my newly awakening sexual appetite'. She decides to take matters into her own hands and seduce some eligible boy from a 'good neighbourhood'. It doesn't quite work out as she planned. Did your sexual plans always work out for you? **Write** about some aspect of sexual conquest or defeat.

- In Chapter 5 of Oonya Kempaddo's *Buxton Spice*, a novel set in a fictional village on the coast of Guyana, a group of girls are playing 'Husbands and Wives'. Afterwards the girls talk about sex, sharing their excitement and disgust at the pictures they see in a book called *Man and Woman*. They examine each other, checking against the book's explicit photographs. Sammy, one of the smallest of the girls, says in disgust, '...de whole business look nasty'. Read the passage. Early sexual understandings and perceptions are often misleading, farcically inaccurate, and hilarious. **Write** a passage of dialogue in which your young characters feel their way towards some uncertain and partial understanding of sex.

- In Chapter 8 of her book Kempadoo explores the notion of gender. Masculinity is espoused in the term 'man-self'; femininity in 'she-self'. The narrator teaches herself 'man-self language' by watching boys. She measures their movements, watches the 'man-self tight inside, coiled, ready to spring'. She dislikes it when the 'man-self' is sloppy, 'hung in flab round they waist'. One boy has his 'man-self' so covered up it is 'confusing'. Rasta called him 'Anti-man'. From her watching and from her practising 'stancing' in front of the mirror, she concludes that 'she-self' has to understand 'man-self' and let it soak into her. She yearns to 'come out of Yan's little sister' skin and be out on the street late at night. **Write** about man-watching or woman-watching. Even man-catching or woman-catching.

- In Chapter 19 of J. D. Salinger's classic novel of disaffected adolescence *The Catcher in the Rye*, Holden Caufield talks to his schoolmate Luce about his sex life. They are in a Wicker Bar, New York, and Caulfield is trying to rile Luce into revealing his secrets. **Write** a man-to-man scene from a film or radio script set in a 'male' environment. Is it a male bonding or male boasting session?

- In *Oranges Are Not the Only Fruit*, Jeanette Winterson describes the struggle between the fundamentalist Christian principles of her evangelical mother and her own growing sense of self and morality. After her lesbian relationship with another member of the church is discovered she is threatened with exorcism, and finally leaves the fellowship. **Write** a fictional scene in which a character comes out and explains to a parent/boyfriend or girlfriend their true sexual identity. For a similar scene written with wry humour read Michelene Wandor's short story 'Meet My Mother' (CC).

- Jeanette Winterson has written in introduction to *Oranges Are Not the Only Fruit*: 'Everyone, at some time in their life, must choose to stay with a ready-made world that may be safe but also limiting or push forward, often past the frontiers of commonsense, into a personal place, unknown and untried.' **Write** about a time when you yourself pushed past the 'frontiers of commonsense' to find that 'personal place' Winterson talks about. Describe the attractions of the 'ready-made world' you abandoned and the rewards of breaking out.

- In the last reflective stages of Winterson's book, Jeanette considers the possibility of going back, going home. 'People do go back,' she acknowledges, 'but they don't survive.' People left behind accuse returnees of being indifferent, 'when you are only different'. What does Winterson mean by not surviving? **Write** the opening scene of a family saga in which a woman after a long period away returns home to see her ageing mother.

- Every group has a scapegoat and a butt. The victim bonds the rest in a common cause, and bullies build their reputation on the foundation of the weakest. Girls no less than boys gang up in shifting alliances excluding and including, rewarding and denying in wilful exercises of power and desire. Read Margaret Attwood's novel *Cat's Eye*. Cordelia dominates the three other girls in the group. But slowly the worms turn. **Write** on one of the following titles: *Bullies, Ganging Up, Gangs, Dares, Forfeits, Fights.*

- In the same novel, the girl gang, now in their early teens, turn their tormenting tongues on a local family. They call them the 'Lump-lump family'. Why does Mrs Lump-lump have a Band-Aid on her face? Because she cut herself shaving is the mocking answer. The sharp-tongued are feared. **Write** a story in which a character tired of being picked on and insulted decides to fight back.

- '...the whole world of girls and their doings...' *Cat's Eye*. Think back to your 'life of girls' or your life of boys. What stands out? **Write** an account of some typical experiences. Attwood spun *Cat's Eye* out of her own life 'of girls'. You could take one episode and render it as a short story.

- The cat's eye of the title is a marble with a striking streak of blue running through its icy clarity. It has magic powers. It keeps the owner safe. It's special. **Write** about such a talismanic possession from your younger days. Say why it was so important, and explain why its power dimmed.

- In Chapter 35 of *Cat's Eye* the bully, Cordelia, irritated that the others laughed at her taking a fall in the snow, seizes the knitted hat of the narrator and throws it down into the 'ravine', a sombre gully throttled with briars and bushes which they pass by daily to and from school. To retrieve the hat she has to go down into the 'ravine'. It's a dreaded place: dank, pungent with cat's piss and the dirty glitter of empty liquor bottles. A stream flows through it from the cemetery, and its murky waters carry the dissolved bodies of the dead. Or so Cordelia says, warning that one poisonous drop of the deadly nightshade growing there in threatening abundance will turn them into zombies. And men lurk there. If the narrator-victim goes down, her mum will go wild. If she doesn't, Cordelia may exact a worse revenge. As she hesitates she remembers her friends putting her in the 'Hole', a deep garden pit, as a punishment. Terrified, she starts to descend into the forbidden dark. Does any of this chime with your own experiences? **Write** about one of them recreating the incident(s) as if they were a chapter from a novel.

Passion and Romance

- In Antonia White's novel *Frost in May*, published in 1933, a young girl, Nanda, joins a convent school near London run by the nuns of the Order of the Five Wounds. She subjects herself to the frigid, authoritarian Catholic culture of the school. Secretly she starts to write a romantic novel. Her heroine has a 'tiny, tip-tilted nose ... geranium red lips and hair of the finest spun gold and huge, limpid violet eyes'. She goes to balls where she swoons in 'the languid ecstasies of a waltz', or stands trembling on the balcony where an admirer presses 'a kiss of burning passion on her scarlet mouth'. Nanda, however, has lavished most of her writer's care on the hero in an attempt to make him as wicked and therefore as attractive as possible, and to make his final conversion to goodness all the more dramatic. He wears a yellow silk dressing-gown embroidered with cabalistic symbols, studies black magic and frequents Chinatown drug dens where he indulges in 'strange narcotics'.

After a surprise desk inspection by the Mistress of Discipline, Nanda's secret chapters are discovered. Her parents on a visit at the time are informed. Her father explodes. 'What filth!' he shouts. Nada is overwhelmed. Devastated. Wretched. Her parents leave. Nanda is expelled. Mother Radcliffe, the Disciplinary one, says it is for her own good: 'I had to break your will,' she says. 'I am...God's instrument in this.' Take *For Your Own Good* as a theme and write a short story exploring its resonances. Loosely base it on an experience of your own. **Write** three or four pages.

- Nanda's novel is energised by the fantasised longings of a young teenage girl. **Write** an autobiographical piece about teen yearnings.

- **Write** a short panting parody of teen romantic fiction.

- Read Jamaica Kincaid's intriguing short story 'What I Have Been Doing Lately' (SS2). This is a cyclical narrative; an adaptation of that oral form of duplicated anecdote that repeatedly eats its own tail. The action of the story is dream-like with both the logic and illogicality of the surreal. The daughter-narrator goes on a journey of self-discovery. After a while she returns to where she began and starts all over again. **Try writing** a cyclical narrative, and allow your imagination to roam where it likes.

- Antonia White's novel ends on a note of despair. Nanda has lost her friends, her reputation, her father's respect and the security of her routined life. She has lost the only home she really knows. **Write** about *Home*.

- In Chapter 5 of *A Boy's Own Story*, Edmund White's central character discusses with his friend, Tom, the nature of friendship. For him friendship borders on the sexual, and he re-cognises this tendency will threaten his male friendships. He learns to suppress the erotic side of his nature. He convinces himself that each time he resists temptation he is accumulat-ing credit somewhere. Each resistance is a snuffed-out flame in a church of votive candles ready to die for their religion. He recognises that he is 'required to deny my love in order to prove it'. Teenage friendships can be intense, exclusive, fraught. **Write** about a too-close friendship.

- Throughout the novel, White explores the interior world of his character: the self-reflections, the resolves, the psycho-logical tactics, the elaborate narratives of self-scripts that shape his social behaviour. **Write** a diary account set in the mid-adolescent years. The diarist has to decide whether to drop an old friendship in favour of a new, more exciting, maybe more dangerous one.

- In 'Araby', a story from James Joyce's collection *Dubliners*, the romance of young love is upon the teenage boy. From his aunt's front parlour he watches Mangan's sister in the lit doorway of the house opposite, entranced by the swing of her dress and the 'soft rope of her hair' tossed from side to side. Her very name, he says, 'is like a summons to my foolish blood'. He promises to get her something from a bazaar called Araby, a train-ride away across the other side of the city.

  At the bazaar he sees the word 'Araby' above the entrance, and the syllables cast an Eastern enchantment over him. He wanders round the empty rooms of next door's uninhabited house trembling and periodically crying out: 'O love! O love!' The trip is a fiasco. At the end of 'Araby', the boy sees himself 'as a creature driven and derided by vanity', and his 'eyes burned with anguish and anger'. Joyce prepares the reader for the final disillusion-ment. The reader first, and then the boy, sees the inevitable failure of the venture marked by a succession of images. These include: the train that 'crept through 'ruinous houses', the 'weary-looking' cashier and the closed stalls, the disinterested waitress flirting with two lads, the sudden dowsing of lights as the fair closes. Read this last page carefully. The economy and concision of the writing is masterly. What is the significance of the badinage of fractured phrasing at the end? What is the point of the two men sitting under a sign of the *Café Chantant*, 'counting money on a salver'? What is the relevance of the boy examining 'porcelain vases and flowered tea-sets'? **Write** a story based on a similar experience of high hopes dashed.

- Read Chapter 17 of Nick Hornby's novel *About a Boy*. Marcus is having trouble with his mother. She goes ape when she discovers that Will, a divorced thirty-something, has bought her son an expensive pair of trainers without consulting her. Bad move Will. Bad move Marcus. **Write** about some of the bad moves you made in your time as a teenager. Use the phrase as a title.

- In Maureen Duffy's autobiographic novel *That's How It Was* Paddy recalls the first time that she felt she belonged somewhere. After years of moving with her consumptive mother between rented rooms and generous relatives, she realised that where she really belonged was the streets of London: '...the lighted shops, the pavements that were splashed with mud and sodden papers, cartons, tissue papers from the oranges around Christmas...I was a Londoner, an East-Ender.' **Write** a piece about belonging. Start with a place and its 'feel' like Duffy does and move out into larger aspects of the topic.

- The opposite pole to belonging is loss and exile. **Write** about one of these themes. It's a commonplace to say that out of loss and suffering some good often emerges. To assume loss has no compensations is to play the victim and to see the world in black and white. Enrich your account with contrary possibilities.

Daddy's Girls, Mummy's Boys

- The Greeks had a word for it. According to the Austrian psychoanalyst Sigmund Freud, sons compete with fathers for the love of the mother. Daughters strive to supplant mothers in the father's affections. These Oedipal and Electral relationships may or may not map the child/parent fault-lines, but it is self-evident that intra- and intergenerational rivalries ferment in the family cauldron. Some of the divisive forces in families are deep-rooted, implicit in the unavoidable intimacies of childhood and growing up. Others seem more calculated, a conclusion of temperament and accident. Unemployment may, for instance, intensify family rivalries, create new rifts, break loyalties. The Freudian oppositional dynamic of family life may be a very false model. Daughters fix affections on fathers for all sorts of reasons, an affection they give in equal measure to mothers. Loving within families creates the capacity for loving outside the family. Sons love fathers, but maybe for recognition and approval not selflessly. Yet this self-centred child-love grows into the selfless thing of maturer understanding.

Read Alison Fell's short story 'The Shining Mountain' (CC). This is a fable about a daughter desperate to earn her father's attention. The father, a famous mountaineer, calls her Pangma-La, a name she is teased about at school. At first, she cries, but her father scolds her. She is Pangma-La, the shining mountain, a name given to distinguish her from all the ordinary Morags and Janets. The father teaches her to climb, and, when the mother worries about her falling and injuring herself he exclaims: 'Let her be, she's tough and hard as nails.' Sometimes children have to carry too heavy a burden of expectation. Daughters may have to be replacement boys in sonless families. A poetry-inclined son of a professional boxer father may have a hard time fitting the masculine template. Have you felt this? Have there been unspoken demands made of you which can never be satisfied? **Write** about it?

- Sylvia Plath wrote a now famous poem 'Daddy', in which her father was depicted as a goose-stepping Fascist. He died when she was only eight years old. Did she unwittingly resent him for this 'betrayal', for his abandonment of her? Was her feeling of loss and rejection and anger loaded onto this vampiric Hitlerian figure? Did hurt change to hate? Did she guiltily try to exorcise the monster? Was she looking for a strong masculinity to force her heart open? Read the poem. Make some notes on the imagery and relentless rhythms of the verse. **Write** your notes into a more coherent response to the poem.

- A more benign, less wrought poem is Seamus Heaney's 'Follower'. As a child he followed the horse-plough worked by his father, admiring the skill and subtle feel for the pull and tug of the turned sods. In the poem, all the young Heaney wants is to follow his father. Now, it is the father who stumbles in his wake. **Write** an affectionate, honest portrait of your father or mother. Start with an image, something concrete. This is not a testimonial.

- His parents are divorcing and he is relieved that he and his sister are to live with their mother. 'It was...a deliverance from my father,' writes the narrator in Edmund White's novel *A Boy's Own Story*. At this moment in his life he recalls going into his father's bedroom as a small child charged with waking him. He remembers being astonished at the size of the man lying down. He was 'like a sea monster beached'. He stares at the gigantic shoes, imagines the lofty shadows of the wardrobe above and the cashmere cardigan hanging there with 'all his discarded but potential selves'. See pages 71–6 for a portrait of the narrator's mother. **Write** about seeing your parents from a different perspective or seeing your parents in a new light.

- Read the opening nine pages of Edmund White's novel where the narrator and his friend, Kevin, go on a midnight boat ride with his father. Kevin was the sort of son the father would have liked. Kevin 'throbbed with the pressure to contend, to be noticed, to be right, to win, to make others bend to his will'. The narrator-son is different. **Write** about being different within the family.

- In the notebook on his play *Death of a Salesman*, Arthur Miller wrote: 'Willy wants his sons prepared for life. Nobody will laugh at them – take advantage. They'll be big men. It's the big men who command respect.' Do you agree with this, or is it an outmoded and disabling notion of manhood? Again in the notebook Miller suggests that Willy's boys are strangled by their father's heroic dreams for them. **Write** a story or poem entitled *Machismo*.

- The Miller notebook again. The playwright trials a Willy Lomond speech in which the salesman comments on his own restless competitiveness and admits it is 'not because it's flowing from me, but because it's flowing against me'. Look at your own life. Does it flow from or against you? Big Question! A tidal metaphor! Think about this observation and jot down some notes. **Write** a continuation of the Willy Lomond speech. Introduce a second character to the scene and continue for two or three pages.

- In *A Boy's Own Story*, the narrator's older sister gives him a hard time. She mocks him for playing volleyball and ping-pong, and not tennis and baseball. She can't wait to tell him he was the only boy she noticed who didn't sit cross-legged in the school gym. She tests him for masculinity. A girl extends her fingers, a boy cups his in his upturned palm; a girl lifts her eyes, a boy throws back his whole head; a girl strikes a match away from her body, a boy toward his. A man never gushes; men are silent or loud. And so on. What details would you add to this list of distinguishing features? Observe men and women chatting, gesturing, stancing in a café, bar, party, et cetera. What gender-specific and gender-defining behaviour do you see? **Write** a scene in which a friend is giving sound advice to someone younger about passing muster in the right company.

- Edmund White's hero fears he is homosexual. He thinks the gay tendency is a result of having a 'surfeit of female com-pany at home', and decides to correct the imbalance by entering an all-male world – a boarding school. His father reluctantly agrees to fund this move to private education and accompanies his son to the welcome interview with the headmaster, who philosophises about manliness over 'a feminine clutter of tea things, tiny pots of marmalade, egg-shell thin cups ...' For the Head, manliness is 'tweeds, trust funds, a polite but chilly relationship with God, a pretended interest in knowledge and an obsessive interest in sports, especially muddy, dangerous ones...'

This is a class-coloured view of masculinity, a particular variant of the condition. Looking back over the years, what do you consider to have been the most formative and determining influences shaping your ideas of gender and sexual identity? Usually the agenda is unspoken, the pressures subtle and implicit. **Write** about anything emerging out of this line of thought. **Write** a poem in which each sentence starts with the phrase: 'Real boys/Real girls'. Complete each line with an assertion of masculinity or femininity.

- Read Jamaica Kincaid's short short story 'Girl'. A mother is giving her daughter a hard time. Do this. Do that. **Write** an harangue entitled *Boy*.

- You've heard of Charm Schools. You've read about college 'How To' courses on 'Flirting' and old-fashioned 'Courting'. **Write** a story entitled *Chat-up* or list as many chat-up lines and clichés from the flirting game as you can think of, and rearrange them into a poem

- Read Margaret Attwood's story 'Significant Moments in the Life of My Mother'(CC). This is a flat, detached picture of a mother/daughter relationship. **Write** a piece under the same title.

- Attwood's mother used to recount the old family stories often to the embarrassment of her daughter. **Write** a story in which a daughter brings home a new boyfriend. At the meal her mother begins a story the daughter would rather not hear.

- By her own admission, Jamaica Kincaid's relationship with her mother was fraught. Read her story 'My Mother' (CC). The narrative follows a series of surreal transformations in which daughter and mother change into geckos, rapacious fish, giantesses, and inhabit caves, large beautiful houses and paradisal bowers. This is an allegory of the changing shape of their relationship. From nourishing and sharing; from being like each other's ghost they grow to be sexual predators, then rivals, then blissful companions. **Write** about the ways your relationship with your mother or father has changed over the years. Move the narrative from stage to stage.

• Michèle Roberts, who has recently published *Impossible Saints*, a book about the father/daughter relationship, has said: 'girls idealise their fathers because their fathers were never there. In conventional families we grew up with fathers who were away trying to be good providers. There was space and into that space comes mythology. Our whole culture, despite feminism, is still based on the idea that men have got to be these glorious creatures. They have to be these heroic, larger than life, mythical figures. A lot of these daddy's girls sooner or later, start to realise the hollowness of the mythology.' Hollow myth! Feet of clay! **Write** about the fall of a god, father or otherwise.

• There's a rich mix of ideas in Roberts's remark above. The word 'girl' suggests that daughters remain permanently juvenile and immature in relation to their fathers. Take issue with her claim that girls idealise fathers, and argue for a different dynamic in father/daughter relationships. **Write** a memo to yourself exploring your ideas on this topic.

• It is a well-documented phenomenon, first noted by Freud, that female patients can develop very close relationships with male authority figures such as psychiatrists or teachers or priests. Is this a transferred father/daughter relationship? Are daughters latter-day Electras who fall in love with any father-figure? **Write** a poem entitled *Electras*. Playing with the word 'Electra' produces such possibilities as Electrance, Electrash, Elect. Such sparks may fire up your poem.

• In Andrew O'Hagan's novel *Our Fathers*, the relationships between the generations of men in the family are characterised by bitterness and wounding. Read Chapter 1 and **write** an episode/scene in which a father and son go on an expedition/trip/visit together. Each character has a mixture of feelings about the other. Explore this mix in the fiction. For a sustained exploration of the son/father relationship read *And When Did You Last See Your Father?* by Blake Morrison. See too *East Bay Grease*, Eric Miles Williamson's compelling novel about T-Bird, the only son of an alcoholic mother and ex-convict father.

- Read Elaine Feinstein's poem 'Father' (PBPBI). It's a simple, loving, four-verse portrait written in quatrains. Emulate **by writing** in quatrains about your father or mother.

- For a more unsettling meditation on parents read Elizabeth Jennings's poem 'One Flesh' (FB). The title is taken from the marriage service. Choose a phrase from the same service and use it as a starter for a poem. In 'One Flesh', the lines rhyme alternately. Attempt a similar scheme in your own version. **Write** under the title *To Honour and Obey*.

- For more family portraits read the following: 'Memory of My Father' by Patrick Kavanagh (RB), 'The Last Words of My English Grandmother' by William Carlos Williams (RB), 'Aunt Julia' (RB) by Norman MacCaig. Dedicate a poem to someone in your family who is no longer living. **Write** honestly.

References

Angelou, M., *I Know Why the Caged Bird Sings* (Virago, 1993).
Ashworth, A., *Once in a House on Fire* (Picador, 1998).
Attwood, M., *Cat's Eye* (Virago, 1994).
Blake, W., *Songs of Innocence and Experience* (Oxford, 1970).
Brock, P., *Indiana Gothic* (Review, 1999).
Carver, R., *A New Path to the Waterfall* (Collins, 1990).
Causley, C., *Collected Poems 1951–1992* (Macmillan, 1992).
Deane, S., *Reading in the Dark* (Vintage, 1997).
Dickens, C., *Nicholas Nickleby* (Penguin, 1994).
Dickens, C., *Great Expectations* (Penguin, 1996).
Doyle, R., *Paddy Clarke. Ha.Ha.Ha.* (Vintage, 1994).
Duffy, C. A., *Selling Manhattan* (Anvil, 1987).
Duffy, M., *That's How It Was* (Virago, 1983).
Freud, E., *Hideous Kinky* (Penguin, 1993).
Galloway, J., *Blood* (Minerva, 1992).
Golding, W., *Lord of the Flies* (Faber and Faber, 1999).
Heaney, S., *New Selected Poems 1966–1987* (Faber and Faber, 1987).

Hornby, N., *About a Boy* (Gollancz, 1999).

Joyce, J., *Dubliners* (Penguin, 1996).

Joyce, J., *A Portrait of the Artist as a Young Man* (Penguin, 1996).

Kempadoo, K., *Buxton Spice* (Phoenix, 1998).

Kincaid, J., 'What I Have Been Doing Lately', in *The Secret Self*, Vol. 2, ed. H. Lee (Dent, 1987).

Kincaid, J., 'Girl', in *Wayward Girls and Wicked Women*, ed. A. Carter (Virago, 1992).

Lee, L., *Cider with Rosie* (Penguin, 1970).

McCourt, F., *Angela's Ashes* (Flamingo, 1997).

McEwan, I., *First Love, Last Rites* (Vintage, 1997).

Michaels, A., *Fugitive Pieces* (Bloomsbury, 1997).

Miller, A., *Death of a Salesman* (Penguin, 1989).

Morrison, B., *And when Did You Last See Your Father?* (Granta, 1998).

O'Brien, E., *The Country Girls* (Penguin, 1970).

O'Hagan, A., *Our Fathers* (Faber and Faber, 2000).

Plath, S., *Collected Poems* (Harper, 1992).

Roberts, M., *Impossible Saints* (Virago, 1998).

Robinson, B., *The Peculiar Memories of Thomas Penman* (Bloomsbury, 1998).

Salinger, J. D., *The Catcher in the Rye* (Penguin, 1994).

Shields, C., *The Stone Diaries* (Fourth Estate, 1994).

Thomas, D., *Collected Poems 1934–1953* (Everyman, 1989).

Trevor, W., *The Children of Dynmouth* (Penguin, 1990).

White, A., *Frost in May* (Virago, 1978).

White, E., *A Boy's Own Story* (Picador, 1983).

Wicks, S., *Claudia* (Minerva, 2000).

Williamson, E. M., *East Bay Grease* (Bloomsbury, 1999).

Winterson, J., *Oranges Are Not the Only Fruit* (Vintage, 1996).

6 | The Language Game

WYSWIWYG – The Way You Say the World Is the Way You Get

- To adapt Jo Paisley's famous football dictum: 'It's not a matter of life or death; words are more important than that.' The word 'Jew' (*Juden*), for instance, sent 10 million people to their deaths between 1940 and 1944. The phrase *Mein Kampf* has chilled the blood and poisoned minds for three-quarters of a century. Primo Levi knew about the importance of words. He was an Italian writer, a chemist and former inmate and survivor of the Auschwitz concentration camp who wrote about the life-threatening power of language in his book *The Drowned and the Saved*. In the *lager*, the network of labour and extermination camps in eastern provinces of the Third Reich, inmates survived only if they knew the language of the camps, the *lager* jargon. This specialist language was a primitive form of German. It was, to use Levi's words, 'skeletal, howled, studded with obscenities and imprecations – and was only vaguely related to the precise, austere language of my chemistry books, and the melodious, refined German of Heine's poetry...'

  Most Italian inmates died within 10 to 15 days of arrival because they could not understand the jargon, could not follow instructions. They did not know where to get food. They did not know how to be subservient and avoid beatings. They did not know how to express repentance. To survive they needed to fit in with the camp identity and exist within the parabola of 'transgression-punishment-repentance'. They couldn't, and they died for want of words. 'They were drowning one by one,' wrote Levi, 'in a stormy sea of not-understanding.'

Astutely Levi observed: 'where violence is inflicted on man, it is also inflicted on language.' Indeed, you first brutalise the language and then you can more easily brutalise the man. The perverted language of the *lager* <u>permits</u> the brutalisation. Thus, the word 'to eat' in Auschwitz was rendered by *fressen*, a verb applied only to animals in good German. And once people are turned into animals they can be beaten and slaughtered without compunction. The *lager* commanders instituted a deliberate policy of degradation by word as well as deed so that the executioners would not feel guilty about what they were doing.

Ignorance of the language wasn't just a threat to physical survival; it struck at the heart of the human being, took away his essential humanity. Each of the executioners could say, like Cassio in *Othello*, 'I have lost the immortal part of myself and what remains is bestial.' As Levi writes: 'use of the word to communicate thought, this necessary and sufficient mechanism for man to be man, had fallen into disuse.' Many accepted 'the eclipse of the word', said Levi writing again about the defeated inmates. They became indifferent and 'drowned'. By 'drowned' here he means either literally died or spiritually withered away.

The survivors of the *lager* protected themselves from their death-in-life, language-barren condition by begging information or by reading scraps of newsprint from garbage bins or eavesdropping on the conversations of the guards. This 'news' of the outside world, these faint echoes of a larger human discourse, made the 'lost legions' of the camps feel less forgotten. The concept of 'the lost' is disturbing. These are the faceless ones, erased from history, never mentioned. They are lost in the sense they have disappeared amidst the multitudes of 'the drowned', and are lost too because the essential word of their being, their name, has been exchanged for a number, a reiterative cipher. It's hardly conceivable that any of us will find ourselves in a *gulag* or *lager*. But some social groups ostracise members, send them 'to Coventry', which like all silencing tries to diminish the self, if not render it invisible altogether. **Write** a story or poem about being silenced.

• History is full of disappearances: peoples, individuals lost to silence. It is estimated that nearly 3 million combatants, or about one third of the British Army in the First World War, were non-British. Over a million Indian soldiers fought on the Western Front. Where are their histories, their voices? They've been erased for want of words. It wasn't only the flower of *our* nation's youth, *our* mother's sons who made the ultimate sacrifice on Flanders fields!

Nearly 200,000 Caribbean volunteers joined the Army in 1914. They weren't front-line troops. They were employed in support units: kitchen staff, orderlies, messengers. Officers were worried that if the enemy saw black troops in action they would feel more confident and might conclude the British had a recruitment problem. The same ingrained racism means that the 20,000 blacks who died in British concentration camps on the South African Veldt in the Boer War of 1899–1902 are nowhere memorialised. Their graves are lost and their identities forgotten. The Boers are preserved honourably in song and poem, history and monument. It follows that if words shape and establish identity then we, who are full of words and able to speak, can, indeed should, use them to find and save those who are 'lost'. Can you think of a 'lost', that is, silenced group or an individual who you could rescue from oblivion by your words? **Write** them back into being and history.

• Language is power. Words have the power to destroy. And they have the power to anaesthetise as George Orwell pointed out in his famous essay 'Politics and the English Language'. The word 'pacification' is a cover-up for the bombing and indiscriminate slaughter of defenceless villages. The expulsion of people from their homes becomes in military language: 'a realignment of frontiers'. And so on. You can gather countless examples of destructive euphemisms. 'But if thought corrupts language,' said Orwell, 'language can also corrupt thought.' Slovenly expression, tired metaphors, dulling clichés, wordiness and abstraction weaken the language and make it easier for us to be foolish thinkers.

Orwell thought we should fight the decay and the abuse of the language. He scorned those who considered language to be an 'organic' phenomenon, and who thought that any intervention was interfering with nature. Language is 'an instrument we shape for our own purposes' he pointed out, and went on in his essay to expose the ways words are degraded.

People who claim that the language is declining mean it is being abused in some way. There are those who are a little pedantic and complain about grammatical niceties being ignored and the decline of the apostrophe. The real problem is with how words shape our attitudes and actions not with linguistic good manners. Start from Orwell's position and collect examples of euphemistic, anaesthetising language and **write** a short up-date of his essay.

- Because words can be powerful they attract the suspicion of authority, and every vested interest has sought to control words, to censor and even burn them. As I write these words, four students are being tried in Iran under penalty of death for writing and publishing a short play satirising the conservative element in the country's political hierarchy. **Write** an open letter to the leader of a military regime or an independence movement or a guerrilla army explaining why it is in their long-term interest to tolerate and promote free speech in their sphere of influence.

- Arthur Quiller-Couch, the distinguished turn-of-the-century critic, novelist, poet and Cambridge professor, argued in his 1913 lecture series for the inclusion of creative writing in the University curriculum. 'Words are,' he said, ' . . . the only currency in which we can exchange thought even with ourselves. Does it not follow, then, that the more accurately we use words the closer definition we shall give to our thoughts?' Examine your relationship with words. Do you treat them carelessly? Do they bite back? Intimidate you? Who's in control? In a poem about 'cancer' a schoolgirl wrote: 'Don't give in to the word. Fight the word.' **Write** about your relationship with words in general or with one in particular.

- In *The Drowned and the Saved*, Levi is scornful of fashionable post-modern theories that say communication is impossible, that we are 'incapable of reciprocal messages, or capable only of truncated messages, false at their departure, misunderstood on their arrival.' The slipperiness of language, so post-modernists claim, means communication is a hit and miss game, distorting reality and deluding the players. To them, according to Levi: 'Discourse is fictitious, pure noise, a painted veil that conceals existential silence; also, we are alone, even if (or especially if) we live in pairs.' To use a metaphor of our time, we are hard-wired for language. To use Levi's terms: 'we are biologically and socially predisposed to communication, and in particular to its highly evolved and noble form, which is language'. Have you come across the idea that beyond the smoke-screen of language there is nothing, only deep-space emptiness, the last zero? **Write** about this idea.

- In his book *The Language Instinct*, Steven Pinker makes some gloomy predictions. Many languages are doomed to extinction. Of the 6000 languages in the world only 10 per cent are destined to survive the next millennium, the rest will die out within a century. Already of the 150 North American Indian languages 80 per cent are moribund. The counts are grim elsewhere. In Russia the same figure for local languages is 70 per cent, in Australia it is 90 per cent – the same percentage for Alaska and Siberia.

  The causes range from the destruction of speakers' habitats, genocide, forced assimilation by education, bombardment by electronic media. Should we be concerned that our linguistic environment is under such threat? Is linguistic diversity as crucial to our survival as bio-diversity? Does it matter that we are about to lose Damin, a ceremonial version of the Australian Lardil language which has 200 words and can be learnt in a day? **Write** a passionate plea for the preservation of language diversity. Focus your argument on the case for saving Cornish, an ancient Celtic language.

- George Steiner, the essayist, philosopher and playwright, has written: 'Language is the main instrument in man's refusal to accept the world as it is.' This is a heroic and defiant view of language. It sees words as the last frontier against the wild. It is *the* essential civilising force. For Ursula Le Guin this is a very male attitude to language. For her it is more a conditional and subjunctive experience. It offers alternatives and hypotheses. It is far more ameliorative and conditional and contemplative and speculative than the Steiner view, which Le Guin thinks is too eager to seize life by the scruff of the neck and shake it to bits.

  According to her, we don't think facts, we think 'maybes' and 'hopefullys' and 'what-ifs'. Our thoughts are not press statements. We think fantasies and rehearse possibilities for ourselves. Imagine yourself in a contemplative mood, day-dreaming if you like. **Write** down the stream of your mental images, your sudden fantasies, the fondest dreams, the wildest imaginings. Let the mental flow dictate the shape of your writing, not the reverse.

- Anne Michaels, the Canadian poet and novelist, has said that there can be 'no poetry after Auschwitz'. Does she mean that the Holocaust is beyond words, so appalling were the atrocities of the time? Is silence the only response to events of this magnitude? Or is there something deficient in poetry itself that it cannot encompass the experience of evil on a vast scale? Does poetic language give a dark allure to the devilish?

  How would you tackle a catastrophe in a poem? As you read this, tribes and terrorists, fundamentalists and freedom fighters, security forces and guerrillas, militias and special operations units, paramilitaries and murder squads, secret police and punishment gangs are fighting, terrorising, shooting, torturing, looting, raping, incinerating, bombing, mutilating, starving, executing innocents – women, girls, pregnant mothers, old men, young boys, babies, refugees, grandfathers, in prisons, gulags, alleyways, cellars, bunkers, camps across 60 different conflicts world-wide.

  Pick up a newspaper each day for a week. Use what photographic material and other information you can gather to **write** something about one of these conflicts. Do you use graphic language, sweeping metaphors? Or do you understate horror to give impact, and work in the miniature? A child's bloodied sandal lying in the dust tells more about war and suffering than a barrage of exploding adjectives and lines booming with distant generalities. For further information check on Amnesty International's website.

- The contemporary notion that language is a smokescreen, a necessary deception to protect us from the horror of the primal void, suggests we live in a faithless and nihilistic age. Whether you regard the so-called 'illusion' of language as an evolutionary defence mechanism against the fear of non-existence, or as a distorting mirror that's fun to play with, there are alternative attitudes on offer. In his poem 'Bifocal' (RB), William Stafford writes, as the title suggests, about two views of the world: the *surface*, which he describes as love, our ability to know and embrace like 'a map of roads/leading wherever go miles/or little bushes nod', and the *'legend'*, which is 'fixed and inexorable'. He concludes that the world:

  > happens twice –
  > once what we see it as;
  > second it legends itself
  > deep, the way it is.

  Words, like those in the poem, shape the way we see the world, but below, another story ('legend') is being told which does not change and which keeps all things, love and knowledge included, in being. Do you have any sympathy with Stafford's ideas about surface and depths? Does he mean by 'legend', old narratives or myths, where the deep truths about human existence are buried? What sense of abiding truth do *you* have, and does language offer any access to it? **Write** about the possibility of mining what Stafford calls 'the darkest mine'. Use this phrase as your title. Or take a myth (see Ted Hughes's *Tales of Ovid* for ideas) and **write** a modern tale of your own based on traditional material.

- One view of language is that it refreshes a tired world. Or rather it wipes away the dull patina of familiarity from our eyes and enables us to see with new vision. In other words, language defamiliarises, eliminates tired thinking and delusions of all kinds. **Try writing** a poem so that every line makes the reader see the object afresh as if for the first time in their lives.

- The Romantics felt the language of poetry offered a unique access to another reality, but twentieth-century writers have seen this business of rewriting the world as an endless attempt to recover 'what has been lost' as T.S. Eliot said. Each new act of writing:

  Is a new beginning, a raid on the inarticulate
  With shabby equipment always deteriorating
  In the general mess of imprecision of feeling…

  Does your own experience of words tally with Eliot's pessimistic assessment? **Write** a poem or commentary using the title *Raiding the Inarticulate*.

- The poet Ann Stevenson says the chief function of poetry is to 'sharpen language'. Over the next few weeks find and record some examples of language where the words have gone blunt. How would you sharpen up some of these examples? **Try writing** about what this research exercise has taught you. Devise a suitable title that plays with the images of sharpness like *Cutting Edge* or *Sharp Practice*.

- In his poem 'The Cool Web', the poet Robert Graves sees language as a way of neutralising the too intense world of the emotions and the senses. We use language to 'chill the angry day' and 'dull the rose's cruel scent'. Were we to cast off this cool web of language, the rawness of the world would drive us mad. In choosing sanity we are also choosing dullness, argues Graves. What do you think the two symbolic phrases – 'angry day' and 'the roses's cruel scent' – mean? Is this how you use language, as a deflection of the real and the raw, as a way of drawing the sting from a situation, as a way of shielding yourself from reality? **Try**

writing a piece that is diametrically opposed to Graves's view of language.

- Anne Stevenson, in accounting for the genesis of one of her poems, recounts how the line 'The Way You Say The World Is What You Get' came suddenly to mind while she was pondering the 'Janus face of language'. Janus was the Roman god of doorways who looked in two directions, back and front, at the same time. The line is a variation on 'WYSIWYG' – What You See Is What You Get – the computer acronym for what you see on the screen is what you get from the print-out. Why is language like a doorway, looking two ways at the same time? And what does Stevenson's WYSWIWYG line mean exactly? From your preliminary answers to these questions **try writing** a piece. Maybe you can use the ideas of looking, of being two-faced, of codes like acronyms, of doubles and mirror images et cetera in your work.

- Language allows us to be evasive and it allows us to hint and imply unpleasant truths without quite facing them. Language can lead readers to the edge of revelation and leave them there more terrified of the fall than of what lies just out of sight. It's like pointing your finger with your eyes closed. Take Ann Duffy's poem 'Mouth, with Soap'. Here words decontaminate the female world. The sanitised woman speaks:

  > She didn't shit, she *soiled* or *had a soil*
  > and didn't piss, passed water...
  > ...though she didn't sweat cobs then,
  > later she *perspired*. Jesus wept. Bloody Nora. *Language!*

  This is language abuse on a grand scale. Here comes 'The Censor clapping a wooden tongue,' says Duffy. A brilliant image! Once language is censored it goes wooden, and the price to pay for this timidity is *'The Big C'* – language, body and self infiltrated and dying. Read the poem carefully. **Write** your own piece about verbal etiquette and/or policing the language.

- The psychologist Adam Phillips has said he is concerned with the 'devaluation of language...through the proliferation of psychobabble'. We have a tendency to pathologise every human state or condition. There's a syndrome or disorder for everything. We can't be miserable because it rains any more; we have to suffer from SAD, seasonally affected disorder. The transient has become a permanent disability. 'Certain words,' says Phillips, 'are very powerful – "shy", "sad", "low self-esteem", "depressed" – and they are very coercive, they don't allow people to have their own thoughts.' So, we've become prisoners of our own language. Over the next few weeks collect some examples of coercive words and psychobabble. The world of the therapist will provide rich pickings. Use this lexicon to **write** something about how language, like some dance club bouncer, intimidates.

- Phillips is interested in 'language that is more productive, language that goes on to produce more language'. This sounds like one of those nuclear reactions that self-generates. What do you think he means by 'language producing more language'? Doesn't this verbal procreation happen all the time anyway? Isn't it just a neat definition of good writing?

  Raymond Carver said writing prose was no more than writing one sentence and then another and then another. Each gives rise to the next in a perpetual motion. Take a phrase like 'self-esteem' and see if you can draw from it more and more words/phrases like a magician might draw an endless stream of silk handkerchiefs from the top hat on the table. The idea is to escape the coercion of the word and move into fresh fields. Out of this exercise, a writing form might emerge. For instance, you could use antithesis as a shaping force opposing negative and positive ideas about 'self-esteem' in the same line or in alternating verses, or you could adopt the extended metaphor as your shaping principle. **Write** ten lines in antithetical form.

- In 'The Language Issue' (NP), Nuala Ní Dhomhnaill imagines her poem as the boat of language placed in the water like Moses in his basket and left to float abandoned on the wayward currents. It's another version of the Paul Celan idea that poems are like ships in bottles left to find their own way into the world. The word 'Issue' in the poem's title hints at the notion of birth, the informing metaphor of the piece. This corporeal metaphor is reflected in other popular expressions such as the 'body of language', the 'mother tongue'. Nuala Ní Dhomhnaill's poem is gently paced and tender. It reflects the sadness of the mother-maker at having to let her creation go. It's like giving up a child for adoption. These thoughts may have triggered your own images and ideas on language. If so, **try writing** about them.

- 'A poet's words are of things that do not exist without the words.' Think about this comment by the American poet Wallace Stevens. It is both a simple and a difficult concept he is expressing, so it might be helpful to make some initial notes in your journal and feel your way towards some kind of understanding. **Write** down your tentative ideas in two paragraphs of reflective writing.

- Poetic language for Seamus Heaney has its spring waters in the pre-verbal. He cites Robert Frost's description of the arrival of a poem: 'A poem begins as a lump in the throat...It finds the thought and the thought finds the words.' Like a diviner, says Heaney, the poet senses a stirring in the mind 'round a word or an image or a memory'. The stirring dilates into a thought or a theme and finally into words. Only then, does crafting into the most apt and right expression begin. A suitable soundbite to describe the process might be – 'thoughts form words'.

  Robert Graves, in his poem 'The Dance of Words', exhorts poets to start with lightning, and not forecast the rhythm nor the choreography, but let raw energy drive the dance of words. Give way to chance and don't force the poem. But how is this done in practice? How do we guarantee a lightning strike? By listening to the man within says Heaney; by attending on things says William Stafford; by being willingly to be in 'uncertainties, mysteries, doubts, without any irritable reaching after fact and reason', said Keats; by running with 'wild mind' says Natalie Goldberg. Steal Robert Graves's title and **write** a poem on language entitled *The Dance of Words*.

- In *The New Poetry* anthology, John Burnside has two enigmatic poems about language, 'Septuagesima' and 'Language' (NP). In the calendar of the Christian Church, Septuagesima is the third Sunday before Lent, and describes the 70 days from then to Easter Saturday. In this poem Burnside suggests that words, names, have obscured the original beautiful, bright silence; 'the winter whiteness' of the world before creation.

  'Language' is a challenging poem about the ways language works. The poet imagines himself wandering 'on the borders of language' looking for names between 'silt' and 'swan' to describe the 'household that stands for the self in dreams'. The word 'silt' suggests the dark deposits of the unconscious mind, and the 'swan', the imagination perhaps, that graceful and instinctual beauty that floats over and transforms the surface of things. Though these two words express opposites they depend on each other for their meaning. We can't have darkness unless we presuppose the idea of light. In every yes there's an echo of no.

  The poet's names (words) arrive only after the world is asleep, the city stilled and 'the fastidious gardens gift-wrapped in dew'. The poem seems to pose the question: where are the words to express the ineffable, the mysterious other? The last few lines of the poem symbolically describe the ordering and arranging function of language in the image of suburban horticulture. Where is its opposite function, its inevitable twin? If suburban gardens symbolise the arranging function of language what symbolises its other function? Does Burnside see the poet's role as a restless wanderer always searching for a fugitive language? **Write** about some aspect of the mystery of words.

- It is the relationship between words and things that Brendan Kennelly explores in his poem 'The Big Words' (EK). He remembers his teacher asking him the meaning of 'transubstantiation'. What a whopper! It knocks his head off, and it rolls over to the mouse-hole where kids used:

  to drop
  Crumbs of bread

Turning to turds
Twice as transcendental
As holy words.

'Transubstantiation' is the Catholic doctrine of the 'true presence'. At the central moment of the Mass believers contend that the wine and water are turned (transubstantiated) miraculously into the real substance of God's flesh and blood. The poem is a protest against how fanciful words betray and falsify the real world of things. They transubstantiate them into jargon and cliché. In the hands of the wrong people, like teachers, such language belittles and blinds and emasculates both user and used. The poet assaults jargon and pretence and the vanity of 'whacking great vocabularies'. Think of an occasion when a word(s) invaded your life and started to bully you. **Try writing** about it. Think of what words do to the real world. Do they transubstantiate in their own way?

- Jargon users may hide behind their puffed-up syllables, but according to W. S. Graham so does a being of a very different species. In his poem 'The Beast in the Space' (EK), he imagines some great animal snorting and growling behind the words of his poem. Eventually it crosses over to the reader who has to look after the temperamental and threatening creature. **Write** a poem placating the beast behind the words or a letter of complaint to W. S. Graham for involving you, an innocent neighbour, in this bestial affair.

- The word 'affair' is a good image to describe a reader's relationship with a poem or any loose paragraph. Imagine having an affair with words or a word? **Write** a witty spin on this conceit.

Word-play and Word-hoards

- All real writers love words, relish and savour them. Natalie Goldberg surrenders to them: 'I have learned to go with words that call me, that have a shivering possibility,' she writes in *Wild Mind*. 'I submerge myself in the pond of darkness and let the electrical animals of thought pass by. If we are awake, the whole world is shimmering and giving us guidance... I have trained myself in one area: to be awake to words.'

Are you awake to words? Or do words waken you? Or do your words awaken the world around you? Goldberg makes some helpful suggestions along these lines. Bite into an apple and write down some strong words. Not 'hard', 'sour', 'sweet', 'sharp'. Wait for some concrete word to come: 'enamel', 'geyser', 'blood'. The idea is to go below the conventional and conditioned response to a deeper level of thinking beyond the discursive. Now combine the word 'apple' with one of these strong words, for example 'apple-blood'. Now you are moving towards comparisons and expressive figurative language. Try more combinations and agglomerations, and see where that leads you. From your many selections and unusual partnerships **forge** a vibrant piece of writing.

- For an exhibitionist verbal display read the extracts from Peter Reading's poems 'Stet' and 'Ukulele Music' (NP). The word 'stet' is taken from the world of printing and proof correction. When written in the margin of a manuscript beside a correction it means that the correction should be overridden and the original 'error' allowed to stand. Under this title Peter Reading has written about his childhood in a series of short verses of great verbal brio. The memories are without censoring and correction, and seem to arrive spontaneously on the page. Try the same form (short bursts of images) and **write** an unexpurgated account of early childhood.

- Sylvia Plath was much taken one day with the name 'Sassoon'. 'It has lots of seas of grass en masse and Persian moon alone in rococo lagoon of woodwind tune where passes the ebony monsoon...' This is a little flexing of the verbal muscles. Runs and riffs. **Try some rapid-fire writing**. Take a name and riff a few lines. Sustain the sound effects as long as you can.

- Goethe, the German poet, made lists of phrases that periodically flashed through his mind. He called them 'splinters'. During the slack times in your day encourage these flashes. Carry a small 'splinter' book with you for instant recording. Here are some 'splinters' that have struck me this week. 'Cramp of frost', 'smear of light', 'a swag of flesh hanging', 'ice grey, laminated slate', 'iris tubers from the garden like tusks', 'blood spots – petechiae', 'from above, the Dome's carapace squat at the end of the dock tongue', 'a woman on the radio says she forgives the murderer of her daughter. Why?', 'a rude jester', 'my Celia...my Celia...mice, miserly' and so on. After you have gathered enough 'splinters' examine what you've got. Turn them into fragments. Assemble the fragments into clusters and **shape these into writing miniatures**.

- By taking polysyllabic words like 'mycelium' (the hair-thread 'root' system of mushrooms and fungi) and freely perming the sounds and syllables, intriguing shapes begin to emerge. Try perming some selected polysyllables of your own and **work** the results into simple poems.

- Horticulturists identify plants by their Latin names. In among the loamy language of their ordinary conversation you'll suddenly come across such exotics as *rosacia convolvularis*. Try and get hold of a list of names for wild flowers, both the latinate and the native versions. Some are richly poetic and expressive. The natives include: 'procumbent pearlwort', 'sulphur cinqfoil', 'fumitory', 'alpine enchanter's nightshade', 'artic mouse ear', 'bur chervil', 'hemp agrimony' and plain 'common dodder'. I've taken this list from Roger Phillips's book *Wild Flowers of Great Britain*. With a bit of ingenuity and lateral thought, using this limited but distinctive vocabulary can yield fine poetic results. **Try writing** a piece based on this sparkling word hoard.

- Just as poetic are the local names for birds. Every region has a special name for the kestrel, for instance. Hopkins called it the 'windhover' in his poem of the same title. In other places it is known as the 'stone-yeller' or the 'wind-cuffer'. Think of some other pairings to describe this falcon. Now, take another bird and coin some new word-pairings for it. Let one idea lead to another till you have enough ingredients to **make a poem**.

- The Scottish poet Don Paterson has written: 'poetry's just a condition of being pathologically sensitive to the weight and texture of words.' Think of some words that have these qualities – weight and texture. Take the word 'rugged'. It's a heavyweight word. It has a particular 'signature' which you could describe like this: 'The opening R growls then deepens with the grunt of the guttural G's, and finally slams itself shut with the uncompromising D at the end.' Or take the word 'ripple'. Its signature might go like this: 'If you roll the opening R on your tongue it chirps, but by the time you hear its sudden wing beat it's gone, and the soft pluck of the P's echoes into the slow note of the dying L.' Choose some examples of your own and **write** a 'signature' for each word along the lines of the above showing how they have both 'weight' and 'texture'.

- It's one thing to know the meaning of a word, it's another to relish the sound and feel of words. To taste and feel them. They are physical. They gargle in the mouth. You can bite on them, gag on them. They hiss back, spit. They have a breathy odour. They are juicy, pulpy. They tattoo on the teeth, resonate, vent their steam, roll on the pitch and toss of the tongue. They sing and they beat out their riffs and endless runs, their sonorities and drum rolls, their pizzicatos and andantes. **Write** a piece that alternates/intersperses fast and slow rhythms, hard with soft-sounding passages.

- Tom Paulin, in his poem 'Sentence Sound' from his collection *The Wind Dog*, describes how as a teenager he was enthralled by the sound of language. Imagining he is entering the attic of the muse where poems are put together 'out of fricatives, labials and peachy vowels...', he says:

> ...the ear
> is the only true reader
> the only true writer...

In the attic, he finds all the traditional tools of the writer's trade, but not the one he is searching for – 'a single file'. From the waste-bin he eventually draws the 'raspy thing', now a worn tongue. He 'licked – no lisped – that smooth file/till it tasted like either hand of a stopped clock.' What a relish word is 'lisped', fricative and faintly plosive!

This poem is about language as a tool which can transform itself and become the object of its own making. One minute it's a file and the tongue itself; next, it's the hand of a clock. Read some of Paulin's title poem. Childhood memories crackle in every aurally-charged line. It is a poem that rejoices in the sounds of words, in the wheeze and bite, the slither and the carillon ring of syllables. Recalling a walk in deep snow he writes of 'the soft quoof/and near crump of it…as our breath spoofs/in the frore air'. This kind of language bypasses dictionaries and gives us more than the feel of things. Take an ordinary activity and **try writing** ear-appealingly, ear-achingly about it.

- When you come across a new word do you go to the dictionary and find out what it means? Do you go to an etymological dictionary and trace its origin? Are words your friends or your acquaintances? Not your enemies surely! **Write** about the unexpected hostility of words, their bloody-mindedness and their betrayals. **Write** about how they bully you, gang up on you, neglect and abandon you. Are they worth the trouble? Or **write** about your 'best-friend' words, those you can trust, who never let you down, and who are always there when needed.

- 'For a writer the language is everything and everything is in the language. Ideas follow language.' Gillian Clarke. At random I pick up a word from the newspaper, for example 'ellipse'. The dictionary tells me it derives from a Greek word meaning to 'come short'. It is a term from geometry, and enclosed in its chill diagrammatic embrace is the sound of lips and the trilling of the tongue. This idea spawns others in my head. Here they are: I wonder now what other harsh geometries have such a soft centre. There's the hard geometry of the skeletal anatomy and the soft enclosures of flesh and the upholstery of muscle. A phrase enters my head: 'the mathematician's daughter'. I don't know why, it just comes. The woman is young, perfectly formed. I see a Renaissance architectural etching, a view of an empty palazzo – all lines and marbled precision. There are axes and fulcra here. The messy computations of the heart balanced against the compassed prescriptions of the head. Are they so oppositional? Now I have the vectors of a poem or a story. Set your fox mind chasing after the hare language. Follow the word-tracks left in the snow and see what the chase throws up. From this material **write** a short piece. Expect the unexpected. GO.

- In his poem 'Ars Poetica' (The Art of Writing Poetry), a title borrowed from the first-century Roman poet Horace, John Heath-Stubbs says: 'A poem is built out of words', but reminds writers that words are not their property. They have been:

  tossed into the caps of beggars,
  and plonked
  On the reception-desks of brothels.

  The advice is to 'make language say/What it has not said before.' The poet must 'Work against language ... Engage in a bout with it.' In the wrestle with words he suggests the poet roll with the punches. One overcomes by not resisting. Heath-Stubbs goes on to warn that words must be cleaned up, polished and worn with style. **Write** your own Ars Poetica.

- Many specialised vocabularies exist. In technology, for instance, there's hackerese and computerese. Sciences, such as astrophysics and geology, have produced their own inventive and poetic cant which includes words like 'wormholes' and 'time-horizon', 'erratics' and 'cleavage fan'. The film industry has its 'gaffers' and 'best boys'. Marketing and business management has its nebulae of gaseous phraseology. Sport – mountain-climbing, skiing, boxing, racing – is riddled with its cult terms. Cooking can 'fricassee', 'drizzle' and 'roux' with the best of them. Collect some examples of these distinctive patois. Specialist dictionaries are treasure houses of exotic and engaging language.

They are like verbal menageries, every corner startles and delights. Using this sort of material, **collage** a poem. Or take a resonant phrase like 'the runaway universe' or words like 'tectonics' or 'air-heave' or 'toadstone' and use them as titles for poems.

- Raymond Carver writes that above his desk he had a postcard on which was a sentence fragment from a short story by Chekov: '... and suddenly everything became clear to him.' Its implications thrilled and amazed Carver. The simple clarity and the hint of revelation, the frisson of mystery. Next time a word or phrase sticks in your mind and won't go away, write it down. Think about it and use it as a title for **writing** a short story or poem

- Sweating at writing was the only way according to Plath. In her *Journals* she describes how one day she sees in the pewter belly of her teapot a silvered and distended world. She wants to discover that miraculous mirrored world. She wants 'to open Alice's door. Work and sweat to pry open the gates and speak out words and worlds.' **Write** a poem entitled *Alice's Door*.

- Try seeing ordinary objects in a new light. Imagine one seen through water, through the eyes of a drunk, reflected in mirrors, caught in firelight, enveloped by snow, fractured, in slow motion, trapped on video, seen from a bird's eye, half burnt, iced over, cubist deformed, bandaged, X-rayed and so on. **Write** about alternative views. Use the title *Through the Looking Glass*.

- Exercises like this may lead writers into being novel and bizarre each for its own sake. As Quiller-Couch points out, it is accuracy of word and thought, and sharpness of eye and ear that is the key. Read Gerard Manley Hopkins's poems 'Pied Beauty' (RB) and 'The Windhover' (RB), or Sylvia Plath's 'Mushrooms' (RB). All these poems delight in words and in their magical ability to make things seem 'realer than real'.

  But these poems are not simulacra. By that I mean they are not copies of the object. They are primarily words, 'verbal symbols', and create their own object, the art-object.

Never confuse words with the real thing! Try achieving the same density and sensuousness of expression that you find in Hopkins. His poems are hymns of praise inspired by his belief in the wondrousness of God's creation. Take a natural object or scene and **write** about it, combining accuracy of expression with a sense of the beauty of things. Try and avoid the conventional response so that you can create a freshened and dawn-new awareness.

- Michael Donaghy recalls some simple objects from his childhood as he attempts in his poem 'Caliban's Books' (EK) to conjure up memories of his father as Caliban, the Shakespearean character he played at school. The zigzag of memory takes him to fishing on Belfast Lough and to his father's schoolroom. Here the poet contemplates his father's books – *The Pocket Treasury of English Verse* and *30 Days to a More Powerful Vocabulary* – but, like the magician's apprentice illicitly trying out his master's spells, he finds himself transported way off course, and he lands, not in Belfast, but in Naples. It is the words: 'Fish stink, pitch stink, sea-spray...' that transport him to the Italian port. To his horror what emerges from below the decks of his anchored ship is something that 'knucklewalks across the dark piazza/sobbing, *maestro! maestro!*' In the poem the Prospero father with his magical books is dead, and some brute ape (the poet as Calibanesqe monster?) walks in his steps. Find some old possessions and zigzag through the memories they evoke. Write down the partner images/words they conjure up. **Conjure a piece of writing** out of this stuff.

- These lines are from 'A Sofa in the Forties' (EK), a poem by Seamus Heaney.

  > The sway of language and its furtherings
  > Swept and swayed in us like nets in water
  > Or the abstract, lonely curve of distant trains
  > as we entered history and ignorance.

  Here the poet recalls turning the family sofa into a train as part of a regular childhood game. The 'sway of language' refers to the language of the wireless, the lingo of cowboy serials, and the pronouncements of the news heard by the passengers and the ticket collectors on the make-believe railway. But what do these images of nets and curves say about the child and language? And why do the riding children enter 'history and ignorance'? In the final verse they pour through a tunnel:

> Like unlit carriages through fields at night,
> Our only job to sit, eyes straight ahead,
> And be transported and make engine noise.

Out of this memory Heaney is drawing out some larger ideas about language, the imagination and childhood. Think of the ways words came to you in your childhood. Were they just background noise? Were you an unlit carriage plunging through the night? When did you emerge from the tunnel? What eventually lit you up? **Write** about any aspect of this. Think about your own make-believe games. Any ideas from these?

- Words are multi-talented. Not only do they talk, they sing and dance. They get together and have a ball. For a rhythmic exhibition read Robert Southey's poem 'The Waters of Lodore' or Hilaire Belloc's 'Tarantella' (RB). For an extravaganza of sound effects read 'Cargoes' by John Masefield or 'Sir Beelzebub' by Edith Sitwell (20WP). But perhaps the best example of a poem that pulls out all the verbal stops, that modulates from lullaby to drum tattoo, from pizzicato to serenade, from the languid to the urgent, from tinkling syllables to gritty gutterals is W. H. Auden's 'Look Stranger'. Find a place – lakeside, tube-station, football match, seaside, swimming pool, computer terminal – and concentrate on the sounds there. **Write** a sound poem in response.

- Peter Reading again. In his poem 'Going On' (NP) he rattles off a long list of taboos or 'Time-honoured creeds' which disbelievers, 'unholy doubters' and antisocials of all kinds break or ignore. This is a wonderfully vigorous, spit-in-your-eye piece against all rule-makers and keepers of sacred cows. **Try writing** a similar swaggering, two-fingers-to-you piece roaring at pretence and pomposity, at petty lawgivers, stuffy custodians and political correctionists everywhere.

- In her autobiography *Once in a House on Fire*, Andrea Ashworth thinks she is being insulted when her Maths teacher tells her she is 'audacious'. But she's delighted to discover the dictionary approves of the word and says it's '*a*. daring, bold'. Her heart swells with pride at the 'heroic-sounding words'. She flicks to the letter 'I' and is impressed with 'impuissant, impugn, impudicity'. Look up a word you've been wondering about for days. Check out the neighbours. Run your finger down the page. You'll probably find a few exotics, a few limousine words, a few no-nonsense ones. Stick with two pages and use this lexical material to **write** a poem. The challenge is to be inventive. You can mate words (compound them), turn verbs into nouns, nouns into verbs, and sound-mix with so many sonorous syllables to hand. Abjure overalliteration absolutely.

- In his poem 'Birth' (EK), Paul Muldoon finds himself in 'scrubs' witnessing the birth of his daughter. Suddenly, in his imagination, the midwives take on archaic roles. They 'ply their shears' like the three sisterly Fates of Greek myth, and haul the baby into the world of:

  > apple blossoms and chanterelles and damsons
  >   and eel-spears
  > and foxes and the general hubbub
  > of inkies and jennets and Kickapoos with their lemniscs
  > or peekaboo-quiffs of Russian sable
  > and tallow-unctuous vernix...

  Here is a list of all the world's wonders in words, exotic and plain. Dorothy Aoife Korelitz Muldoon is born into the word-world, and after a 'quick rub-a-dub' is 'whisked off to the nursery'. **Whisk up a poem** full of the verbally off-beat and ordinary, the expressive and the effervescent. Check if your local library has a dialect dictionary for your county. Use some of the phrases or words from this word treasury. Think of some other 'treasuries' such as *Brewer's Concise Dictionary of Phrase and Fable* or Tony Thorne's *The Dictionary of Contemporary Slang* or *Cassell's Dictionary of Slang*. See also Bill Bryson's *Made in America*. Alternatively, borrow some words from the world of your grandparents or the world of science or from another language.

- Read W. N. Herbert's poem 'First Fit' (FPB) written in the language of Tayside and **try writing** your own dialect poem.

- In his essay about how he became a poet, called 'Feeling into Words', Seamus Heaney writes about composing his first poems. They were more than mere words, he realised. In them he 'felt he had let down a shaft into real life'. In childhood proverbs and playground chants he senses the founding moments of his poetic vocabulary and, in the writings of other poets, the echoes that were to resound in his adult writing. These echoing sounds he felt had flowed into him, and his first step as a writer was to imitate them. Gerard Manley Hopkins was thus a major 'influence'.

  His first poetry was all pastiche of the Victorian writer, but it was also the exercise yard where, through these 'trial-pieces', he learned his skills. By now Heaney says he was in love with words and getting a sense of their 'crafting', and he recalls how words, 'as bearers of history and mystery' in particular, began to appeal to him. He loved the verbal music of church litanies and the nightly catalogue of the BBC's weather forecasts for Britain's coastal areas. Can you **write** the history of your word-love, your logophilia?

- Heaney's language is rooted in the physical world. He was born a farmer's son and his writing reverberates with the daily experiences of rural life. Unlike writing in the English Romantic Tradition, which aspires towards the ethereal, Heaney's delves downwards into the brown turf and below into bog and the squelch of ditches and ponds, into the 'thick slobber' of frog-spawn and the slimy kingdom of the rat. He gives to words what the critic John Carey calls 'weight and texture'. Think of five hard and resistant objects, and five soft and giving objects. **Write** a poem about one, some or all or them using an appropriate language to describe each.

- Words have a physical presence, a materiality in themselves. They can hiss, sibilantly. They can be breathed and murmurous. They can growl gutturally, sneer nasally and lisp on the lips. One critic writing about the poetry of Basil Bunting says the reader experiences his poems 'much as one might any other bodily sensation. Certainly they ask to be fondled with the tongue, to feel the roughness of the consonants, taste the flavour of the vowels.' This is close to Heaney's requirement that poetry involves 'a conscious savouring of words...' **Try writing** an experimental piece that uses only sound words and echoisms. Use aspirants and labials and dentals and fricatives and exclamations. And make the writing flavoursome, grainy, full of taint and tang. The best way to feel your way towards expression like this is to taste good writing, rolling the lines round your tongue till you can recognise the vintage, the real bouquet.

- In her autobiography *Once in a House on Fire*, Andrea Ashworth writes about the 'feelings we got – velvety, spiky, watery, like fire – just from words'. Whenever she read poetry she could sense 'words gathering and buzzing inside me'. **Write** an account of how poetry affected you in the past and how it affects you now. For Andrea Ashmore, 'Lit-ter-atch-yoor' was a sanctuary. What has it been for you?

- Such is the potency of words for Andrea, she imagines letting them loose on her violent stepfather whenever he pokes her in the chest and tells her she is 'good for nothing'. They will have a 'beautiful sting', she says. **Write** a song of revenge using words that have a 'beautiful sting'.

- In one of Ashworth's English lessons the class is discussing Robert Frost's moving poem 'Out, Out – '. In a timber yard, a boy loses his hand to the spinning saw and he dies from the shock. It's heart-flutter writing. The boy holds up the hand with a 'rueful laugh'. What does 'rue' mean, asks Andrea's teacher? 'It is the ache you feel,' says Andrea, 'when you wish things could be re-wound, even though you *know* it's too late, to make it turn out differently.' The girl is thinking of the atmosphere at home, full of threat and fear, dangerous and wounding as a spinning blade. Has your reading mirrored real life like this? Have someone else's words expressed or revealed your true feelings for yourself? **Write** about the time when words fused with feeling.

- Words hurt. Insults bruise each time they are uttered. They lie beneath the skin throbbing dully. But words can also caress and kiss and smooth the troubled spirit. They can send shivers up your back. Read 'Out, Out – ' for back-shivering words. Think of a word that either bruises because of its personal associations or which caresses because of its intimate place in your life. **Write** a poem about it. A close and elderly relative of mine recently spent two months in a hospital convalescent ward. She hated its careless intrusions into privacies, its forced jollities, its smells and decrepitude. She refers to it now as 'That Place'. She can only talk about it in code. The phrase 'That Place' puts it beyond naming, the anonymity sanitises the experience, and eventually the memories will be expunged altogether. Lovely word – 'expunged'.

- There must be times when you wished you could rewind events and start again. It's always going to be different next time, we think. **Write** about something you rued and still rue.

No Words but in Things. The Language of Poetry

- Charles Tomlinson started writing poetry in the late forties when the rich rhetoric of Dylan Thomas dominated the poetic landscape. He rejected the thickened metaphors and dramatic verbal flourishes of Thomas. Instead, he went to William Carlos Williams for a more modest but truer 'voice'. He wanted to cut through the Freudian swamp of symbolism, avoid 'wrapping the whole thing up in rhetoric', and reach out for a clean-cut, unobtrusive language. **Write** a William Carlos Williams-like poem – unadorned, unobtrusive, but true to its subject.

- The French symbolist writer Stéphane Mallarmé wrote that the real function of the poet was to: 'purify the dialect of the tribe'. What do you think he means? Write some notes about this provocative remark. To the pragmatic English, the French are notorious for wanting to keep their language 'pure'. Borrowings from other languages, especially American-English, are regarded as contaminants by the Académie Française, the custodian of the tribal tongue. Words like 'picnic' and 'stop' and 'weekend' they want to ban. Can you ring-fence words? Isn't language a hybrid by definition? Why are the French really so protective? **Write** a stiff letter to the President of the Académie pointing out the stupidity of their protectionist policy.

• I like the great Samuel Johnson's magisterial riposte to the stuffier linguistic embalmers of his day: 'Academies have been instituted to guard the avenues of their languages, to retain fugitives, and to repulse intruders; but their vigilance and activity have hitherto been in vain; sounds are too volatile and subtle for legal restraints; to enchain syllables, and to lash the wind, are equally the undertakings of pride, unwilling to measure its desires by its strength.' This shapely utterance is from the Preface to his 1755 *Dictionary*, a monumental project and milestone in the development of the English language. Look up Ambrose Bierce's *Devil's Dictionary* for another eccentric lexicon. **Write** a one-page primer on hacker slang, the argot of the electronic freebooters. Or any other slang/cult lexicon.

• Alfred Gilder, who sits on the French government's Commission de Terminologie, has just published 'En Vrai Française and le texte', a list of 8000 unwanted anglicisms. It includes 'start-up', 'debriefing', 'brainstorming', 'bodybuilding', 'shopping', and Gilder wants to replace them with real French words. Like all languages, French is changing, and changing fast. But it's not government officials nor academicians that are responsible; it is the *banlieusards*, young out-of-work second-generation immigrants from desolate suburbs whose flexible approach to the language has produced a new variant on French called *verlan*, a once secret street code which is now filtering into all corners of French life. In *verlan*, the trick is to reverse any word to create a new vocabulary. So, *frère* (brother) becomes *reufré*, and *métro* (tube) becomes *trome*. Reversal is only one linguistic flick. In *verlan* the word for cigarette – a French word 'borrowed' by English – is *nuigrave*, a compression of the government warning on cigarette packages: 'Nuit gravement à la santé'. Using compression and reversal and repetition create a new vocabulary and use it to **write** a love poem.

- Edwin Morgan, a great experimenter and word-juggler, wrote a poem entitled 'The First Men on Mercury' (PBPBI). An expedition from earth meets a deputation of locals and in customary imperial fashion demands to be taken to their leader. In the conversation that follows the Earthlings acquire the language of the Mercurians, and vice-versa. In the exchange, there is a point where both sides speak a hybrid of each other's language, a compromise lingo before completing the swap. ' – Stretterworra gawl, gawl...' says the Earthling at the end. 'Of course', is the Mercurian reply, 'but nothing is ever the same,/now is it? You'll remember Mercury.' What is the poem saying about language if anything? **Write** the Mercurian report on the incident explaining the significance of this unusual planetary encounter.

- Each writer has a distinctive vocabulary, a characteristic ring to their word treasure. Seamus Heaney's has risen out of the muddiness and dark bog-depth of his native Irish rural upbringing. He was always interested in wells and sluices and troughs and butts and ditches. Someone from a flat and dry landscape might have a very different interest and selection of words. Have the landscape and the contours of your upbringing led to a characteristic vocabulary and way with words? Maybe you've chosen a particular language voice already. **Write** about this aspect of your language.

- The American writer William Carlos Williams was very clear about what constituted a desirable language for poetry. In his poem 'Raleigh Was Right' (RB) his message is blunt. The language of the past will not do in this modern age. Writing about the loveliness of the wild violet suited a rural past when country people had 'flowering minds'. The unforced language we need now is evident in his first verse:

What can the small violet tell us
that grow on furry stems in
that long grass among lance shaped leaves?

Nothing fanciful here. No words like the fine Victorian sentiment of a word like 'loveliness'. For Williams, writing in the 1920s and 30s in New Jersey, the voice of poetry is the language of ordinary speech and the stockyards of the city's industrial heartland. Williams rejected the rhetoric of the past. He favoured a language that came *from* the world, not one that imposed itself *on* the world. Poetry was not the place to be confessional and inward and subjective; was not a trumpet for truth and morality and the 'big' themes; was not an aesthetic object existing outside reality. It was a nest of words drawing its authenticity and rationale from *things*. 'There's no idea but in things', was Williams' precept.

Thus, the effect of his poems depends upon the slow unveiling of the object as each brief line succeeds the previous. Read these three poems: 'The Red Wheelbarrow', 'I Have Eaten' and 'Poem'. **Write** a 'thin' poem of your own using the same structure as 'The Red Wheelbarrow' or 'Poem'. This latter piece is about a cat and brilliantly captures the movement of the animal. How does it do this? **Write** a similar shaped poem about an animal.

- For a very different attitude to poetic language read 'The Names of the Hare' (RB) translated by Seamus Heaney from a Middle English poem. This is a farrago of words, inventive and exuberant where Williams is spare and tight. Naming brings things into being, and this poem calls up the hare in all its flamboyance and mystery. Many of the terms are compounds, like honorific titles. **Try writing** a similar flurry of words to describe an animal, using your imagination to create exhilarating compounds and a muscular idiom.

- Words are promiscuous. On the one hand, they have a respectable public face and are partners for life to objects in the world; the word 'cat' sticks faithfully with the real ginger through thick and thin. The word 'cat' *denotes* the real thing, the real Macavity. On the other hand, words form secret and dangerous liaisons once they get together. They have *connotations*! Each connects with others suggestively. 'Rose' suggests blood, sexual love, beauty, fragility, the England rugby team, my old Aunt Rosie and so on. It is this rich night-life of words that gives writing its texture and complexity of meanings.

Take G. M. Hopkins's poem 'Spring' (RB). 'What is all this juice and all this joy?' asks the poet seeing the bloom and blush of pear-tree leaves, and gives an immediate answer: 'A strain of the earth's sweet being in the beginning/In Eden garden.' The word 'strain' is multivalent here connecting ideas and images surfaced and sunken in the rest of the poem. It relates to the word 'juice' in the previous line and hints at wine-making as if the primal world is being sieved and purified in each new spring. It means *kind* or *variety* as in a 'strain' of apple and, in combination with the phrases 'sweet being' and 'Eden garden', returns us to the fecundity of paradise, and then reminds us of the persistence of genetic character. It means exerting, straining to break free of hindrance, and is, therefore, emblematic of the budding and bursting of spring energies. So Genesis and genetics are intimated in one word, and give rise to a progeny of meanings.

These various denotations form the surface contours of the poem, the intricacies of cross-referencing words, but they also interconnect below the surface like latticing mycelia, to construct the more diffuse and mysterious world of connoted meaning. Words then come with various aliases and ambiguities, and good writers exploit this fluidity. **Collect some poems** and separate the denoted from the connoted in some of your examples. Try and detect some of the verbal threads that the poets have woven into the texture of the poem.

- 'The Hook' (NP) is a poem by Duncan Bush. The poet describes a knife as a scimitar but the owner, an 'old man', corrects him and calls it a 'hook'. In a succession of short verses the tool is described in all its hookness, its functional harshness and pitiless edge. Scimitars are emblematic, hooks are real. Hooks are implements. In the second part, the poet addresses another 'beautiful' word – 'swathe'. The gutturals and the dentals of the first part give way to the soft sibilants, the labials and fricatives of the second. You can hear these sounds in the phrase: 'tall, green, slender seeded grasses'. Here the musical descent at the end of the phrase echoes the slow fall of the stems under the knife. The two successive monosyllables – 'tall, green' – hold the line back and accentuate thereby the slide into the smoothness of 'slender seeded'. The phrases: 'their stems fell sheaved' and 'like armfuls of bluebells' are musical, and slo-mo the action into something approaching the elegiac.

No wonder the line: 'the blade was wet with sap', startles with the suddenness of a slap after the relaxing liquid sounds of the previous lines. **Write** about an object or activity so that you interleave the soft with the unforgiving, the chilled with the warm, the fast with the slow, the accelerating with the braking, the impeded with the free-running. Cutting fruit, scrubbing skin, sawing wood, climbing a rockface, making jam, ploughing, cars crashing, playing music are a few topics that suggest possibilities for rhythmic and aural variation.

Mugging the Queen's English – Argots, Slangs, Cant and Codes

• In a sense anyone who writes on behalf of the dispossessed gives the silenced a voice. Consider writers who have spoken for ethnic minorities. Read Frantz Fanon, Linton Kwesi Johnson, James Berry, John Agard, Benjamin Zephaniah, Fred d'Aguir, Merle Collins, Grace Nicholls. All these writers champion their own language as the measure of their ethnic and racial identity. Read John Agard's poem 'Listen Mr Oxford Don' (PBPBI) where the poet refuses to comply with linguistic prescription, and acknowledges that 'mugging the Queen's English/is the story of my life'. In the poem Agard imagines himself as a fugitive from justice, a 'man on the run' for doing-in donnish English, the custodial voice of the BBC and the Establishment. Choose an alternative dialect to 'educated' English. It might be a 'street' language, a regional dialect, a youth cult variant, school slang, cyber jargon. **Write** a protest song/poem in one of these 'languages'.

• Some people think that dialect is a dying artefact; a curiosity much like a museum exhibit. It bears no relation to the business of modern communication. **Write** a letter to the local newspaper pointing out the value of dialects. Focus on a few selected examples to show why it is necessary to preserve their usage. You can try the 'heritage' argument, but there may be stronger arguments elsewhere.

• Louise Erdrich, the American novelist and poet, has written: 'there is an inalienable bond between what you express and who you are ... self and language are so much the same.' How has your writing established and sustained self? What difference would it make if you ceased to write? Imagine you have a sceptical friend for whom all this talk of writing and the self is mere narcissism. To them writing is a public act, and should be about entertaining the reader not about running a self-help course in behavioural correction. **Write** a letter to your friend demonstrating the truth of Louise Erdrich's assertion about words and self, and repudiating these comments about narcissism and therapy. Draw evidence from your own writing showing how language has helped shape and make you the person you are.

• In his group of poems printed under the title *School of Eloquence*, Tony Harrison explores the connections between language and self, between words and self-respect. At school his flat northern accents were regarded by one teacher, T.W., as barbarous, and he was encouraged to adopt RP, received pronunciation. His mouth 'stuffed with glottals', he was forced to 'E-nun-ci-ate' and say $\wedge$s not UZ. Eventually he rebelled. With real language he decided to occupy 'your lousy leasehold Poetry'. 'I chewed up Litter-erchewer', he says defiantly going all native, and 'used my *name* and own voice.' Finally, he asserts: 'RIP RP, RIP T.W./ I'm *Tony Harrison* no longer you'. The reassertion of his native Yorkshire tongue was an assertion of self. Out went Anthony, in came Tony. See 'Them & [UZ]' (PBPBI). Has language been a site of conflict and rebellion for you? If so **write** about the experience.

- Demotic speech, the language of the people as opposed to the language of the academies, has always had a reputation for being the vigorous root of language. It has a mongrel tenacity and vigour when compared to the aesthetic lexicon of 'literary discourse'. This latter phrase is the sort of posh phrasing that passes for educated expression!

  Renewal of the poetic language has been the periodic ambition of writers for centuries; Sidney's *Defence of Poetry* and Wordsworth and Coleridge's *Lyrical Ballads* being the most celebrated attempts at revitalising effete language. In the introduction to their ballads the two Romantic poets aimed to return to the common language of men. But there is not just one single common language in English. There are many Englishes, such as Standard English, Scottish English, Yorkshire English, Caribbean English, et cetera, and against the dominance of Standard English the other 'dialects' protest at times. See John Agard's poem above.

  Take Caribbean English. It has localised variants – Barbadian, Jamaican, and so on. It exists alongside Standard English and is primarily oral. Or was. Its volatility and vitality and closeness to ordinary folk and life make it an attractive medium for writers wishing to assert their own identity free of the subject status and imperial governance embodied in the use of the Queen's English. 'The Third World as a whole,' writes the Caribbean poet Edward Braithwaite, 'is acutely concerned with language. We regard words, word play, word power as an essential part of our personality.' Thus writers in Jamaica and in Britain, dub poets for instance, have chosen not to write in the English of the elite, the governing and the educated classes, but in Jamaican creole, a primarily oral language but which now, through the pen, is establishing itself in written form and coming out from under the shadow of English and

American English. If you belong to the black community in Britain write in your local patois or **write** a dub poem. Read some of Benjamin Zephaniah's work for inspiration.

- Anita Desai, the Indian novelist, has written about the problem of being caught between two languages, her native Indian and English, the lingua franca of empire. She studied the European literary tradition and read Dickens, Tolstoy, Proust, et cetera. This literate language had little to do with the life she led, and she tried in her writing 'to bend the English language, to bring in the tempos and rhythms of the spoken languages around me'. Desai acknowledges that though English is a very flexible instrument much of Indian life eludes its grasp.

  This problem of inadequacy is also a familiar one for Tom Leonard, a Scottish writer who is very interested in the sound of the Scottish language and its spoken character. He is also very aware of the politics of language. In a poem from 'Unrelated Incidents' (PBPBI), he challenges the prerogative of received pronunciation, RP, to voice BBC news. **Write** a dialect piece designed for performance. Choose a lofty subject or public occasion so that you maximise the gap between form and content, and create satiric or comic effects.

- The prefix Fitz- derives from Norman French and means 'bastard son of'. Centuries after the Norman Conquest Fitz-this and Fitz-that families are respectable. In the same way slang terms become respectable and enter the broad church of the English language. Typical social climbers are words like 'clever', 'fun', 'sham', 'banter', 'mob', 'stingy', 'bully', 'junkie' and 'jazz' – all once disreputable slang. Create your own slang-lang for a Clockwork-Orange world and use it to **write** the opening of a short story.

- Inventing an argot is not an uncommon practice for writers. Russell Hoban, in his novel *Riddley Walker*, created a post-nuclear hybrid of fractured and poetically degenerated English. Other writers have done the same for the chemical generation. Irving Welsh's *Ecstasy* and some of his short stories in *The Acid House* and Geoff Dyer's *Paris Trance* are recent examples. Even more topical is *Boxy an Star* by Daren King. The language here is derived from drug culture. Read some of these novels and from your knowledge of youth culture, the club scene, and the E generation **write** a 'chemical' story involving two teenagers, one experienced, the other innocent or stupid.

- Roger McGough's poem 'The Jogger's Song' is based on a true incident reported in the *Evening Sentinel*. Here he turns the clichés and self-serving platitudes of male aggression against the rapist narrator who has attacked a young woman when she appealed for his help after she had been raped by two men already. The poet demonstrates the place misogynistic language plays in the perpetration of violence against women. Working with a partner, make a list of phrases and words that demean women or racial minorities. 'The Jogger's Song' (note the ironic attribute – 'Song') starts off with the line: 'Well, she was asking for it'. Heard that before! Start with this notorious phrase and add as many others as you can. Use your material to **write** a poem or short radio script or performance piece. You could use a newspaper item as the occasion for your piece of writing.

- Scene: coffee bar. A young woman sits at a table already occupied by X. Neither has met before. X is suffering from hagiophrasis, a rare psycho-neurotic condition in which the subject is unable to censor his thoughts. Whenever he speaks he says what he thinks. A listens more to herself than to others and can talk the hind leg off a donkey. She suffers from a condition known as periphrasis! **Write** the scene between the young man and woman in the café.

- Most words are long-lived, though they do change personalities over time. If you want to get better acquainted with words, it's worth studying their individual histories or etymologies. Use an etymological dictionary and track down the meanings of some. Try an ideological dictionary like Jane Mills's *Womanwords* and look up 'gossip', 'bird', 'girl/girlie', 'pornography', 'woman', 'spinster', 'nice', 'lady', 'pin-money', 'blue-stocking'.

This exercise will convince you, if you needed convincing, that words are ideologically coloured and a product of their times. The history of our words is indeed the cultural history of our nation. Look up the word 'apple' in as many different types of dictionary as you can find in the library, including Brewer's *Dictionary of Phrase and Fable*. From your findings **write** a portrait of 'apple', a sort of verbal still life. You can, of course, do this 'portraiture' for any number of words.

- There are many examples of invented languages. They range from the internationalist Esperanto to 'argy-bargy', a kid's secret code engagingly depicted in Keith Waterhouse's novel *There Is a Happy Land*. Did you use/devise the equivalent of 'argy-bargy' as a child? If you did, try using the language in an imaginative adult way to **write** about some aspect of childhood. It would be interesting, for example, to write about an adult topic in the play language of children for the ironic discomforts it would produce.

- 'Nobodaddy' was William Blake's coinage to describe the misconceived view of God as an aloof patron. It is a compression of the words 'daddy' and 'nobody'. Tom Paulin uses 'fortogiveness' in one of his poems. Try experimenting with compressions and mergers and **write** a short poem. Other examples of such techniques can be found in Lewis Carroll's 'Jabberwocky' and in e. e. cummings's 'flotsam and jetsam' and 'Buffalo Bill's'.

- A distinctive feature of Scandinavian and Anglo-Saxon poetry was the kenning; simple metaphoric expressions to give descriptive colour to the narrative. 'The swan's road' or 'whale's way' = the sea; 'battle-light' = flashing sword. **Try writing** a poem using simple kennings

- In her letter writing, Sara Coleridge, the wife of the poet, devised her own language which she called 'Lingo Grande'. The poet Liz Cashdan was so struck by this private code that she used it in a poem as the 'voice' of Sara herself complaining about the way her husband neglected her:

Oh, Esteesis, he's my thumper, my undoer
my cutter-up, full of the detesty of opium.
It has snatcherumped our love...

Invent your own secret language. In the safety of this
code **write** to your best friend revealing secrets you've
told no one else.

- Imagine a child writing a diary in simple code. It's a mix of
  Standard English and invented words. It has to be because
  the text must be reasonably accessible to the reader! **Write**
  some of the entries. One wants to ask why the child has
  chosen to disguise her thoughts in this way. Does this
  innocent game mask hidden motives? Are they hinted at
  in the entries you are inventing?

References

Ashworth, A., *Once in a House on Fire* (Picador, 1998).
Auden, W. H., *Selected Poems* (Faber and Faber, 1979).
Bierce, A., *The Devil's Dictionary* (Wordsworth, 1996).
Bryson, B., *Made in America* (Black Swan, 1998).
Carroll, L., *Selected Poems* (Fyfield, 1995).
Carver, R., *A New Path to the Waterfall* (Collins, 1990).
Cashdan, L., in *Delighting the Heart*, ed. S. Sellers (The Women's
  Press, 1989).
Coleridge, S. T. and Wordsworth, W., *Lyrical Ballads* (Penguin, 1999).
Duffy, C.A., *Selling Manhattan* (Anvil, 1987).
Dyer, G., *Paris Trance* (Abacus, 1998).
cummings, e.e., *Selected Poems 1923–1958* (Faber and Faber, 1969).
Goldberg, N., *Wild Mind* (Rider, 1991).
Graves, R., *Selected Poems* (Penguin, 1992).
Green, J., *Cassell's Dictionary of Slang* (Cassell, 2000).
Harrison, T., *Selected Poems* (Penguin, 1985).
Heaney, S., *The Government of the Tongue* (Faber and Faber, 1989).
Heath-Stubbs, J., *Collected Poems* (Carcanet, 1988).
Hoban, R., *Riddley Walker* (Picador, 1992).
Hughes, T., *Tales from Ovid* (Faber and Faber, 1997).
King, D., *Boxy an Star* (Abacus, 1999).

Kirkpatrick, B. (ed.), *Brewer's Dictionary of Phrase and Fable* (Cassell, 1995).

Levi, P., *The Drowned and the Saved* (Abacus, 1989).

Masefield, J., *Selected Poems* (Fyfield, 1984).

McGough, R., *Selected Poems 1967–1987* (Cape, 1989).

Mills, J., *Womanwords* (Virago, 1991).

Orwell, G., *Collected Essays and Journalism*, Vol. 4 (Penguin, 1970).

Paulin, T., *The Wind Dog* (Faber and Faber, 1999).

Phillips, R., *The Wild Flowers of Great Britain* (Pan, 1977).

Pinker, S., *The Language Instinct* (Penguin, 1995).

Plath, S., *Journals* (Ballantine, 1982).

Poe, E. A., *Selected Tales* (Penguin, 1994, 1981).

Quiller-Couch, A., *The Art of Writing* (Fowey, 1995).

Sidney, P., *Defence of Poetry* (Oxford UP, 1971).

Southey, R., *Poems* (Woodstock, 1997).

Thorne, T., *The Dictionary of Contemporary Slang* (Bloomsbury, 1999).

Waterhouse, K., *There Is a Happy Land* (Sceptre, 1992).

Welsh, I., *The Acid House* (Vintage, 1995).

Williams, Carlos W., *Selected Poems* (Penguin, 1976).

Zephaniah, B., *Face* (Bloomsbury, 1999).

SECTION 3
THIS WRITING ART

7 | Beginnings

Standing on Giants' Shoulders

- Behind a writer's personal ambition lies a larger obligation to the republic of letters. I like to think the past has handed on a baton to all writers, new and old. For the sake of Shakespeare and Dickens, we need to write as well as we can and insist on our best. We owe it to those guys. They began what we continue. We owe it because they have given us the templates and set the sights for us. You want to write a sonnet? Thank Shakespeare and Milton and Wordsworth because they were the trail-blazers. You want to write ballads? Then honour the unknown Scottish balladeers of the fifteenth century and Coleridge and Tennyson and Charles Causley. You want to write science fiction? Then thank pioneers like H. G. Wells and Zamyatin or acknowledge Huxley and Orwell because it is their prophetic visions that showed us where to start writing fantasy. Thank Hopkins and Dylan Thomas for showing us the intense colouring of words. Thank Carlos Williams, Zen haikuists and Ezra Pound for distilling the image, and Eliot for our modernist sensibility. Above all, thank Chaucer for settling us into that rich sorcery of French and Anglo-Saxon that has sustained the written language for 500 years. And above that again, thank William Tyndale and others for the Authorised Version of the Bible, and Thomas Cramner for the Book of Common Prayer that grafted plain speech with high-mindedness and set the standard of English prose style for centuries. Thank Bunyan for his plain fare and Shakespeare for his prodigality; Dickens and the nineteenth-century novelists for their range and radical passion, Hardy for his gloomy destinies, Joyce for making us conscious of consciousness and for turning over the inexhaustible tilth of language, and Woolf too and Darwin and Freud and ... and ...

From an anthology of English verse select any form – ballad, sonnet, lyric, elegy – and **try writing** a pastiche. Select a modern subject but try writing in the style of the time. The rationale for this kind of historical reconstruction is that it develops a sense of verse technique. The strictures of form push the writer into rebelling against it and force ingenuity. So avoid slavish copying, and try to reshape the form in small but significant ways.

Here are some possibilities:

1 Read the first few pages of Edgar Allan Poe's tale *The Fall of the House of Usher*. **Write** a description of a location – castle, abbey ruin, gloomy forest, remote monastery – in typical 'gothic' style. It's worth reading some of Angela Carter's stories in *The Bloody Chamber*. She reconstitutes folk material and gives the old tales a luscious gothic make-over.

2 Carol Ann Duffy continues the modernising approach in her collection *The World's Wife*. She takes famous men's wives and, speaking in their voices, gives the woman's side of the story. Mrs Faust, for instance, adopts a casual contemporary idiom and confessional tone for her monologue. You can imagine Duffy's Euridyce, fag hanging from the corner of her mouth, skirt hitched up, sitting on a bar stool telling her life story at a girls' night out. Choose a historical celeb wife and **write** her version of the story. Select a style that fits the character you are creating and write for performance. Think of pausing, timing, pacing the piece, and be aware of the voice as your medium.

3 Read any poem from A. E. Houseman's collection *The Shropshire Lad*, such as 'The Welsh Marches' or 'Bredon Hill', and **write** three or four rhyming verses on the rural idyll.

4 Read Tennyson's lyric 'Song' with its celebrated opening line: 'Now sleeps the crimson petal, now the white.' Each verse hangs by a similar verbal thread in its first line. Use the same device of repetition to help structure a song about solitude. Choose a suitable setting for this poem.

5 Read the opening pages of Virginia Woolf's novel *The Waves*. Use the same approach, but imagine your characters as four passengers sitting in a tube train. **Write** four pages.

- In some areas of contemporary culture great emphasis is placed on originality. Distinction lies in difference. There's a certain irony here, given our fondness for facsimile, our preoccupation with disneyfied, window-dressed versions of the past, and technology's infinite capacity for replication. Some writing shares this progressive tendency. The past is old hat. The present is the future. Everyone is looking for new voices on the block. Breaking with the past, purring new-style prose for the catwalk is a good marketing posture, but innovation has to be radical not faddish.

  William Gibson's cyber-punk fiction broke new ground in popular literature, but, if its style and vision matched new electronic realities, the story lived by the same narrative urgencies as always. Suspense, moral uncertainties, self-seeking and retributions still characterised the plot. Old emperor, new clothes ... again! **Write** the beginning of a 'virtual reality' novel. To the new cyber generation – cyber-surfers – writing is itself a cultural redundancy, and this task is typical of regressive tendencies. Ignore such barbarian attitudes and write the opening paragraphs.

- All writers have an ambivalent and wary attitude to past writings. No one wants to write like Shelley or mimic Thomas Gray's *Elegy in a Country Churchyard*, though in the chintzy verse of some home magazines echoes of tolling bells and lowing herds still faintly sound o'er the lengthening column inches. On the other hand, the literary achievement of the past casts a diminishing shadow across our own attempts. Leaving the past is like leaving home for the first time. You have to break with family and make your own way, but it is a wrench. Most writers start by modelling their work on the masters of the craft. Raymond Carver admired the Russian writer Anton Chekhov whose work was a model for his own short stories. Wilfrid Owen's early work, sub-romantic lyrics, was heavily influenced by John Keats.

What writer has most influenced your work? Exactly what techniques have you learnt? Have you developed a vision, a way of looking at the world as a result of your reading? Maybe you have admired but not imitated. **Write** a short letter to your 'mentor' saying what you have liked about their work and what you have learnt and put into practice in your own writing.

• Writers look to the past for a start, but in the course of their writing life go their own way. Some are more innovative than others. The poet and critic A. Alvarez has pointed out that Sylvia Plath was one writer who found the old forms no longer adequate for what she wanted to say. It wasn't that she wanted to experiment technically, but that making it new was the only way to explore her own inner world – to go 'down into the cellars and confront her demons' as Alvarez puts it. Other writers have sought new ways of expression. After the great modernist shifts of Woolf and Joyce and D. H. Lawrence, after the surrealist experimenters of the 20s and 30s, came the Beats of the 50s.

One of the central figures of the Beat Movement, Alan Ginsberg, shook more than the San Francisco scene when he performed his stinging, vibrant, vatic poem 'Howl' in 1954. In their work Ginsberg, Lawrence Ferlinghetti, Gregory Corso, Jack Kerouac and William Burroughs all sought belief and value in a post-war world they considered mean-ingless, self-interested and banal. Ginsberg was particularly influenced by the poetry of William Blake and the idea of the visionary and the irrational element in life. So celebrat-ing, reaching beyond the mundane, liberating the spirit through the incantatory and affirmative power of poetry for instance, became the essence of the Beat experience.

Ginsberg's writing developed an incandescent style that caught up the audience and worked them into excitement or anger. Powerful verbal energies and fierce convictions drive through his writing, and make readers begin to sense a vibrant other world beyond the immediate and the diurnal. Read any of the following celebrated poems: 'Kaddish', 'Howl', 'Sun Flower Sutra'. **Try writing** a sutra of your own modelled on Ginsberg's poem, for example *A Sunset Sutra, A Sutra for a Stormy Night, A Shipwreck Sutra, A Sunset-Strip Sutra, A Rain Sutra*. And so on.

- Most artists, writers included, see the past as a vast junk shop littered with goodies to be borrowed at will. Indeed contemporary theorists see this borrowing as an unavoidable consequence of language and as a legitimate compositional strategy. Recycling material has become an accepted modernist and post-modernist narrative procedure. T. S. Eliot's seminal work *The Waste Land* reconstitutes literary fragments from world literature. In itself, this fracturing is something of a metaphor for the fragmentation of the old humanist coherence. In the stunned world that succeeded the trench slaughter of the First World War, things indeed had fallen apart as Yeats said, looking across the emptied no man's land of decades. **Write** a piece that 'borrows' material from past literatures and put together a verbal collage, cutting and pasting from the past. Take a grand apocalyptic view of humanity in the twentieth century. The tradition is generous; it will readily yield treasure. Read any anthology of English verse or prose. Go to your own private haul of books and cull without compunction.

- Imagine standing on a cliff top looking across the vast plains of past centuries. What you can see is the intriguing geography and landscape of literature. Imagine climbing down and travelling into the undergrowth. You follow the paths and discover ruins – abandoned workings, luxuriant plants, exotic animals, bizarre lifeforms, prophets, wanderers and minstrels. **Write** about your trek through the kingdom of writing.

- A piece of writing that is made up of quotes from other writers is called a *cento*. An example is Tom Paulin's poem 'The Wind Dog'. This work is not so much a patchwork – *cento* means a garment made up of patches – as a series of echoes, and a great deal of original material too. **Write** your own cento about your locality, your patch! Your patchwork of 'borrowings' could include street names, billboard blurb, shop names, quotes from local newspapers, local sayings, overheards, family sayings and so on. Topics for centos are endless.

- *The Oxford Book of English Verse* contains approximately 35,000 lines of poetry. Borrow phrases at random and compose and recompose into a coherent piece. This is a game to play with a partner. **A** selects words and whole lines for **B**, and vice versa. Out of the instances **shape** a composite poem modifying tenses and endings, adding connector words as you see fit.

- Max Brod, companion and confidante of Franz Kafka, the early twentieth-century Czech writer, published his friend's diaries. They are full of chance phrases, passages of wild speculation, strange fantasised images, fragments of ideas, hard nuggets of information, prosaic details. Take any page in *Kafka's Diaries* and, from its bric-à-brac of words and images, **create** an assemblage. The entries may tempt you into interesting verbal exploits of your own. Follow your whim, take a few alleyways, be prepared to be startled.

Style – Dressing up for the Occasion

- 'Words somehow arrive', says the Scottish poet Robert Crawford. 'A phrase sticks in your head and others accrete round it.' Iron filings to the magnet. Have any words 'arrived' in your head recently? Has a 'magnet phrase' been richocheting round there? Write it down.

  Sit still. Wait. You're in a hide. Alert. Watching for the appearance of a rare animal. It will come, suddenly, out of the darkness. It does. There it is – timid, hesitant, suspicious. Wait. Others will come. Be patient. Bit by bit the words are gathering, nudging and nosing each other into place. You have to time your intervention and begin to shape them and shuffle them without stampeding the lot into rhetorics. The poem is coming into close-up. Look at it suspiciously. Be on your guard. You don't want to frighten the thing off. **Noose** it gently. Calm it down. Tether it, but let its wild heart beat.

- 'Style is the dress of thought,' wrote the Reverend Samuel Wesley in 1700. He added that it should be a 'modest dress, neat but not gaudy'. What austere puritan attitudes this definition reveals – a worthy man does not draw attention to himself, for unobtrusive virtue earns its own reward in a more lasting kingdom. But the dress image is instructive. It has the disadvantage of suggesting style in writing is a surface effect, something you deliberately put on for public show. True style is more than skin-deep; it comes from the core; it is inherent and integral to the subject. But the metaphor can be usefully extended. Just as dress accommodates occasion – dressing up for one, down for another – so style is adjusted to suit context and purpose in writing.

In August 1945, weeks after an atom bomb had devastated the city and killed upwards of 50,000 inhabitants, the American journalist John Hersey visited Hiroshima. He had been commissioned by the *New Yorker* magazine to write an article about the effects of a nuclear attack on the civilian population. His article/book *Hiroshima* is written in an unobtrusive, low-key style. The events he witnessed and the evidence he gathered from survivors was so horrific he would have been forgiven had he written in a graphic and even lurid fashion. But he chose an undemonstrative, modest style. Why? Because understating horror can bring out its true nature more effectively; the prosaic casts an unrelenting eye. Writing that screams, loses respect. It looks like it's playing to the gallery. It is the quiet accumulation of simple but telling detail that gives *Hiroshima* its chilling taste.

However, the lethal and forensic calm of the prose style serves other purposes. First, the calmness gives the voice authority and therefore lends authenticity to the account. There's no frenzy and hysteria here – just a persuasive dignity in the expression. Second, this simple dignity of language is culturally appropriate because it exemplifies and honours the quiet dutifulness and acceptance of fate that is a part of the Japanese character. Read some of Hersey's book. If you have witnessed any distressing scene: a car accident, a brawl, a storm, **try writing** an eyewitness account in a subdued and matter-of-fact tone and style.

• Other subject matter may demand a richer, more charged language. Read Cormac McCarthy's *All the Pretty Horses* for high-octane expression. This is the epic style suited and suitable for large canvases and grand themes. McCarthy is writing about the American West, the vast aridities of desert, the horizon-stretch of lightning storms, the throttling heats of gulches and arroyos, the careless brutalities of frontier life. The metaphoric intensity and rhythmic sweeps of his prose create his mythic landscape which contrives to be both real and supra-real. Read some of McCarthy's work. Recall some landscapes/seascape that for you suggest immensity and intensity. **Try writing** in the epic style. Try and be accurate in your observation. Wagnerian verbal flourishes do not necessarily make for a compelling grand style. Paint the picture, not the picturesque. Choose a subject suitable for your style.

• Plain-speak style has its critics. The American novelist Lynn Schwartz has taken issue with those writers she calls 'minimalists'. 'They have ennui and despair...they refuse to allow the richness of life...they are passive and victimised...life just keeps hitting them over the head...' Uhhm! She claims that such utilitarian writing is a male thing, an avoidance of 'the emotional and the existential'. 'Minimalist books,' she asserts, 'are a kind of escape from actually living...' Do you agree with this diagnosis?

Michael Crichton, whose thrillers of international espionage and adventure have sold 100 million copies worldwide, has a simple policy on style. From the beginning of his career he admits to being 'anti-literary' in his writing. He wanted a style: 'shorn of all ordinary fictional devices ...and devoid of all stylistic procedures'. He wanted an invisible style that drew no attention to itself, and suggested the factual not the fictive. Imagine you are starting your latest novel. You want to give the work a sense of *actualité* and *factualité*; a documentary-like authenticity. Using a spare, colourless style **write** the first three pages.

- George Orwell, the great proponent of plain English, thought style should be as transparent as a pane of glass. In other words the best style is unobtrusive and does not impede a clear view of the subject. But style doesn't have to be so retiring. You can turn it on, strut your stuff. Read some of Tom Wolfe's New Journalism writing from his collections *The Electric Kool-aid Acid Test* or *The Kandy-kolored Tangerine-flake Stream-line Baby*. Here is motor-mouth writing; rapid-fire and exhilarating. Try some for yourself. Imagine you visit an indoor sports event (karate practice session, basketball game, stepdance hour) or a speciality club meeting (pony-club meet, triathlon competition, fell-walk race) and **write** a Tom Wolfe-style fast-track commentary on the scene.

- Wilfred is the dutiful and cloddish writer in Stevie Smith's epistolary poem 'The Jungle Husband' (20WP). Write a poem in the same mould. Possible titles might include: *A Plumber Husband* or *An Office Husband* or *A Politician Husband* or *An Accountant Husband*, or *A DIY Husband*. And so on.

- A bus queue waits. When the bus arrives there's a rush and a man has a button torn off his coat. This is the simple scenario with which Raymond Queneau, the French experimental writer, begins his book *Exercises in Style*. He offers over a hundred versions of this one incident, each presented in a different style. There is the verbless account, the parenthesis account, the adjectival account. There are accounts in the style of the blurb, the recipe, the military despatch, the office memo, the legal document. There are erotic versions of the bus-stop episode, slang versions, biblical versions, textbook versions and headline versions. And so on. Take a simple occurrence from your day's chronology and **write** some Queneau-like versions of the event. Try a dictionary definition of the event, an instructional version, a prayer version, a drunken version, a bird's-eye view version, a child's version, a monosyllabic version, a surreal version et cetera.

- The ultimate minimalist style is telegrammatese. An Italian cinema poster for an erotic thriller summarised the film with exemplary brevity: 'Kiss. Kiss. Bang. Bang'. **Try writing** a story or a poem in 'kiss-kiss-bang-bang' style. It looks like verbs are the number one word in this mode, but you could use nouns to broaden your options.

- For an opposing voice and beat seek out some of the great masters of English prose style. Try reading Edmund Burke, the eighteenth-century political orator and polemicist, or Jonathan Swift's *A Modest Proposal* or any essay by William Hazlitt or any example from *The Oxford Book of English Prose*. Choose an example from this anthology to imitate, and see if you can **clone** a sonorous and lofty voice from the past.

- Voices come no loftier and ringing than from the King James Bible, The Authorised Version (1611) based on William Tyndale's translation of 1530. This book, The Book of Common Prayer (1549) and John Bunyan's *Pilgrim's Progress* (1678) have set the standards for English expression right up to our own times. Their perfect fusion of solemn and homely expression, the faultless rhythms and harmonies of the phrasing, should be in the hidden inventory of every writer. These texts are the templates of all modern expression. **Read** some sample pages from the King James Bible.

Digging and Divining

- When writers are asked where they get their ideas from the answer should be: 'I don't get ideas'. Stories don't start with ideas. Neither do poems nor plays nor film scripts nor novels. Read the following comments:

  1 'He didn't write *Death of a Salesman*,' said film-director Elia Kazan of Arthur Miller's play. 'It was there inside him, stored up waiting to be turned loose.' (Kazan was probably thinking of Miller's difficult relationship with his father and all the humiliations and emotional warfare of his childhood.)

2 'There are certain stretches of road over which the diviner's rod will come to life,' wrote Seamus Heaney.

3 Ursula Le Guin, in her essay titled 'Where Do You Get Your Ideas From?' wrote: 'The story-beginning phase (of writing) ... arises in the mind, from psychic contents that have become unavailable to the conscious mind, inner or outer experience, that has been "composted" ... The stuff has to be transformed into oneself, it has to be composted, before it can grow into a story.'

4 Tamsin Winter, a student writer at Manchester Metropolitan University, in a piece entitled 'My Beginning as a Writer', wrote: 'I am forced to confront my feelings. With the help of my writing I can say what I cannot speak.'

5 Edith Wharton, in her book *The Writing of Fiction*, advised would-be writers to walk round their subject and 'let it grow slowly in the mind'. This sounds very much like Le Guin's notion of 'composting', an image she borrowed from the poet Gary Snyder. **Try writing** your own response to the question, Where do you get your ideas from? What conclusions do you draw from your thinking?

- 'Every story is an *inside* story.' What do you think this means? Is there such a thing as an *outside* story? Write up some ideas in your journal. **Write** the beginning of an *outside* story.

- Have another look at Seamus Heaney's remark above. What are 'the stretches of road' in your life that make the divining rod tremble? In an early poem Heaney sees the poet as akin to the water diviner. Both have a mysterious capacity to contact hidden energies by intuition rather than by reason or research. **Try writing** two pages using the title *A Stretch of Road*.

- So, stories begin inside the writer. The trigger may be external – a phrase glimpsed, an overheard remark, a newspaper story, an anecdote, a gesture – but the energy driving it comes from within. You need the energy of the dancer to inform the choreography, and both to create the dance. You need the psychic energy of the writer to shape the narrative pattern, and both to create the story.

Chapter 2 above explored the idea of the hidden self as the storehouse of story, and Seamus Heaney's image of 'digging down' best describes the relationship between this hoard and the writing process. Others have tugged at the same metaphoric line. The French feminist theorist Hélène Cixous, in her book *Three Steps on the Ladder of Writing*, argues that every writer must descend into the self. Just as Christ in the Harrowing went down into Hell to confront souls in despair, so the writer has to confront his/her truth in the same spirit of quest and courage. She writes of 'unearthing' the hidden, an image that carries a whiff of exhumation and consequent terror. It is fortunate that writers are rarely aware of what they are unearthing as they write, and many insist that there is always a mysterious other in the poem that the words can point at but never explain. In 'Dance of Words' Robert Graves describes words dancing to metre and music: 'Until only lightning is left to puzzle over'. Here lightning is the mysterious core energising the poem. If you have written a poem or prose piece where the raw lightning of it strikes you, or where you feel you have unearthed something unexpected and maybe unnerving, **write** about the process of its composition or even its 'composting'.

- The puzzle of existence itself confronts all writers, all humans, but particular dilemmas or mysteries exercise individual imaginations. What set Ann Michaels on the long trek to *Fugitive Pieces* was her desire to 'fathom the laughter of torturers'. This strong moral vision informs her writing. It is a process, she says, that 'helps her learn how to live better'.

Not all writers start so definitively. Indeed, most of us start with a very muddled plan, but, as we have seen, the act of writing itself can discover our true purpose, and therein lies the 'secret'. Subjects are not given, they *emerge*. And the best advice to someone who wants to know where ideas come from is to say: 'trust the writing and the "ideas" will come.'

So forget ideas, start with image. Recently, I asked a workshop group to start a piece emphasising the importance of image and insisting they wrote about something they disliked doing. One writer still unsure of where to start was told by a friend to write about how he hated washing up after his flatmates. Sounds trite? It triggered a story about his Cinderella-sense as the youngest in the family: the drudge role he felt life had dealt him; his powerful sense of fairness which he acknowledged was strongest in those who suffer even minor discrimination; his recognition that servile behaviour (washing up) was a way of ingratiating himself and winning group approval; his anger at himself – displaced by smashing plates – for being so craven at heart. These are the 'psychic contents' Ursula Le Guin talks about above, out of which real fiction grows.

The psychological strata of this story only became apparent subsequently, and only in the probing and reconnaissance of group discussion. These ideas had not pre-dated the story; they impelled it during the process of writing much as a deep sea current impels the craft above. Think of something you dislike, a minor irritating feature in your life. **Write** a short, short story about it using the first person narrative voice. Just because you use this voice doesn't mean it has to be *your* voice. You can invent an alternative one.

- When I talk about fiction 'growing', I'm offering an organic view of the writing process. When I suggest you start a story with a particularising image, I'm suggesting that out the content (image) the form (story) emerges. Samuel Taylor Coleridge, the Romantic poet and critic, distinguishes in his essay on Shakespeare between mechanical and organic form. 'Form is mechanical,' he argues, 'when on any given material we impress a predetermined form, not necessarily arising out of the properties of the material; as when to wet clay we give whatever shape we wish it to retain when hardened. The organic form, on the other hand, is innate, it shapes, as it develops, itself from within, and the fullness of its development is one and the same with the perfection of its outward form.'

The notion of organic form is at the heart of Ted Hughes's celebrated poem 'The Thought Fox' (PBPBI) where the subject and the language seem to give birth to each other spontaneously and simultaneously. The animal emerges in the shaping words – out of the dark garden and out of the fecund dark of the poet's imagination, step by step, word by word together. **Write** a poem entitled *The Mind Cat* or *The Thought Shark* or *Dream Boy*. Of course, it's possible to parody this idea with a title like *The Thought Food-Mixer*!! Or to write about the emergence of the poet in the fox's imagination!!

- As any writer knows, a fluent collaboration between subject and form is rarely won without effort. Raymond Carver, in his short narrative poem 'The Painter and the Fish', tells how a painter, after a day's work, calls home from his studio. His wife is unimpressed. Over the phone she sneers at his efforts. Unnerved and distracted by her response, the painter wanders the streets aimlessly, his creative spark dimmed. But some things register – the 'soft rain', 'the smell of fresh-cut lumber', the lightning breaking across the sky 'like memory', a fish in the water under the jetty standing 'on its tail'. Suddenly he is exuberant, elated. The leaping fish has changed his mood completely. It is all there, the writer's subject:

> Lightning, water
> fish, cigarettes, machinery,
> the human heart, that old port.
> Even the woman's lips against
> the receiver, even that.
> The curl of her lip.

The artist's material is everything and everywhere around us, says Carver; every image, painful and benevolent, is the province and the provender of the writer. Get it all in, he enthuses. It is this 'variousness' of the world as the poet Louis MacNeice describes it, that delights and confirms and nourishes the writer in his/her endeavour. **Write** about an occasion when you were particularly aware of the 'variousness' of the world and when you found your faith in writing surprisingly confirmed and enhanced. What was the 'sign' that, like Carver's leaping fish, triggered in you the feeling of elation described in 'The Painter and the Fish'?

- Read Lawrence Ferlinghetti's poem 'Don't Let That Horse' (RB). The jouissance of creativity and the artist's playful disregard for convention and propriety are gloriously caught in the free-rein phrasing and the excited pacing and imagery of the piece. Ferlinghetti is writing about the surreal world of a Chagall painting, where the inevitabilities of gravity and time are suspended, and where generosity and instinctive kindliness rule, not precept and ordinance. Choose a Chagall painting and, using it as your inspiration, **write** a free-rein poem or prose piece in the manner of 'Don't Let That Horse'. Ferlingetti's enthusiasm breaks the grammatical protocols of syntax and punctuation to lead his reader on a wild horse-chase. Try writing impulsively, letting your imagination go walkabout, and letting the verse gallop along.

- The American poet Denise Levertov is exhilarated and a little scared by how ordinary things confront us with their 'marvellous truth'. In her poem 'Matins' (20WP) she says it dwells 'At every turn,/in every guise . . . ' It is in the kitchen, in steaming bathrooms, in ordinary streets, in our 'crowded hearts'. She prays that its terrible joy will 'thrust' its smile close to her. The poem ends with this intimation of predatory sexual knowing, a humming echo of the dynamo driving the world around us.

  Look in your 'crowded heart'. What's centre stage there now, or what makes a regular appearance in the repertoire of your inner life? What image or setting do you associate with this emotion/feeling? Starting with this image, **write** a piece that expresses the 'terrible joy' that Levertov wants to energise her writing. The word 'terrible' originally had religious connotations. It was associated with fear of the divine, with a 'trembling joy' in the presence of the Lord of Hosts. Today we have dumbed down and emasculated the word. It is now a mere emphatic, a holdall word meaning 'bad'. If you read some of the poetry of Emily Dickinson you will get a sense of the word's original force where it carries the intimidating power of divine and elemental presence.

- Sylvia Plath was thinking along the same lines when she wrote in her journal:

  > We must fight to return to that early mind – intellectually we play with fables that once had us sweating under sheets – the emotional, feeling drench of wonder goes – in our minds we must recreate it... A god in-breathes himself in everything: Be a chair, a toothbrush, a jar of coffee from the inside out: know by feeling in.

  Recall a time/moment/incident which was full of the 'emotional, feeling drench of wonder'. **Try and write** about it, re-creating the experience, as Plath suggests, by getting 'inside' it and releasing the 'god' there.

- The word 'confront' in Levertov's poem is aggressive. Have you been 'confronted' by a 'Marvellous Truth'? It may have been a moment of shock, a heart-thumping instance. Or it may have been an interval of deepening awareness and trepidation. Extreme sports – bungee-jumping, parachuting, climbing, deep-sea diving, caving – do create such moments. So do religious services, moonlit walks, stillnesses and wildernesses. I'm not talking about being stunned by fear, as when a large dog bristles and snarls in your path. I'm thinking of something deeper, felt and sensed along the blood and in the soul, as Wordsworth might have said. **Write** about such a moment or passage in your life when you were confronted by the inexplicable, the profound, the transfiguring even.

- 'Write what you know' is the customary advice offered to new writers. Sounds sensible. But it is dubious counsel. 'Just gibberish,' Ian Sinclair has said. Writing is discovery and exploration. You are better off writing about what you don't know. When he wrote *Espedir Street*, his novel about the popular music business, Iain Banks knew nothing about his subject. He explained that his 'research' was a skip through *The Guinness Book of Records* for the titles and dates of a few hit singles. From there on he 'winged it', and wrote from the imagination unimpeded by the weight of researched knowledge, unhindered by personal experience. Since writing is about escaping the familiar the advice offered to novices might be better phrased: '*Start* with what you know, then get off the beaten track – ASAP.' Do some superficial research on a topic you know little about and use it to '**wing**' through the opening scene of a novel/short story.

- Start a piece of writing from familiar territory, a childhood memory for example. Let the writing carry you along, incorporating new memory flashes as they occur, and drift with the reminiscent currents wherever they take you. When you land on some strange or forgotten shore, stop, stand and reflect. Now concentrate on recreating these new surroundings in a more controlled fashion. Less drift, more plan. Just **write**.

- This kind of 'setting sail' into writing is possibly what Herman Melville, the nineteenth-century American novelist and author of *Moby Dick*, meant when he used the mining metaphor in advising writers to 'mine deeper'. And one writer who did focus on the buried life, the hidden strata of the psyche, was a French woman called Nathalie Sarraute. She was born in 1900, was a friend of the existentialist writer Jean-Paul Sartre and wrote her first book *Tropismes* in the 1930s. 'Tropism' is a biological term to describe the reactive, almost imperceptible, movements that organisms make towards or away from whatever impinges on them. So, for instance, the term 'phototropism' describes a plant's tendency to move towards light; hydrotropism, its tendency to move towards water.

  Sarraute's tropisms examine human reactions, the buried, never quite conscious to-ings and fro-ings of the psyche that accompany all social contact. Her dialogue delves into the unspoken and sometimes unspeakable subsoil of polite conversation and it shows that politeness is no more than a glittering and merciless polish masking aggression, disguising anxiety. Imagine scenes at a party. **Try writing** some on-the-surface dialogue that also shows the egoisms that swim just below the formulaic exchanges.

- 'From the Frontier of Writing' by Seamus Heaney is a poem whose immediate subject is a night-time checkpoint interrogation on a Belfast road. The same tension and 'quiver in the self' that accompanies the occupants of the stopped car also attend the writer driving 'on to the frontier of writing'. Is this about the obligatory self-searching that every writer goes through before they reach their true destination? What guns are trained on the writer? What things in the writer's life, in the creative process are the checkpoint equivalents? Try using some of the images associated with frontiers such as customs, barriers, surveillance, station, watchtowers, checkpoint, searchlight, guards, et cetera, as openings for **writing** about starting writing.

- Just as Sarraute observed the human habitat in the salons of Paris, you've probably, over the years, done your own examination of male and female behaviour. Weaker characters placate stronger, roll over like dogs to expose their vulnerable stomachs, offering themselves. Others respond to the glow of approval, others flourish best in limelight. Some stiffen and swell with jealousy, some push upwards towards a lofty moral superiority.

  Sartre, at the end of his autobiography *Words*, quotes the story of the Greek, Philoctetes, who gave away his bow without condition. 'You can be sure,' says Sartre, 'that, underneath, he expected his reward.' Even altruism, if it seeks the sun, especially if it seeks the sun, has its hidden inclination in selfishness. **Try and write** some 'tropiste' dialogue. Base the writing on what you know about the reactive behaviour of our species, about the subterranean to-ings and fro-ings of social exchange.

- Here is what the Canadian writer Anne Michaels says about how poems start. 'A poem arises out of a central metaphor or a cluster of images.' It is like a net catching something, and 'it takes a while to understand what exactly is in that net'. Presumably, the next process of revising and reflecting begins to reveal the contents of the net. The third stage is to let the poem sit for a long time. Sometimes they ferment, sometimes rot. Sometimes they dry up, says Michaels ruefully. Leaving the poem to 'ferment ' (to 'compost' as Gary

Snyder would say) is crucial because it gives the writer enough distance to be ruthless in editing. 'You're hoping to catch something through hard work and discipline,' Michaels says. 'Something that is quite mysterious.' The net image reminds me of 'dream-catchers', small cross-threaded wooden hoops used by Native Americans to trap flying dreams. Research dream-catchers. Use the word as a title and **write** a poem about writing.

Dream-Catchers and the Big Bang

- Draw a four-inch diameter circle – the 'catcher' – on a piece of paper. Now relax and let images flow through your mind. Once they are flowing freely, freeze them and write down in the circle what you've trapped and frozen on the screen of your mind. You should fill the 'catcher'. Examine the entrapped material and begin the Michaels' approach. Rearrange, supplement, pair off words into unexpected combinations, chop up phrases, string them out, cluster images, get a beat going, compose short runs of musical phrasing. Leave to rise in an empty room for a week or two. Then return and edit, **whisking** till smooth and tasty.

- When asked how he started a short story Raymond Carver said he first wrote a sentence and then another and then another, building up layer upon layer until he'd finished. After three pages he had a wall of fiction. This chain-reaction approach may seem a flippant or even mechanical, lego-brick way to write, but it can work. After all, each sentence should give rise to the next either as a complement or as an antithesis. Once again, it may be a question of the writer being the willing instrument of the imagination, and skilfully following the master plan. What seems accidental is in fact being guided by an invisible hand. **Write** down any sentence taken at random from any novel on your bookshelf. Write the next sentence and the next and the next till you have filled a page. Some overall idea will emerge fairly soon in the construction, and you can let this guide your writings.

- In his essay on writing entitled 'You Are Adam and You Are Eve', the American teacher and writer George Garrett outlines the four main stages of composition. First is pre-vision, second vision, third revision, fourth review, and all practitioners when talking about their craft reiterate these central categories. Mulling and idling is how Garrett sees the first stage. It's about leaving the deep processes of the mind to their secret fermentings; it's about the rituals that distract the censor mind. 'Trust darkness,' said the Welsh poet Vernon Watkins. At this stage Gillian Clarke, another Welsh poet, sees intimations only, a sense of excitement, a blurred image, not quite discernible lines, words too dark to be read, an unclear vision declaring itself. These for her are the inevitable assurances that a poem is being prepared for and can be written. Can you recall such presentiments in your own work, the first moments of creation of a particular piece? **Write** about the occasion and the intimations.

- After pre-vision comes the vision, when, says Don Paterson, 'poems arrive in the form of words, not ideas'. The word 'arrive' suggests they come of their own accord, uninvited, knocking. Many practitioners have attested to the unsolicited nature of the first moment, the Big Bang of the poem. Poets don't choose poems, they say poems choose them. (Good title that – *The Big Bang!* As an alternative to the posh title *Ars Poetica* which is usually accorded to poems about writing poems.)

  Prose writers talk about this same sense of destiny; a sense that they have been singled out. The American novelist Louis Erdrich says writers cannot stock up on their material: 'they have to let the door open and whatever chooses you, chooses you.' Go with the flow! Open the door of your memory and let whatever wanders by come in. Let the memory speak, and as it does, write down the words. After a while examine your record. Divide the material into short 'scenes', some set in the past, some in the present. Now arrange them into a sequence. This is your storyline. Just **write**. At any time you can develop these first steps into full-blown fiction.

- The first spark is sometimes called inspiration. Michael Longley claims it is an old-fashioned notion. He defines it as 'the breathing into the mind of some idea, the suggestion of an emotion or impulse from outside the confines of your own body and personality. I live for those moments,' he enthuses, 'when language takes over the enterprise, and insight races ahead of knowledge.' This out-of-body experi ence is the incorporeal Muse calling. In ancient times the muse was the embodiment of the creative mystery. Don Paterson thinks muses still exist. We ignore them at our peril. In this cynical, rationalistic century they've been exiled to some dull verbal gulag or etherealised into an impossible heaven, but they're still there for the calling. **Write** a piece entitled *Muse* in which she appears either as bag-lady or personal trainer or webpage master.

- These verbal flashes or sparks, these germs are what Don Paterson calls the 'Given' of the poem. Helen Dunmore, poet and novelist, refers to the same idea when she talks of how a poem emerges out of 'primitive map-making', where 'one or two fully-formed phrases . . . embody the essential music of the poem.' By map-making she is referring to first doodles, the pen idling over the waters in those pre-visionary, mul- ling lulling moments before the lightning strike of the Word.

  These one or two fully-formed phrases are the DNA of the poem, Paterson's 'Given', from which the whole piece can be developed. Keats had a similar view of creation. He wrote: 'Unless poetry comes to the poet as naturally as leaves to the tree it had better not come at all.' It's not that Keats is against conscious craft, far from it. Rather, he wants to emphasise the mysterious and divinatory well-spring of poetry as Seamus Heaney has described it. Can you recall a phrase that you couldn't get out of your mind? Maybe it's one that keeps coming back. It could be the name of a place, a street, an object like the enigmatic sledge etched with the word 'Rosebud' in Orson Wells's film *Citizen Kane*. From the sea of memory try hauling in these forgotten words. Was it something you overheard, read or were told? Mull over it. **Write.** If anything comes up, snare it in a web of language and write a piece appropriately.

- Tom Paulin, the Irish poet, critic and broadcaster, writing about his collection of poems *The Wind Dog*, describes how his memory is littered with words and persistent phrases: lines from Hopkins and MacDiarmid encountered as a schoolboy, dialect words like *skelf* and *dag*, words that have been carried on the wind from distant histories, like the Jewish word *shetl*. These are his pedlar's pack of 'trifles', the magpie glitter that he weaves in and out of his poetry. Magpie, because like all poets he is a generous borrower, taking a phrase from Shakespeare here, one from John Masefield there, something else from popular ballad and song. Then he tacks them to the sturdy mast of his own poetry. Paulin calls this linguistic hoard his 'archive', and out of it many poems are sustained if not born. Look at your own 'archive'. Unearth from the sludges and sediments of memory some of the glitter and record what you find. Can you start a poem from these sudden bright appearances? **Try writing**.

- By now you will have become uneasy about what I have been saying about true/real poetry emerging as a bright verbal fragment, unbidden, like a bolt from the blue. You will be arguing that the problem with inspiration is that it puts the writer at the mercy of the muse. You could be sitting there for months waiting! Then you will ask yourself, very sensibly, what's the value of doing exercises that ask you to ignite the fire when lightning is supposed to do it for you. If creation is spontaneous how can it come from calculation?

  One answer is the asteroid shower argument. Fire enough ideas at planet imagination and some will get through and shoot flashing poems across the face of the earth. Another is the Shelleyan argument – a poet can blow the dull embers of the imagination into heat by his/her own concentrated effort – no divine agency is necessary. What turns a glow into a flame varies for every poet, but the effort of expiration (breathing out) can substitute for inspiration (breathing in). Hopefully the suggestions in this book will at least help you take in air (inspiration) and enthuse you into flame. Expand on these ideas and **write** them down in your journal.

- When a poem starts to come, writers must realise what they have on their hands. Unless they *listen* to what the poem is starting to utter, the thing will go dumb. Listening means letting the poem speak, not forcing, not imposing or demanding that it tell truths, carry BIG ideas, perform verbal acrobatics. So it is wise to wait upon a second mulling, a subsequent ferment, that allows the words to settle down and slowly bubble.

To change the metaphor and borrow another from Michael Longley, we can say poems sometimes lie 'buried like a shattered vase waiting to be reconstructed. Chance leads you to the fragments which you relate to each other and piece together.' That the form (vase) of the poem is there from the beginning, waiting discovery, does make the poet more of an imaginative renovator than an originator. But the value of the analogy lies in its emphasis on the importance of craft in making an original whole again. But how do you relate the fragments?

This is the Willed bit as opposed to the Given bit where the conscious mind takes over and begins the revision, the re-seeing of the poem, casting new lights on the original words. The art is to craft the rest of the poem so it sounds as spontaneous as the Given and seamless with it. For this revision stage to be successful, according to Gillian Clarke, you have to develop the original into 'something much more, longer, deeper, more satisfying', and she recommends intense concentration and research. Research means using dictionaries, reading in allied fields, scouring the memory for associated material. This is sideways thinking, looking at things askew for a new way in. If you believe Pascal's axiom that chance favours the prepared mind, then searching in hope will bear fruits. So, if the image of a vase seems to be at the core of the poem, then finding out about glazes and clays and firing techniques may offer fruitful ideas.

Helen Dunmore identifies an interesting feature of this revision stage, where she sees a transition kind of writing going on, exploratory forays – 'writing which is done for the sake of getting somewhere else'. This writing is lost, edited out in the final drafting process, but, like scaffolding, it meanwhile holds up the poem and allows the structure to reach its true dimensions. Take a phrase at random from the newspaper. Let it be one that you find striking. For instance, yesterday in a poetry magazine article I came across the phrase 'deep time'. It hit me again today – a newspaper article explained that the concept is used by palaeontologists and geologists to describe those tracts of time so large they reach beyond the mind's grasp. Take a phrase, like 'deep time'. Imagine it releasing a stream of ideas and images. Record this stream as quickly as you can. Now pan out the dross so the striking material shines clearly. Set these glitters in a poem. **Write.**

- Nothing at this revision stage quite matches the seismic moment when the poem first quaked its presence and shook the poet awake. But the graft stage does throw up exhilarating aftershocks as you play with words and try to fit them into their allotted place. A new word may be touchpaper to another and torch a dull line into incandescence. Try taking some lines of your own and introduce some rogue words taken at random from another poem. See if you can **light up the line**, turn a squib into a sparkler.

- Reviewing is the final stage of the compositional process. It's a kind of dedicated housekeeping, where the poem gets cleaned up and the lines polished. It is also the occasion for stepping back and getting a sense of the work as a whole. The American novelist Marge Piercy says that the major deficiency of young writers is their inability to see the work as a whole. When she writes novels she gets the 'architecture' right first and claims that the rest follows. It makes sense. You don't design the wall-lights before the walls, the bricks before the building. Look at some of your work-in-progress. Is the architecture right? How would you change it? **Try writing** the outline of an alternative structure for one of your short stories or scripts.

Templates – the Killer and the Carrier-bag

- What poems and stories need is form. Often poems find their own form. The 'Given' lines turn out to be iambic, and this offers a rhythmic template immediately. The poet's predisposition to looser forms may produce free verse structures based on the phrase, not the metric line. The poet's delight in sound effects may create complex musical patternings as the cohesive principle of the poem. So by a co-operation of accident and design, the poem gets into shape.

But there are other ways. Literature offers a variety of ready-mades, templates to get the beginner and the expert going. Pre-formed, they allow poets to work against a grain and, in the friction, generate considerable energy. Don Paterson sees form as 'doggy-chew' for the left side of the brain that distracts the intellect and allows the imagination an unimpeded run at the poem. Other writers see form – the villanelle, the sonnet, the quatrained lyric, the Keatsian ode, the coupleted ballad – as ritual motions which, like incantations, call up unexpected ideas and sometimes the devil of a poem.

If you have tried rhyming you will know how the enforced search for the punning end-of-line syllables discovers surprising gems. The discipline of form loosens serendipities on the writer and the reader! **Try writing** a ballad of six rhyming couplets about someone you regard as a bit of a 'character'. Avoid doggerel where the rhythm becomes dog-trot. Experiment with half-rhyme, masculine and feminine rhyme, and polysyllabic rhyme. Use run-on to weaken the tyranny of the rhyming sounds, and criss-cross the lines with assonantal runs and internal rhymes. If all this sounds too technical then read some of Charles Causley's work or a selection of Roger McGough's poems, and let the technical aplomb of the writing sink into you so it instinctively instructs your mind and ear.

● John Gardner, author of a number of books on writing, sums up his advice to new writers with customary brevity and point: 'Expand, develop, think harder, make a design.' So far, this section has been about expanding and thinking harder. Now we need to think about 'design'. To understand how stories work try this. With a group of friends get in the mood by swapping family stories. Talk about recent events and happenings in the office, on the road, at the doctor's, et cetera. Trade gossip. Take turns to be the story-teller. Those who listen should try and work out the simple story-telling techniques being used: repetitions for emphasis, pauses for dramatic effect, metaphoric colouring, dialogue to enliven, exaggeration for effect, rhythmic patterning. And so on. The group should discuss the various narrative devices being used, and draw up a repertoire of them. **Try rewriting** one of the stories heard in the session, and tell it in the voice of the original teller improving on the dramatic qualities where you think fit. Share the results with the group.

- In fiction the underlying narrative shape has been dominated by one particular model – the linear conflict-crisis-resolution pattern of plot whose roots are in the ideal defined by Aristotle in the *Poetics* as having beginning, middle and end. Chekhov's remark that his stories were 'like tortoises, all middle' shows that even within this frame great variation is possible. Read some short stories and try and discern the underlying pattern. Often there is a main character(s) impelled/motivated by some ambition, a desire to achieve or realise some plan or objective. This leads to conflict. Here's an example. **A** wants to expand the family business and move to new premises nearer his main markets. This means going south. **B,** his partner, doesn't want to move away from a sick mother. Dilemma! The mother is a majority shareholder in the company and has loaned her daughter a substantial sum to buy the house of her dreams. Mummy has power. Dilemmas all round. Whatever decisions are made or deferred here, there will be fall-out. **Continue** this story-line. Write about two sides showing how the various characters face up to the obstacles hindering their different ambitions. Bring the plot through a series of crises to a final resolution.

- This view of story has been called 'gladiatorial' because it centres on conflict. It has been regarded as a very masculine model. Anything that progresses from rising action to climax and declines into denouement looks like an analogy for the male sexual response! This is not the only way to satisfy readers. Some stories, for instance, revert the order by beginning with the climax, and then work through the aftermath because the writer is interested in survival not conquest. See Kafka's 'Metamorphosis'.

The conquering all-action hero of traditional narratives was derided by Virginia Woolf in the preparatory notes to her book *Three Guineas*. She regarded fictional heroism as a form of 'botulism', a pervasive poison in the literary body. Heroes are violent; they fight with sword and spear and gun. This is the 'killer' view of narrative. It is summed up in the laconic film poster caption: 'Kiss. Kiss. Bang. Bang.'

Ursula Le Guin proposes a more civilised metaphor with her 'carrier-bag theory of fiction'. The 'killer' story, since it deals with weapons, decrees that it shall start here and go straight there, BANG; a time's arrow view of narrative trajectory. The 'killer' story decrees that it shall have conflict, that it will have a hero to cope with conflict and that it will re-establish order after narrative mayhem. The 'carrier bag' story wanders and doesn't necessarily have a hero-saviour (that old throwback to the dependencies of feudalism). It is flexible and tolerant of many shapes because it is concerned not with antithetical energies – rupture and disruption followed by settlement and consolidation – but with process and change and development, with frayed ends and digressions and narrative loops, with circularity and unexplained discordances.

Take, for example, Amy Hempel's story 'In the Cemetery Where Al Jolson Is Buried'. This has been described as a 'mosaic'. She provides bits and pieces of scenes that the reader has to put together. In this particular 'mosaic', the narrator recounts her visits to a friend dying in a cancer ward. She tells stories to her friend in an ineffectual effort to give comfort and solace. These stories are some of the 'bits and pieces' and fill the larger bag of the overall narrative shape. 'Shape' is hardly the word because, like an amoeba, the story seems to bulge out one way then contract only to propel a stubby finger of itself in another direction. The uncertainty and lack of conclusion in the story is very different from the 'neat' knot ending of the classic Aristotelian plot. Kempel leaves the reader in no man's land, hinting that what we have read may be just the 'bearable' version of what actually happened. The real truth she has omitted. She suggests that she has lied about the whole thing and that she may have to retell the story of how her friend died.

This is a trick. The story is about the narrator's inability to face up to death and loss, and her guilt at not being able to help her friend when she most needed it. Just as the narrator shies away from the horror of death, so the story circles the topic, darts in, eyes closed, recoils and never really touches the dark centre. This succession of mini-stories darting in and out suggests evasion and procrastination. Thus, structure embodies theme, subject determines structure.

Stories have always been procrastinatory. *The Arabian Nights* contains all the thousand and one tales told by Scheherazade to entertain her husband and thereby distract him enough to stop him carrying out his plan to kill her. **Try a 'mosaic'** of your own. Think of some preoccupation you have at the moment. Encircle the experience with tangential stories, snatches of dialogue, narrator reflections, and bit by bit approach the core of the experience.

- In her essay 'Breaking the Rules of Story Structure', Diane Lefer suggests writers should think carefully about what interests them about stories. If a writer is interested in re-creating the feeling of an event and not just its telling; is principally concerned with the inner life; is more interested in a character's thoughts than in plot twists; is aware of writing as discovery; is in the habit of ordering events according to emotional or psychological links not chronological; is interested in inferring and hinting at truths rather than asserting them; is interested in the rhythmic and musical effects of language then, Lefer says, he/she is more likely to find the classic plot structure of traditional fiction unsatisfactory. Think about what kind of fiction you like to read and what kind you like to write. Are they the same? Test your preferences against the criteria listed above. Try and get your thoughts going on this by writing. In this re-evaluation, consider some examples of your preferred stories and say why they appeal to you. **Write** about two pages.

- Diane Lefer also suggests writers ask themselves the question: 'Do I take pleasure in what Franz Kafka called "the mind revelling in its own keenness"?' What do you think Kafka means by this phrase? Does he mean the self-delighting qualities of the mind, seeing keenly and being perceptive, playing with language, toying with ideas? Think of what you delight in, what your mind revels in. List down some examples and **write** a poem or a journal entry based on these reflections.

- Jean-Paul Sartre, in his autobiography *Words*, recalls the adventure stories he wrote as a young boy. They were full of impossible single-handed heroics, satanic villains, murderous monsters from the deep, exotic far-flung settings. They were utterly derivative, dependent for plot and stereotype on the second-hand comics he bought from stalls on the quais beside the Seine, and which he devoured almost daily. Sartre regarded his early writing as 'monkey tricks' designed to impress his family and bolster his reputation as a genius with the adults in his life. Did you try and impress? Do you still? Remember the first story you ever wrote? Remember your teen years' stories? In note form, summarise their main features. **Write** a few pages of a putative Writer's Autobiography in which you describe and analyse this stage in your evolution as a person and as a fiction writer.

- Here is some long-standing advice: 'Break the rules'. That was the poet Angelo Poliziano writing in 1491. More recent and more gnomic is the advice to simply 'let go'. In other words, as the Australian novelist Janet Turner Hospital has said: 'Trust your instinct. Trust it. Trust it.'
  Now this laissez-faire attitude is all very well, and I have been advocating this approach to writing throughout this book, but what is appropriate for the early stages of composition may not be for later stages. Across all writing genres – poetry, novel, short story, drama – the nature of composition does seem remarkably similar. It is commonplace to describe the process in terms of stages, but this enforced and simplified symmetry misses the subtle variations and hidden shaping forces in the creative process.

To recap: writing follows a four-stage process which involves pre-vision, vision, revision, review. Pre-vision is that idling, mulling over period so many artists have recognised as the mysterious but necessary precondition for creating. Next is the vision, the moment(s) when lightning strikes, when an image quickens you with possibilities. Trust this impulse. Trust it, trust it, as Janet Turner Hospital says above. This is the best advice you will get – anywhere. Without vision the story will never live.

After vision comes revision. This is where you broadstroke, craft and shape the original impulse, knocking it into some kind of form. It is hard work, hard thinking, and gives rise to a fallacy and common excuse among new writers, namely, that the act of revising and editing (the fourth stage) is counter-productive because it kills with effort the original intuition. The paradoxical truth is, that it is this effort and labour that ultimately creates the impression that the work has been effortlessly conceived and artlessly shaped. Ursula Le Guin sees this as the crucial stage in the whole compositional process. It is *concentration* that guarantees success she says, *concentration*; which means keeping a single-minded and obsessive eye on the object, and includes a capacity to shut out the world and just write and write and write. The Japanese call this focusing, 'getting in the can'.

Decisions about structure and style and point-of-view and chronology are not easy for any writer, let alone new writers. Two points here. First, if you know what alternatives are on offer, making decisions is easier. If it's first person narration or third, at least there's a concrete choice. So, learn about all the alternatives. Read this book, for instance! Second, if you want remedies to problems, you have to diagnose difficulty. In other words, you ask questions of the text. As always it's not just any old question. You have to learn to ask the right questions, and this is another writing skill learnt through practice. Here are some of the BIG questions to stop and ask of yourself and your story:

What is the story about?
Why has it got the form it has?
Why does it start where it starts?
What's at stake for the characters?
What drives them to behave in the way they do?

Answer these and the revision process can begin. It's not all about 'finding a voice', which sounds all very messianic, but about hard-nosed professional practice where you learn to interrogate yourself. Take any story or poem which you consider to be either unfinished or failed or 'stuck' and ask it some BIG questions. **Write** down some of the answers so you sustain and advance this self-critical debate. See if you can rewrite the piece more confidently after this diagnosis.

- To ensure the progress of a novel, Edith Wharton's advice to writers was to include 'illuminating incidents' at frequent points in the narrative. They are the 'magic casements of fiction' she says – 'scenes that shed a circle of light far beyond the incident recorded'. Her examples include: Arabella flinging the offal across the hedge at Jude in Hardy's novel *Jude the Obscure*, Emma losing her temper with Miss Bates at the picnic in Jane Austen's *Emma*, Stephen Guest dazzled by the curve of Maggie Tulliver's arm as she lifts it to pick a flower for him in the conservatory, in George Eliot's novel *The Mill on the Floss*.

  These pivotal moments enrich all fictions, short or long. Joyce coined the term 'epiphany' for those self-illuminating moments where characters are stopped in their tracks and which leave the reader uneasily voyeuristic. Recall a significant moment witnessed by yourself. Use the scene/image as the centre round which you circle a story. **Write** on.

Writing with a Camera

- In television drama they talk about the 'hits' in a story. These are emotional hotspots that quiver the viewer. A typical 'hit' is the embrace scene. In a soap, girl and boyfriend make up and hug each other. Camera CU shows her eyes-closed and a satisfied smile on her lips. Switch shot to boyfriend head in her hair, eyes wide open and frowning. Something's up. Something's not quite right. Something's going to spoil this scene . . . very soon. He has something to tell her.

In the classic crisis-resolution model of plot, there needs to be a succession of crises to drive the momentum of TV drama. If you are interested in scriptwriting, then you write the story-line as a succession of scenes in which dilemma and crisis egg each other on and in which accident and miscalculation deflect the course of characters' lives.

To teach yourself the basics of scriptwriting watch a week's worth of TV drama – soaps, serials, one-offs. Do the following:

1 **Make notes** on how the story is told. Try answering the following: How do serials begin? How is the viewer 'hooked'? How is the action paced? How are characters presented? What is the relationship between words and visuals?

2 Video some examples. Select a sequence without speech and **write** down a short description of each scene.

3 Turn down the sound for a few minutes and **write** the dialogue for the character(s) on screen. See how yours matches with the video script.

• Take a simple scene. A person is sitting alone in a café. Use this as your lead-in for a script. To prepare the script do the following:

1 **Write** a profile of each character who will appear. A profile contains info on age, sex, social class, occupation, marital status, education, ethnic origin, disposition and temperament, values, habits, interests and idiosyncrasies. Know your character better than he/she does.

2 Decide the genre – psycho-thriller, human interest, comedy, police drama. Decide the theme/treatment – reversal of fortune, stalker and chase, bid for independence, possession/obsession, revenge. **Write** a short statement of theme.

3 **Write** a brief (two paragraphs) synopsis of the story.

4 **Write** the first three pages of the script, starting with the scene in the café. You don't have to launch straight into dialogue. TV is primarily a visual medium and good scriptwriters think visual. If you want to convey your character's distress, for instance, think carefully before you introduce a concerned onlooker to ask if she's alright. If the camera has done its job the viewer knows the reply already. Write with the camera and show your despondent character aimlessly stirring her coffee or screwing up another tissue.

- Read the script extract below.

> Scene: Café Solitaire. *Man enters and goes to counter.*
> Man : Bacon buttie and a cup of char please.
> (*Owner behind counter ignores him*)
> Man: Bacon sandwich and cup of tea. (*Pause*) Please.
> Owner: Sorry.
> Man: What's that yer doin'?
> Owner: Going through my accounts. Bad month. I
> don't know where it's all going to.

The story is about a café on the skids and how the owner tries to save his business. There are good and bad things about this script. What are they? Make some notes. **Try rewriting** the scene 'with the camera' and continue for two pages. Avoid 'ping-pong' dialogue, where two characters feed lines to each other and which do not advance the action or reveal character. Avoid 'caption speak'. This occurs when a character, in effect, tells the viewer what is obviously going on or says something which would be better implied and left for the audience to deduce for themselves. Is there any 'caption speak' in the script fragment above?

- Andrea Ashworth's autobiography *Once in a House on Fire* describes her upbringing in a house of parental violence. One day, during one of her vicious stepfather's absences, she is peeling potatoes in the kitchen. She whispers to her Auntie Jackie and asks if she thinks her mother is missing 'him', her Dad. Jackie sneers under her spectacles. 'If that silly arse tries any of his famous performances, he'll have me to answer to,' she says, flourishing the kitchen knife. 'Silver flashed, swooped and sliced through raw spuds,' writes Ashworth. This is 'camera writing'. Can you explain why? Imagine a kitchen scene. Mother and teenage daughter are preparing a meal. The daughter is strangely silent and the mother tries to get her to talk. Write the rest of the scene using the rituals of cookery as imagery to heighten and advance the drama.

- Recall a school outing. Write a sketch of the day's events and the central figures of the action. Divide the day into a succession of scenes. On the bus. Fairground. Amusement Arcade. Teacher losing temper. Sandwiches in the park. Lost! Bunking off with best friend. Caught! Riot act. Fags confiscated. Purse stolen! Back on bus. Use this material as the basis for a TV script adopting the following sequence.

  1 Arrange your 'scenes' in a running order.

  2 Now devise a story 'thread'. For instance, one of the teachers and one of the pupils dislike each other and their simmering resentment agitates the story until it breaks out in embarrassing confrontation. OR one of the characters secretly fancies another and spends most of the trip trying to get their attention. OR two of them fancy the same person. OR one pupil has something dangerous in his bag – a Polaroid camera.

  Write the opening scene using description of action and camera views only, no dialogue. Write the scenes on the bus: setting off, the journey, the arrival. They should capture the authentic 'feel' of school trips, establish the characters, set up the rest of the story. See if you can write with a 'camera's eye'.

- Write a film adaptation of Ted Hughes's 'The Rain Horse' (MBSS). Take the first two pages only, and convert the text to film narrative, that is, choreograph for the camera. You will be faced with the challenge of capturing the mood and feelings, the interior world of the silent walker. And how do you shoot the appearance of the horse? Sudden gallop of hooves; sound first then visuals? Or close-up of horse's wide eye, looking through leaves, rain dripping from lashes? Will you use a leitmotif? A recurrent image such as long shot of man in vast landscape with drifting curtains of rain to show his vulnerability and diminishment in face of inscrutable and alien forces of nature? How will you build up the tension as horse hunts man, as city-dweller-man comes face to face with the primitive? For a real imaginative challenge, **try writing** the screen adaptation of the first two pages of Dylan Thomas's story 'The Burning Baby' from the same anthology.

- 'Radio is a visual medium.' Write some notes exploring this apparent contradiction. Here are some ideas/situations for radio drama that allow you to exploit the unique possibilities of the medium. A patient drifts in and out of consciousness, fragments of his/her exploded past come into focus then dissolve. A marketing manager for a brewery, married with two daughters, comes out as a transvestite. A man is kidnapped in the mistaken belief he is an informer. In a bio-tech laboratory a research team has managed a genetic fusion of living plant tissue with DNA from vegetable material preserved for 100,000 years in a frozen Siberian asphalt pool. A Eurospace star-liner returning from an asteroid mining expedition finds its robotic pilot has changed its course. Two sisters decide to do something about their dull marriages. A child runs away and finds he has a strange guardian angel on hand. A woman finds that she has an irresistible urge to tell the truth at all times.

  Try writing the opening scenes for any one of these scenarios. Use sound effects to establish the mood (sombre, light-hearted, threatening, eerie, mundane), setting (building site, office, hospital ward, cavern, train), space and scale (intimate, close-up confined, oppressive, distant, vast), time and pace (slow, relaxed, frenetic, recollective, dream-like). Avoid 'caption speak' – 'As you crouch in the doorway is that a gun you are holding and pointing across the room at my chest?' You have to use language and SFX more inventively than this to write good radio scripts.

- After June's elderly mam goes to a Pentecostal meeting she starts speaking in tongues and is soon having visions and hearing voices. June is alarmed, and thinks her mother should be put in care. Her son thinks his nan is a religious phenomenon. His wife thinks the old lady is a nut case. Spin a story-line out of this scenario. Shape the material into scenes for a radio play following the classic pattern of exposition/dilemma/crisis/resolution. **Try writing** the first five minutes of the script. By the end of this section you should have introduced the 'voices', your four main characters, and established the theme and central dilemma for the family.

Despising the Inexact

- Vaporous expression and nebulous emotion are the tell-tale signs of uncommitted writing. Examine this passage:

  The moon's reflection was emaciated, hollow and dull. Its persona had been dampened and its frailty whined like a dying memory. The last sip of light, which had been so eager to illuminate last night's festivities, seeped into the sinister cracks of the land drowning by its own fear.

  Ursula Le Guin describes this kind of writing as 'bellowing and plunging and kicking up a lot of dust' and never getting out of the corral. The critic John Middleton Murry put it more elegantly, but no less effectively, when he wrote this about rhetorical flourishing:

  instead of defining and making concrete your thought, by aid of your sensuous perception you give way to a mere verbal exaggeration of your feeling or thought. Instead of trying to make your expression more precise and true, you falsify it for the sake of vague impressiveness ... you try to replace quality by quantity and forget that all quantities to an infinite power are all the same. By pounding the keys with a hammer you merely break the strings.

Despite off-loading emotions onto inanimate objects, despite substituting quantity of words for quality words, despite the verbal exaggerations, the 'moon' passage above does contain at least one striking phrase – 'The last sip of light'. It could be salvaged from the elaborate wreck. But, on the whole, it's 'victim' writing, feeling sorry for itself, striking plaintive attitudes, and posturing.

Writing needs engagement, which comes with a sense of a *particular* character caught up in powerful feelings at a *particular* time and in a *particular* context. It's the *particularity of image* that is the antidote to mere emotionalism. To repeat Ezra Pound's dictum – 'Fundamental accuracy of statement is the ONE morality.' OR to remind you of Rilke's injunction: 'Despise the inexact.' Other Ezra commandments are relevant here. His famous Don'ts contain the following advice: 'Go in fear of abstraction. Don't babble worn out poetic expressions such as "dove-grey hills" or "pearl-pale". Don't use such an expression as "dim lands of peace". It mixes an abstraction, "peace" with the concrete "lands".' Now **write** an alternative description of a moon-lit scene without any 'verbal exaggeration'.

- Here's a situation. A teenage boy and his father are in the lounge standing about vaguely discussing the problems of the gas-fire. They are uneasy, awaiting the wife's return from a hospital appointment. They both hope the news will be good. Suddenly they hear the key in the front door. It scrapes open. It always did catch on the parquet. It seems ages before the lounge door opens. The two watch her standing in the doorway, hoping for a smile perhaps. She takes off her gloves, slowly. Then she puts them back on. She takes them off. Puts them on again. Silence.
  What telling imagery!!
  After a particular vicious 'domestic' in which her step-father batters her against the wall and half throttles her mother, Andrea is left at her Auntie Agnes's watching colour TV. 'Cops scooted about, setting off sirens, clutching guns in their praying fists.' How precise this last image; the trained posture of armed officers entering a dangerous building, the classic Mel Gibson moment – back to wall, both hands

praying a gun, waiting to confront the door, kick it down and burst into the empty room. But this image closes the chapter in Andrea Ashworth's book *Once in a House on Fire* with a disturbing ambiguity. Violence and pleading are united in that final phrase, just as they are in their painful domestic life. The image is both a visual fix and an icon.

Later in the book, the stepfather is sitting on the settee holding up a spirit level, steadying it and trying unsuccessfully to centre the air bubble. How is this image iconic? Images have an immediate impact, defining and particularising the moment, the place, the appearance, the state of mind and heart. And they invoke the larger contours and intensities of human life. Can you think of a family image that brings the immediate reality of domestic life into play and yet suggests broader, deeper currents at work? It may well be something small like a gesture, like a marble. **Try writing** a story where this image is significant, even symbolic.

- Other verbal images are leitmotifs. By repetition they take on a larger meaning and act as a shorthand for a cluster of meanings in a book. The cat's eye marble is such a leitmotif in Margaret Attwood's novel *Cat's Eye*. It is both the talisman of the child and the symbol of the unsullied self, the untouchable core of being, her self-belief. Imagine visiting an old aunt. After years of silent enmity her sister has sent you to try and reconcile the two of them. You enter the twilight world of ageing auntdom. **Write** the story of what happens, opening with a tell-tale image that recurs throughout the account and which acts both as a sensory pointer and a symbolic motif.

- While her mother lies in bed suffering one of her regular consumptive attacks Paddy asks her about Hell. Her mother reaches for the tin of Nippits before replying. Not unsurprisingly, she thinks 'heaven and hell are here and now'. This is at the closure of Chapter 17 in Maureen Duffy's *That's How It Was*. The last sentence reads: 'Outside the window a bird chirped lustily for a moment then was silent. Sunlight lay across her legs that made hardly any hump in the bed; her restless fingers puckered the sheet into tiny regular gathers.' **Write** a commentary on these final images and how they close down onto a minute detail. Are they just a way of rounding off the chapter, photo-framing it? Or do they serve other purposes as well?

- Obviously, you can have too much of a good thing. As Edith Wharton notes in her guide *The Writing of Fiction*: 'Most beginners crowd into their work twice as much material... as it needs.' Too much detail sinks a story and leads to 'the indolent habit of decorating its surface', she adds. And there you have it. The art is to deploy image and particularised description and action sparingly and to timed effect. Find a piece of your writing which, on reflection, you feel is decorative in parts. **Expunge** such passages or strip them of their fine feathers. Examine your images and see if you have made the best use of them.

- Ursula Le Guin argues that stories have to have 'strong ideas' as well as 'strong feelings'. If the mind doesn't work along with the emotions you have 'a bathtub of wish fulfilment (as in most mass-market romances) or anger (as in much of the "mainstream" genre) or hormones (as in porn)'. The remedy, according to Le Guin, is to read widely, think hard and develop your vocabulary. Otherwise, writers are attempting to play complicated music on an instrument for which they have not even learnt the fingering. So, keep it simple. Find the image. Don't blather. Start by plucking a few strings only. **Write** a short and simple story about two friends who go for a walk and find the weather is changing for the worse. Try writing from the third person point of view, the so-called 'omniscient author' point of view. Then do a version in first person, the 'I' narrative voice. Then do a version from the point of view of one of the characters, but without using the 'I' narrative voice. It's worth remembering that stories don't have to follow the classic plot trajectory of complication, crisis, resolution. The narrative can be a jigsaw of pieces that readers are invited to assemble for themselves.

- All stories start as babies. They come from a small germ and gradually grow. At first they burble and stumble to find their feet and then repeated practice begins to make them perfect. So, you start from not-knowing and, by making sounds, you begin to shape a life. Getting going can be hard. The American crime writer Edward Bunker had an answer. He wrote and wrote and wrote. Nothing worked. Eventually he tried something different – he wrote in the first person and it worked for him. Then he cut out every spare word, unnecessary description and loose sentence and he had a clear way ahead. For successful ignition, change the angles; for lift-off, keep writing and writing. Take a simple situation as the basis for a story and **write**. Start with a dialogue opening. Open with a description of a person or a place. Try a third way – internal monologue. Try an action sequence. Think of a fifth and sixth alternative and try them out.

- Put at the heart of your next story a simple incident. Focus on this only. Now try and create some kind of contrast, some light and shade. For instance, you might have two mismatched characters involved in your single episode/moment, as different as white and black, or two characters who have very different perceptions or misperceptions of each other, or two whose difference lies in externals, in age, sex, class, nationality and the cultural distinctions these incur. Light and shade may be a matter of style. A story may be frothily romantic or richly poetic or darkly realistic or cerebral or colloquial. Imagine a common situation, like a woman going to select a wedding dress. Take a simple related image/incident. **Write** the story in terms of light and dark: the white organza against a storm-darkening sky, the glitter of the shop against the drabness of the street, the glossy magazine shots against the overweight bride-to-be, the chatter of the overenthusing mother and the cool talk of the arch assistant against words from the marriage service in The Book of Common Prayer.

- The novelist Jane Rogers has written a spoof of the Mills and Boon school of woman's fiction. Her three-part story is written in two contrasting styles – gritty realism and frothy romantic. The antithesis in style exposes the vacuities of romantic fiction. **Try writing** a spoof that depends on collisions of style. In the M & B spoof, divide the story into three sections entitled: 'First Date', 'The Kiss', 'The Morning After'. One of these titles is more suited to the 'gritty' voice than the other two! Write each version alongside the other, selecting tone, language, names, settings and subtitles appropriate to each style.

- **Try writing** a spoof 'aga-saga' using Jane Rogers's device of running two contrasting styles in the same story. Set the 'aga' style/conventions against documentary style. Do the same for an Agatha Christie-type narrative, running it alongside an Irvine Welsh-type narrative. There is also dynamic energy to be gained from setting style against subject. For instance, **try composing** a manual on car maintenance in an erotic style or write a valentine in slang, a chiller in Janet-and-Johnese.

- David Harsent, in his poem 'From Marriage' (NP), lets sparks fly by striking flinty words against softer ones, technical against homely. 'Fish' clenches into 'fistula'; the quick music of 'flensing' glances off the heaving phrase, 'flub of gut' in the next breath. Such sensory and rhythmic collisions are the very stuff of good poetry. Browse through a good anthology, keeping an eye out for unexpected pairings of images, dissonances, counterpoint and all the pull and tug of dynamic writing. **Write** about preparing food with an eye and ear to creating sound and sensual clashes and harmonies. Push at the limits of your vocabulary. Don't be afraid of using 'technical' terms. Exoticise language. If you are writing about food, remember it's your fingers that are cutting, slicing, rolling, stretching, kneading, peeling, pithing language, flensing the flab to the hard white bone of poetry.

- Read some of Medbh McGuckian's poems. It has been said she uses language, metaphors in particular, in a distinctively 'feminine' fashion because her images connect by association not by logic. Comparing a cocoon to a bandage is 'logical'. To compare a cocoon, as McGuckian does, to a car-wash is not. Male critics have read her work as no more than verbal wash, made up of randomised images, a metaphor in itself for women's 'butterfly' minds. But in juxtaposing seeming incompatibles, the poet pushes the reader beyond the surface into a world of ideas and sharper angles. Read 'The Butterfly Farm'. Start with the implications of the title. Madame Butterfly and factory farming come to mind. Then consider the poem's strange relations – Japanese tea-houses and car-washes, artificial sun and the Indian Moon Moth. **Try writing** a piece that exploits 'illogical', but purposeful, associations, that strikes unexpected but resonating notes.

- Your opening paragraph, so they say, should hold the germ of the whole story. A quick check on some stories you know well will confirm this truth. The opening paragraph, like a door half-opened on a dark room, throws in a blade of light that shows its depth but not its details. Look at successive openings of your short fiction. What is the function of the opening paragraphs? Do they disquiet, signal the theme, foreshadow the future? **Write** the opening three paras in which weather foreshadows future events in the story.

- Here's a useful take on story starts. Adopt a cinematic approach. Open with a close-up, follow with mid-shot or tracking shot, and complete opening sequence with a distance (long) shot. OR reverse this order. Which order you try will depend on your fictional objectives. If you start with a shot of horizon lightning and a darkening sky, then move to the white clapboard house, then to a close-up of hands over-vigorously rolling pastry, you are saying something about pent-up emotional energies by siting the story in a private world of family where domestic explosions are a real possibility. If you start with a woman's face looking through a window at the distant strike, and then let the paragraph pan over fields till the reader sees the dark lift of the Black Mountains, we know we are in for a different kind of story. Take a simple situation and **write** two versions of the opening sequence, starting the first from close-up, the second from long shot.

- Varying the distance is a structural device in both film and fictional narrative. Successive enlargements and contractions set up patterns of movement in stories. Surging and stalling and retarding the pace of the fiction is an accomplished narrative art that the 'cinematic' approach helps to develop. Robert Wells's poem 'Five Sketches' (FBP) shows how seeing stories in terms of snapshots, key scenes or frames, creates a distinctive narrative structure. Wells has written a narrative of a love affair in five scenes. Take the same subject and divide it into five 'sketches'. **Write** up each 'sketch' till you have a story.

- The novelist Ann Lamott got going at writing by sitting down, day after day, five days a week, to practise. It was just like 'you practise piano scales'. But she felt she had nothing to write about, so she kept her hand in by writing vignettes – portraits and end-pieces. Only when her father became sick did she find in his illness something to write about, and that was the real beginning.

  If you feel there's nothing in the tank, then use time productively by writing vignettes or miniatures – character sketches, five-minute scripts, mini-sagas, topographical pieces, articles, 'stream of consciousness' fragments, journal/diary entries, diatribes, polemics, and so on. These are the equivalent of the artist's notebook, and out of the seeding something may come to full term. **Write** four miniatures: the first, out of 'overheards' (eavesdrop in the supermarket and make a shopping list of them); the second, out of 'frozens' (images that flash across your vision as you look up at house windows or down the street and which become fixed in the mind); the third, out of dream 'left-overs'; the fourth, from 'jigsaws', where half a dozen images from the day are stitched together.

It's Just One Sentence After Another

- Once you begin, write quickly and, while the iron's hot, strike and strike again. And you don't need to worry about the quality – at first. Writing's like curry, the more you reheat it the better it gets. But you do have to cook it time and again. Scott Fitzgerald's first drafts were, on his own admission, poor. That is, dull and uninspired. But he was a great second-time cook. In the first draft of the *Great Gatsby*, he used the phrase: 'fairy blue' to describe the bright Mediterranean sky. Second-time round he wrote that the sky was 'blue honey', a far more sensorily complex and startling phrase.

The truth of the matter is that rewriting is where the real gold begins to glister. Here is what the great Italian poet and novelist Cesare Pavese said about second-phase writing: 'They say that to create while actually writing is to reach beyond whatever plan we have made, searching listening to the deep truth within us. But often the profoundest truth we have is the plan we have created by slow, ruthless, weary effort and surrender.' If you have a first-drafted story, start the slow and ruthless reworking of it . . . NOW. This is no tinkering. This is beating it, annealing it into shape. This is getting glitter in the phrasing, edge in dialogue, bite in the descriptive passages. Go for it. **Write** out the stale and the lazy phrasings.

- One way to review your opening paragraph is to see if it ventriloquises the reader. By this I mean, does it make the reader ask questions? One page and the reader should be puzzling over what's going on, should be asking who these people are, should be wondering why they are behaving in the way they do. The first page should 'hook' the reader, as they say in television. The opening sentence of *Once in a House on Fire* runs like this: 'My father drowned when I was five years old.' Some hook! Jane Austen opens *Pride and Prejudice* with these celebrated lines: 'It is a truth universally acknowledged, that a single man in possession of a good fortune, must be in want of a wife.' Thus is lit the slow fuse of the novel.

  Like everything, if you strain for notice, you get the wrong kind of attention. The art is to lead readers, not shake them breathless. Everyone will recognise over-eager openings as an uncritical application of the hook-the-reader ploy from the How-To School of Creative Writing. However, reconsider some of your fictional openings. Do they draw readers into the story by intriguing and making them want answers? If you think they could be rewritten and given a stronger magnetic attraction, **rewrite** them.

- The reward for the travail of writing that Pavese identifies is sensing the truth. And before revising, it's worth thinking hard about what the first haul has brought up. Ask yourself just what is this stuff I have written all about? The answer may be a resounding blip. Only when the rewriting starts, does any faint glimmer of an answer emerge, and maybe not even then. Michaelangelo thought of his subject as being interred in the marble block he was about to carve. His job was to release the imprisoned form from the restraint of stone.

  Whether the subject is exposed or kept as a hidden presence in the writing, is partially a matter of genre, partially a matter of individual vision. A fable wears its subject/theme on its sleeve as it were; a short story intimates its presence and avoids overexposure. **Write** a ghost story. Imagine something is breathing behind the images. Work out what it is and write a short piece that signs its presence, but does not fully reveal itself. In writing the supernatural it is often better to understate and resist Gothic excesses. M. R. James was a master of the genre. The creature in his story 'Oh Whistle, And I'll Come To You My Lad' has 'a face of crumpled linen'. That's all the reader is given. The rest is left to the imagination. It is masterly restraint. Less is more – as always. Chose a single image to describe your supernatural presence, and work with a suitably ghostly, but cliché-free setting. Emptied places are suitable. But hooting owls and clanking chains are not. For a modern ghost story read Susan Hill's *The Woman in Black*. It's a slow chiller.

- Edward George Bulwer-Lytton was a popular early Victorian writer whose novel *Paul Clifford* was published in 1830. The opening sentence goes like this:

  It was a dark and stormy night; the rain fell in torrents, except at occasional intervals when it was checked by a violent gust of wind that swept up the streets, for it is in London that our scenes lie, rattling along the housetops, and fiercely agitating the scanty flame of the lamps that struggled against the darkness.

Now that's bad. Quickly analyse this faux-elemental gush. If you think it's worth trying, write a bad opening sentence. Here's the winning sentence from this year's *Bulwer-Lytton Fiction Contest*.

Through the gathering gloom of a late-October afternoon, along the greasy, cracked paving-stones slick from the sputum from the sky, Stanley Ruddlethorp wearily trudged up the hill from the cemetery where his wife, sister, brother, and three children were all buried, and forced open the door of his decaying house, blissfully unaware of the catastrophe that was soon to devastate his life.

Compare with this –

On the veranda overlooking the garden, the drive and the gate, they sit together on the creaking sofa-swing, suspended from its iron frame, dangling their legs so that the slippers on their feet hang loose.

(*Fasting and Feasting*, Anita Desai)

Write a bad Bulwer-type opening and then transform it by radical revision. It may not be possible to recover it! The Bulwer-Lytton opening may be long, but compared with the head sentence of *Tristram Shandy*, which is 145 words long, it's positively gnomic. Read Thomas Pynchon's opening to *The Crying of Lot 49* and try writing a very long opening sentence.

• In a newspaper article, Blake Morrison considered the problem of hooking the reader and suggested various strategies for the undecided writer. Writers can try The Plunge opening which takes the reader straight into events, as in Graham Greene's *Brighton Rock*; the Shocker, as in Kafka's 'Metamorphosis'; the Intriguing Narrator, as in Gunter Grass's *The Tin Drum*; the Epigram, as in Jane Austen's *Pride and Prejudice*; the Cosmic, as in Margaret Attwood's *Cat's Eye*; the Self-referral, as in Italo Calvino's *If on a Winter's Night a Traveller*.

Check out some fictional openings and see if you can fit them into any of Morrison's categories. The Israeli novelist

Amos Oz has written that the writer must 'seduce' the reader in the first pages of a novel, or all is lost. Try using any four of the above strategies to **write** the opening of a short piece of fiction. The idea is to snare, importune, seduce the reader. It is possible you will seduce yourself. If you get so involved then continue and conclude the affair.

- It's all so easy! And so ordinary! As Raymond Carver said all you do is write one sentence and then the next and then the next. You can do no better than work on sentences, just like a gymnast or dancer or actor works continually on simple routines. The routines of sentences are like Lego – you can build complicated structures from single components. 'The cat smiled' is a **simple** sentence. Glue another bit on with the adhesive 'and', so it reads: 'The cat smiled AND licked up the milk'. Now you have a **co-ordinate** sentence. Other adhesives include 'but', 'yet', 'because', 'then' and so on. You can accessorise the cat with all kinds of feline additions. 'The cat, who was black, smiled and gently licked up the milk till she was so full she rolled over and drifted into a gentle, fur-lined sleep on the soft, pale carpet' is a **complex** sentence because it has a number of additional units bolted into position, like the word-group, 'who was black'. This unit is called a subordinate clause. (What do you expect from a cat?) Phrases like 'fast and fur-lined' and 'soft, grey' are modifying word-groups.

And *subordination* and *modification* are what give variety and power to written sentences. What sentences gain from these two processes is pace, rhythm and drama. Take the demo complex sentence above. The last nine words are a succession of mainly monosyllables interrupted by commas, and as a result they read very slowly. Their sounds are not unimportant. Because they are dominated by long vowels and breathed and labial sounds the effect is languorous. Thus the sentence mimics its meaning. After the busy pace of the first half, with its precise dental and harsher guttural sounds (t's and k's), it slows down, lulling the reader with its softer tones.

If the cat is then frightened by a falling pan on the tiled floor of the kitchen nearby, any description of its response should be in short, even staccato terms. Short sentences after long ones, if nothing else, add variety to writing. To learn the art of writing good sentences, first read some good sentences and see how they work. Consider their sequence and how they alternate the long (subordinated) with the short (simple); how they invert normal syntax (word order) periodically; how they set polysyllabic words against monosyllables, harsh sounding against soft sounding; how they brake and accelerate; how they end strongly with an image and not with a nonentity of a word; how they play with the silent music of words.

For examples, read and analyse the opening paragraph of James Joyce's story 'Eveline' from *Dubliners*, the last paragraph on page one of Frank McCourt's *Angela's Ashes*, the opening three paragraphs of Chapter 17 in Maureen Duffy's *That's How It Was*, the opening sentence of Maxim Gorky's *My Childhood*, the opening paragraph of E. M. Forster's *A Passage to India*, the first page of Charles Dickens's *Bleak House*, the last page from James Joyce's story 'The Dead' from *Dubliners*, the opening paragraphs of Angela Carter's short story 'The Erl King' from *The Bloody Chamber*.

Now practise. **Write** two paragraphs about a race. Think about the momentum of the piece. Does the pace hot up? When? OR do a Dickens and write about a snowstorm in a city street. Bustle gives way to the soft paralysis of snow. How do the sentences reflect this transition? A windy hailstorm would demand a different sentence performance. It would bristle with abrasive sounds, jerk and snatch and never settle into any rhythm.

References

Ashworth, A., *Once in a House on Fire* (Picador, 1998).
Attwood, M., *Cat's Eye* (Virago, 1990).
Austen, J., *Emma* (Penguin, 1994).
Austen, J., *Pride and Prejudice* (Penguin, 1994).
Banks, I., *Espedir Street* (Abacus, 1990).
Book of Common Prayer, 1662 (Cambridge UP, 1992).

Bunker, E., *The Bunker Omnibus* (No Exit, 1999).

Bunyan, J., *Pilgrim's Progress* (Penguin, 1970).

Calvino, I., *If on a Winter's Night a Traveller* (Minerva, 1992).

Carter, A., *The Bloody Chamber* (Vintage, 1995).

Carver, R., *A New Path to the Waterfall* (Collins, 1990).

Causley, C., *Collected Poems 1951–1992* (Macmillan, 1992).

Cixous, H., *Three Steps on the Ladder of Writing* (Columbia UP, 1994).

Clarke, G., in *How Poets Work*, ed. T. Curtis (Poetry of Wates Press, 1996).

Coleridge, S. T., *Biographia Literaria* (Everyman, 1997).

Dickens, C., *Bleak House* (Penguin, 1994).

Dickinson, E., *Selected Poems* (Colombia UP, 1994).

Duffy, C. A., *The World's Wife* (Picador, 1999).

Duffy, M., *That's How It Was* (Virago, 1983).

Dunmore, H., in *How Poets Work*, ed. T. Curtis (Poetry of Wates Press, 1996).

Eliot, G., *The Mill on the Floss* (Penguin, 1994).

Eliot, T. S., *The Waste Land & Other Poems* (Faber and Faber, 1972).

Fitzgerald, S., *The Great Gatsby* (Penguin, 1994).

Forster, E. M., *A Passage to India* (Penguin, 1998).

Garret, G., in *Letters to a Fiction Writer* ed. F. Busch (Norton, 1999).

Ginsberg, A., *Howl and Other Poems* (City Lights, 1956).

Gorky, M., *My Childhood* (Penguin, 1990).

Grass, G., *The Tin Drum* (Minerva, 1997).

Graves, R., *Selected Poems* (Penguin, 1992).

Greene, G., *Brighton Rock* (Penguin, 1998).

Gross, J. (ed.), *The New Oxford Book of English Prose* (Oxford UP, 1999).

Hardy, T., *Jude the Obscure* (Penguin, 1998).

Heaney, S., *Selected Poems 1966–1987* (Faber and Faber, 1990).

Hempel, A., *Reasons to Live* (A.A.Knopf, 1985).

Hersey, J., *Hiroshima* (Penguin, 1990).

Hill, S., *The Woman in Black* (Vintage, 1998).

Holy Bible: Authorised Version (Harper Collins, 1992).

Houseman, E. A., *A Shropshire Lad* (Penguin, 1999).

Hughes, T., *The Complete Poems* (Oxford UP, 1998).

James, M. R., *Collected Ghost Stories* (Wordsworth, 1992).

Joyce, J., *Dubliners* (Penguin, 1999).

Kafka, F., *Metamorphosis and Other Stories* (Penguin, 1992).

Kafka, F., *Diaries* (Schocken, 1988).

Lefer, D., in *The Best Writing on Writing* ed. J. Heffron (Story, 1994).

Le Guin, U., *Dancing at the Edge of the World* (Paladin, 1992).

Longley, M., in *How Poets Work*, ed. T. Curtis (Poetry of Wales Press, 1996).

McCarthy, C., *All the Pretty Horses* (Picador, 1993).

McCourt, F., *Angela's Ashes* (Flamingo, 1997).

McGough, R., *Selected Poems 1967–1987* (Cape, 1989).

McGuckian, M., *Selected Poems* (Wake-Forest UP, 1997).

Michaels, A., *Fugitive Pieces* (Bloomsbury, 1997).

Paulin, T., *The Wind Dog* (Faber and Faber, 1999).

Poe, E. A., *The Fall of the House of Usher and Other Writings* (Penguin, 1986).

Pynchon, T., *The Crying of Lot 49* (Vintage, 1996).

Queneau, R., *Exercises in Style* (Calder, 1999).

Radcliffe, A., *The Mysteries of Udolpho* (Oxford UP, 1999).

Ricks, C. (ed.), *The Oxford Book of English Verse* (Oxford UP, 1999).

Sarraute, N., *Tropismes* (Flammarion, 1980).

Sartre, P., *Words* (Penguin, 1967).

Sterne, L., *Tristram Shandy* (Penguin, 1997).

Swift, J., *A Modest Proposal* (Prometheus, 1994).

Tennyson, A., *Selected Poems* (Penguin, 1992).

Wharton, E., *The Writing of Fiction* (Touchstone, 1997).

Wolfe, T., *The Electric Kool-aid Acid Test* (Black Swan, 1989).

Wolfe, T., *The Kandy-kolored, Tangerine-flake Stream-line Baby* (Picador, 1981).

Woolf, V., *The Waves* (Penguin, 2000).

Zipes, J. (ed.), *The Arabian Nights: A Selection* (Penguin, 1997).

8 | The Practice Ground

Found Writing and 'Abandoned' Texts

- Take any two lines at random from a published poem. Continue **writing** from where they leave off, until you have at least ten more lines. Feel no guilt about this thieving. Paul Valery, the French symbolist poet, said no text is ever finished, it is just 'abandoned'. Well, you are just recycling what others have left by the wayside. Alternatively, take a phrase from an established poem and use it as a title to kick-start writing.

- Another option is to update the past. For example, some contemporary writers have 'translated' well-known 'period' poems. Gavin Ewart's witty reworking of Thomas Wyatt's famous sixteenth-century lover's plaint 'They Flee from Me That Sometime Did Me Seek' (OBV) is a good example. Ewart renders the original in modern-day idiomatic cliché. The title becomes: 'The chicks that went for me/in a big way...' Peter Porter is another recyclist. He develops a variety of spins on Arnold's phrase: 'Its melancholy, long, withdrawing roar' ('Dover Beach') in his poem 'Divisions'. **Try your hand at revoicing** and rebranding a poem or line of traditional verse. Instead of the small change of club and media chat or disc-jockey patter you might adopt psycho-babble or management-speak as your contemporary voice. Another example is Tom Leonard's take on William Carlos Williams's celebrated poem 'This Is Just to Say'. Leonard's

247

is another idiomatic rendering, and is titled 'Jist to Let Yi No' (FB).

- Study a large-scale Ordinance Survey map and list the unusual, the startling place names. Near me there are two villages, one called Cold Overton, the other Burton Lazars. What resonant terms! Out of your material shape a list poem. There are plenty of models. Michael Longley's 'Trade Winds' for one. Each of the four quatrains in this poem consists of a short catalogue – the names of locks on the River Lagan, of apples from County Armagh, of clay pipes made in Carrickfergus, and of fishing smacks in Portavogie harbour. We are all collectors of trifles; it's a common pleasure.

  Here are some other fruitful collections: the common names of wild flowers, herbal remedies, birds and moths and butterflies, varieties of eating apple; the specialised languages of trade and profession; the names of Aegean islands, tropical fish, local streets and roads; nineteenth-century Staffordshire coal-mines; brand names for perfume, beer, cars; pet names from personal ads and valentine pages; terms from weather forecasting and the names of meteorological coastal areas. And so on. **Write** a 'collection' poem.

- Even in the unlikeliest of places poetry flourishes. From a newspaper page, cull some telling phrases and jostle them into unlikely and revealing combinations. Pages from Franz Kafka's diaries are particularly inspirational, so impromptu and ragged and surreal are his entries. Other 'found' material includes 'overheards', the verbal refuse of the day. **Collage** this into intriguing free-verse moments or **snatch** phrases from the airwaves and start up a bounding hare of a poem.

- The words 'crossed lines' describe a cross-threaded conversation where two sides are talking at odds. It also describes a writing technique of splitting up lines and re-pairing the bits. Try this technique. It can lead on to better things if pursued. **Collage** a piece called *Cross-lines*.

- In her 'Waste Land Limericks' (20WP), Wendy Cope quarries Eliot's poem for references and phrases, and out of the shards shapes her five-limerick poem. Quarry any example from the canon of Eng. Lit. and **recast** it in a simple form. Cope is undermining the airy, literary and possibly male style of the original by adopting a popular comic form, the limerick, and by deliberately mouthing an idiomatic, anti-intellectual voice.

- Reworking traditional material such as nursery rhymes has become part of the poetic heritage business. Many of these rhymes started as adult street songs and satires, but in Victorian times they were scrubbed clean and sneaked into the nursery by working-class maids and nurses. Some have been given a twentieth-century makeover. 'Ring o' ring o' roses' is one example. The last two lines take on a new and disturbing twist and now read: 'Hiroshima. Hiroshima/We all fall down.' Try your hand at renovating nursery rhymes. **Rewrite** two or three famous ones. Imagine you are returning them to their scurrilous and sardonic original.

- Working with a partner, collect some proverbs. Use this common property to **create a poem**. Counterbalance each proverb with a saying of your own or extend each one into a second line with a particular example. For some ideas, read James Berry's poem 'Folk Proverbs Found Poems' (PBPBI). Also look up Don Paterson's 'Proverbs' from his collection *Eyes*.

- **Try writing** your own aphorisms. Here are some examples. 'Hope is trying to bribe the future.' 'Hope is halfway to hopelessness.' 'Hope heals.' 'Hope is the procrastinator's virtue.' 'Hope is giving glasses to the blind.' Start with *Love is.. or Loneliness is...* or *Touch is...* or *Home is...* or *Guilt is...* And so on. Write ten lines

- Read Peter Reading's poem 'Axiomatic' (FBP) for a sequence of axioms about ageing. Choose any topic – youth, winter, maps, candles, sickness – and write a sequence of related axioms.

- The American poet W. S. Merwin has also written aphorisms. They are like pebbles, small poems tossed into the mind that make a little splash and ripple suggestively through the consciousness. Here are four examples. 'Thief/plans even his naps.' 'Don't curse your wife/at bedtime.' 'Sudden/like a spear from a window.' 'Tree grows the way it wants/That one they cut down first.' **Try writing** some *aphorisms.*

- The poet Simon Armitage says that fellow poet Paul Muldoon showed him how you could use ordinary speech in poetry – clichés, proverbs, idioms – 'rubbing phrases up the wrong way, making then pull a bit more weight, using the puns within them'. Read work from both these poets and see how they rub up words and give the small change of language new shine and sharpness. Go on a cliché hunt. Collect them from newspapers, magazines, radio, TV. And then play around with the results till you are ready to **write** a piece, either full of old clichés, or full of reconditioned ones.

The Great Hat Project and Erotic Alphabets

- Riddling is at the heart of language; both describe one thing in terms of another. Take Wallace Stevens's poem 'Pineapple'. Here are eight ways of puzzling the fruit. Or look at Sylvia Plath's 'Here' (RB), a crossword with ten clues and one answer. Take any object and **riddle** it so it's wrapped up like a present for the reader to untie. Use 'Pineapple' as your model.

- For another take on the disguised, oblique view of objects read Elizabeth Bishop's poem '12 O'clock News' (OBV). The items on her desk are described as if they form a vast landscape, and are presented in the language, tone and pitch of broadcast news. Take any common object, camouflage it and **write** in a borrowed style/voice. Imagine the contents of your desk as different kinds of properties being sold or appraised by an estate agent. Or the features of your body being described by a street-trader as if they were goods on a market stall. Or imagine your body as items of food being described as part of a cookery demonstration. Or body parts as art objects being described by a connoisseur or gallery guide.

- Alphabets are a good bet. Read Edward Lear's 'Animal Alphabet' (RB) and **write** one of your own, rhyming a couplet for each letter. There are Erotic Alphabets and Lovers'Alphabets. There are Christmas Alphabets and Space Alphabets and Slang Alphabets. There are alphabets for foodies and shop-a-holics and alphabets for the environment. There are anti-alphabets and body-part alphabets. **Write** an alternative alphabet.

- 'Thirteen Ways of Looking at a Blackbird' is a celebrated poem by Wallace Stevens. The formula can be applied to any subject under the sun. **Write** a Ways-of-Looking poem about a cat, a kettle, a storm brewing, a baby, a kite flying, an idea forming, a kiss, you, a grandma, a shadow, a dream and so on. The Ways-of-Looking formula allows the writer to invade the subject and seemingly reach into its secret meaning. Use the title *Ten Ways of Looking At...* (Enter object) Consider Matthew Caley's poem 'Eight Ways of Looking at Lakes' (FBP). From the binocular sweep of the lake in section one to dark immersion and dying bubbles in the eighth 'Way', the poem takes the reader gradually into the watery heart of things. Or consider Pamela Gillilan's 'Three Ways to a Silk Shirt' (FBP) where the factual material is poeticised into a powerful statement about how the natural world pays for our pleasures.

- Finding a new way of looking is what good writing is about. It makes the reader take a second look. It riddles the world. Read Craig Raine's poem 'A Martian Sends a Postcard Home' (PBPBI). The familiar mechanical world is seen through the distorting but revealing eyes of a visitor from outer space. **Write** a poem made up of two-line 'postcards' that offer a view of our familiar world through very different eyes – a robot's, a child's, God's, the Devil's.

- Instead of being a Martian poet you could transform yourself into an animal and see things from yet another point of view. Read Jo Shapcott's poem 'Goat' (FB). Choose any animal and get inside its skin and **write**. See too Peter Didsbury's poem 'A Bee' (EK).

- Laments and *In Memoria* can be lists too. Look up Nick Drake's poem 'In Memory of Vincent Cox' or Robert Minhinnick's 'Twenty-five Laments for Iraq', both in FBP. Using these poems as models, **write** your own lament or *In Memoriam*.

- Other comparable litany poems include 'Touching the Peter' by Peter Porter and 'My Cat Jeffrey' (RB) by Christopher Smart. Each free-verse section of the Porter poem is made up of six short lines. Invent your own loose form for this piece of writing. **Write** a list poem using the Touching-the-Peter formula. Think of other keywords to substitute for 'Touching'.

- These last two poems are pro-cat. They are catophilic. Peter Porter also has an anti-cat poem; a sort of catophobic catalogue of their less than attractive habits. It's called 'Mort Aux Chats' (OBV). **Write** an anti-something poem.

- Read Vernon Scannell's 'Six Reasons for Drinking' (OBV) in which his alter ego, no doubt increasingly inebriated, justifies his behaviour to a 'constable'. **Write** a dialogue between yourself and an increasingly cynical listener listing the justifications for a habit/obsession of yours.

- Poems of praise are frequently enumerations of virtues. In the Navajo poem called 'The War God's Horse Song' (RB), the 'Turquoise Woman's son' honours his horses with a roll call of praise. Give yourself an honorary name and **write** a litany in praise of something or someone you value immeasurably.

- Read Ken Smith's poem 'The Great Hat Project' in which he memorialises the hundreds of hats he has encountered in his lifetime. **Try writing** your own Hat Project or Girl-friend Project or Auto Project or Shoe Project or Chat-up Line Project. And so on.

- **Write** a litany-poem made up of quatrains and entitled the *Four Seasons*. Each line should itemise a distinctive but not stereotyped image. No abstractions. See what Keats does with Autumn's attractions in his famous ode. For other list topics consider – days of the week, the planets, months of the year, deadly sins, horsemen of the Apocalypse, ages of man, signs of the zodiac.

- Doctor Faustus, in Christopher Marlowe's play of the same name, meets the Seven Deadly Sins. Each announces itself in a speech of suitable tone and style. Anger splutters so much every sentence is disrupted and exclamatory. Sloth has neither the energy nor the inclination to finish a sentence. Imagine the *Seven Deadly Virtues* doing a self-promotion. **Write** their introductory speeches to an amazed audience.

- Naming the parts. The ritual titles of deities and divas, sovereigns and saints make intriguing reading, as anyone who has read the Marian litanies will know. 'The Names of the Hare' (RB) recites, with reluctant admiration, the antics and attributes of the animal. **Write** a naming poem, along the lines of the hare example, about someone or something you half-admire, half-fear.

- Fearing leads to cursing. An excellent get-it-off-your-chest curse is Ian Duhig's 'Hepstonstall'. In this piece the poet vents his spleen iambically and in a single sustained and emphatic rhyme. 'Come all you demons, hear my call,' he prays, conjuring misfortune for the unfortunate village. Start with a similar invocation and **write** a curse that gratifies your feelings of anger and indignation. 'The Rattlebag' (RB) shows you the way. Here the poet shakes a rhetorical fist at the 'bloody nuisance', at 'the field-keeper, the comrade of straw' who frightens off his girl. And the anonymous Gaelic poet, who curses his enemies in 'The Wicked Who Would Do Me Harm' (RB) with similar virulence, is no verbal slouch either.

- Curses are to anger as charms are to hope, and as spells are to both. **Write** a wishful charm or a spell. Make it fill in the future.

- Make a list of memories associated with each day of the week or each season of the year and turn them into a seven-verse poem or a four-verse poem. Do memory-associations for any or all of the following: a household object, a personal possession, a particular place or person, an episode of illness. **Shape** the memories that surface into a piece of writing.

- Ian Duhig has also recast the haiku. He calls them 'instants'. Here's one example:

  Catching the moonshine
  the signature of a snail,
  a streak of lightning.

  Instead of writing a number of isolated haiku or 'instants', try writing a sequence. **Write** a set of household haiku or hiking haiku or water haiku or seduction haiku or getting-up-in-the-morning haiku, or weather haiku. And so on. See too Vicki Feaver's poem 'Ironing' (FB).

- **Write** a duet with your partner. One of you writes down a question, the other writes an answer. Focus the material by first agreeing a subject. Start with the concrete image – water, candle-flame, make-up, photographs. Ask both obvious and 'wilder' questions, whatever comes to mind. Answer as directly or as deviously as you want. Alternatively, write a duet between yourself and a historical person in which you play the role either of the daughter or the son, the mother or the father or the lover of your chosen character.

- Take the title *Yes's and No's* for a piece about an animal. The first lines could be: 'The Yes of a snake is its shimmer./The No of a snake is its bite.' And so on, alternating Yes and No lines. Try a Yes-No version of *Red* or *Yellow* or *Black* or *White* or *Peace* or *Sex* or *War* or *Apples*. The list is inexhaustible. This formula can cover any subject under the sun (including the sun). In the same way, the words 'but' and 'yet' create counterbalancing forces in writing. Try an 'Ifs and Buts' poem.

- From the following list choose a topic to write on: Falling Out, On the Spot, Compromised, Between the Devil and the Deep Blue Sea, Let Down, An Incomplete Man.

- In his poem 'A Consumer's Report' (EK), Peter Porter is product-testing 'Life'. **Write** your own consumer's report where you product-test *Love* or *Religion* or *Politics* or *Race* or *Capitalism* or *Consumerism*. And so on.

- To fix up your deflated life what would you put in the puncture repair kit? Make a suitable list. **Write** ten lines.

- **Write** a Domesday poem in which you list all the disturbing, harrowing, distressing events of recent times. Simon Armitage's 1000-line millennium poem 'Killing Time' is a suitably apocalyptic model.

- Read 'Gaelic Stories' by Iain Crichton Smith (PBPBI) where, in 18 short self-contained imagist verses, he camera-snaps some of the distinctive features of Gaelic life. Choose a familiar and loved place and **snap** a sequence of verbal shots. Arrange in groups of three lines.

- In her poem 'Telegrams', Carol Ann Duffy traces the progress of a love affair in the abbreviated language of the telegram. Try using this truncated form of expression and **write** about other aspects of human relationships. Another Duffy poem, 'Postcards', wittily manipulates the stilted language and pictorial possibilities of the postcard as a meditation on the nature of courtship. **Write** your own postcard poem, or shopping list poem, or even Visa Statement poem. The fancy names that credit companies use to market their plastic opens up a number of poetic possibilities.

Body Work

- Read Matthew Caley's poem 'Colander Man' (FBP). It's an exuberant celebration of a flamboyant body that undoes itself. The poem plays with the idea that flesh and skin, sinew and muscle make up a gorgeous garment. **Write** a celebratory piece about the body.

- Ever since Eve ribbed Adam, we've admired our body parts. In 'The Legs' by Robert Graves (RB), in 'The Nose' by Iain Crichton Smith (RB), in 'To the Foot from its Child' by Pablo Neruda (RB) the poets meditate and fabulate on parts. Choose a bit of you, a bit part: teeth, eyes, breasts, bottoms, hearts, feet, fingers, genitals, back, bones, skull, odours, warts, moles, skin, et cetera and **write** about it.

- **Write** about one of the following: sleep, exercise, eating, dressing, tattooing, piercing, anorexia, catwalks, make-overs, body-painting. Read Gillian Clarke's poem 'Horse Goddess' (FBP). Take birth as your subject and **write** about it.

- Awareness of the body comes into slow focus for us all. **Write** about a time when you became particularly conscious of your own body or someone else's. It may be helpful to read a poem like Vicki Feaver's 'Rope' (PBPBI) or Thom Gunn's 'Touch' (PBPBI).

- Body image preoccupies our self-regarding world. Collect photos of bodies from fashion magazines, art books, family albums. Reflect on the images and begin to **write** something in response.

- The fashion for trimmed, tanned, tinted, toned and tested bodies has driven people into fitnesses and fads. List down the names of beauty products, slimming programmes, fitness machines and accessories, alternative exercise regimes, health foods and supplements, and, selecting from this melange, **write** a poem.

- What's the difference between 'nude' and 'naked'? Is one a model body? Read Nuala Ni Dhomhnaill's poem 'Nude' (FB). **Write** about an admired, desired body.

- In his poem 'My Beloved Compares Herself to a Pint of Stout' (EK), Paul Durcan enjoys the elaboration of the figure in the title – the physical and the literary figure – and relishes sending-up the traditional form of amorous address in which poets used to idealise the attributes of the loved one. e. e. cummings has a similar extended metaphor in his poem 'she being Brand', in which getting a new car going for the first time is a metaphor for making love. Complete the following title: *My Beloved Compares Herself/Himself to a* . . . Now, **write** a poem to go with it.

- One of the finest poetic contemplations on the human body is Andrew Marvell's 'Ode to His Coy Mistress'. **Write** a Marvell-type ode for our times, one that with irresistible reasoning, smooth persuasions, breathless murmurings and fierce declarations seeks to seduce the woman or the man into bed. It should use the full range of ploys and platitudes and come-ons.

- An ode is a longish poem in full-dress – DJ, the lot. So, it's a little formal, but with fashionable flashes like a bright silk cummerbund or jazzy bow tie. It can handle the idiomatic if you wish. Try **writing** a cool, chic ode. On the other hand, you might like to **write** a real down-market seduction poem, a coarser version of the elegant Marvell original. Experiment with the full range of ad-man rhetoric and sales technique.

- Making love is an ambivalent joy in Heather McHugh's poem 'Coming' (EK). **Write** about the ambivalences of sexual pleasure. Adrienne Rich describes the same mix of elation and perplexity at the experience in her poem 'Two Songs' (EK).

- SSSIs are Sites of Special Scientific Interest around the country and are protected under law. The body too has its SSSIs – Sites of Special Sexual Interest. **Try writing** about the pleasure points of the body. *SSSI* is a possible title!

- Read Carol Anne Duffy's poem 'Small Female Skull' (EK). Jot down the ideas that the words 'skeleton' or 'bone' suggest to you and out of the fall-out compose a piece of writing. You've possibly found bleached animal bones on moor or beach. You've probably seen skeletons in exhibition cases in natural history museums, and sherds and fragments unearthed in archaeological digs. If so, use the memories to **inspire** a poem. Read 'Bone Dreams' by Seamus Heaney. Heaney has also written poems about the Danish bog people. The titles 'Bog Queen' and 'Grabaulle Man' refer to the bodies, over a thousand years old, found perfectly preserved in the peat bogs of Denmark. His evocative language gives a new corporeality to peat-tanned skin and the bric-à-brac of broken bones. See also his poem

'Punishment', which is about a young bog girl garrotted in a ritual sacrifice.

- We take our bodies for granted until they splutter and misfire and we are ill. Then we notice them. Les Murray in his poem 'Travels with John Hunter' (FBP) describes his emergency admission to the John Hunter Hospital, in Newcastle, New South Wales. **Write** about a time when you were ill or hospitalised or being scanned or were anaesthetised or were hurt in an accident.

- Animals, their bodily shape, movement and habits, fascinate humans. We imitate and envy and eliminate them. Read any good poem about an animal. They are always based on astute and acute observation. And an instinctive sympathy that tries to get to the essence of the creature. For starters read George Macbeth's 'Owl' (EK) and compare it with Sylvia Plath's poem also titled 'Owl'. Or compare Ted Hughes's 'Thrushes' with Norman McCaig's 'Ringed Plovers by the Water's Edge' (OBV).

Wild Country

- The environmental writer Richard Mabey has written: 'We become imprinted by places ... We plod our private routes, touch trees and mark (in our imaginations, at least) our special spots – a bend in the road, a gate to lean on, a face glimpsed in a trunk.' **Write** about one of your 'special spots'.

- Dante's Inferno is a place of deep circular ditches or bolgia. In each ditch a particular class of sinner endlessly enacts its appropriate punishment. Create a modern version of the Inferno. **Write** in prose or verse.

- In Yvgeny Zamyatin's celebrated science fiction parable *We*, the city is made of glass. Given the dominance of glass in contemporary corporate architecture this is a prescient image. Describe the sprawling metropolis of the future. Will it be like the city in *Blade Runner*, where new technology runs alongside the antiquated? Or will it be glassy, glossy and dirtless, sighing with pneumatic release and riven with laser light? **Write** the opening page of a sci-fi novel which describes the new urbia.

- Maps are shorthand geographies. Study any OS map and use the names you gather to **write** a poem.

- *The Songlines* by Bruce Chatwin explored the Australian Aboriginals' myth maps that define both space and time. Here topography is not inert, not a matter of surveyors' grids and co-ordinates and theodolitic readings. Billabongs and river beds, rocks and boulders are the vitalised narratives of dreamings, stories of tribal and human origins. Every place has its secret life, its songlines, its cache of memories, its patina of the past. **Write** about the secret life of a place you know well.

- Every tribe has its sacred places, often barbwired with taboos and fortified with ritual. But have these survived modern times and attitudes? Are we so enquiring now that everything has to be explained and nothing left to mystery? If we have contemporary sacred sites where are they? **Write** a reflection on the idea of 'the sacred'.

- Fictional places often have a significance beyond their physical reality. They are not just settings or backdrops for the action; they are deep presences in the narrative. Examples of such symbolic power include: Egdon Heath in Hardy's *Return of the Native*, the Fens in Grahame Swift's *Waterland*, the Marabar Caves in Forster's *A Passage to India*, Dublin suburbs in Joyce's *Dubliners*, the sea in Virginia Woolf's *The Waves*, the lake and the rocks in Wordsworth's *The Prelude*. The list is endless. **Write** the opening to a short story where you describe a town at night, and suggest in the writing larger and wider associations for your image.

- The wilderness writers like Barry Lopez and E. O. Matthiesson are particularly conscious of open space and placeless places. One of the wilder and most remote regions on earth is the Arctic, and Lopez's *Arctic Dreams* is one of the finest evocations of this part of the earth. Read Chapter 6 entitled

'Ice and Light' for remarkable descriptions of vast ice rafts and their different structures and formations, including sea-ice, shorefast ice, grey ice, pancake ice, candle ice, pack ice, grease ice. The rafts are pocked with permanent open pools called 'polynyas' and threaded with 'flaw leads' – cold rivers that serve as highways for marine mammals. The drawing power of Lopez's writing is that it is based on acute observation and a real understanding of the natural environment. Share your own understanding and knowledge of a wilderness in a piece of sympathetic writing. Interpret the word 'wilderness' imaginatively. A subway or a cemetery at night is as wilderness-like as a deep pothole or a tent on stormy Dartmoor. **Write** sharply, alert to every detail, using specialised terminology where appropriate.

References

Armitage, S., *Killing Time* (Faber and Faber, 1999).
Chatwin, B., *The Songlines* (Picador, 1988).
Dante, A., *The Divine Comedy* (Oxford UP, 1998).
Duffy, C. A., *Selling Manhattan* (Anvil, 1987).
Duhig, I., *Nominies* (Bloodaxe, 1998).
Forster, E. M., *A Passage to India* (Penguin, 1998).
Hardy, T., *The Return of the Native* (Penguin, 1994).
Heaney, S., *New Selected Poems 1966–87* (Faber and Faber, 1990).
Joyce, J., *Dubliners* (Penguin, 1999).
Kafka, F., *Diaries* (Schocken, 1988).
Keats, J., *The Collected Poems* (Penguin, 1973).
Longley, M., *Selected Poems* (Cape, 1998).
Lopez, B., *Arctic Dreams* (Picador, 1986).
Marvell, A., *The Complete Poems* (Penguin, 1991).
Muldoon, P., in *How Poets Work*, ed. T. Curtis (Poetry of Wales Press, 1996).
Plath, S., *Collected Poems* (Harper, 1992).
Paterson, D., *The Eyes* (Faber and Faber, 1999).
Porter, P., *Collected Poems* (Oxford UP, 1994).
Smith, K., *Wild Root* (Bloodaxe, 1998).
Stevens, W., *The Collected Poems* (Faber and Faber, 1955).

Swift, G., *Waterland* (Picador, 1994).
Williams, Carlos W., *Selected Poems* (Penguin, 1990).
Woolf, V., *The Waves* (Penguin, 2000).
Wordsworth, W., *The Prelude* (Penguin, 1995).
Wyatt, T., *Poems* (Everyman, 1999).
Zamyatin, Y., *We* (Penguin, 1993)